Power, Crime,
and Mystification

LiJ/SJL

Tavistock Studies in Sociology

General Editor: FRANK PARKIN

STEVEN BOX

Power, Crime,
and Mystification

TAVISTOCK PUBLICATIONS
LONDON AND NEW YORK

First published in 1983 by
Tavistock Publications Ltd
11 New Fetter Lane, London EC4P 4EE

Published in the USA by
Tavistock Publications
in association with Methuen, Inc.
733 Third Avenue, New York, NY 10017

Photoset by Rowland Phototypesetting Ltd
Bury St Edmunds, Suffolk and printed in
Great Britain at the University Press,
Cambridge

British Library
Cataloguing in Publication Data

Box, Steven
Power, crime and mystification. –
(Tavistock studies in sociology)
1. Crime and criminals
I. Title
364   HV6030
ISBN 0-422-76400-0
ISBN 0-422-76410-8 Pbk

Library of Congress
Cataloging in Publication Data

Box, Steven.
Power, crime, and mystification.
(Tavistock studies in sociology)
Bibliography: p.
Includes index.
1. Corporations—Great Britain—
Corrupt practices. 2. Police
corruption—Great Britain.
3. Police—Great Britain—Complaints
against. 4. Rape—Great Britain.
5. Power (Social sciences) 6. Female
offenders—Great Britain. I. Title.
II. Series.
HV9647.B69 1983   364.1'0941
83-9194
ISBN 0-422-76400-0
ISBN 0-422-76410-8 (pbk.)

Contents

For Cassius and Blossom

.

Preface

The germ of this book infected me on Trent Park underground station nearly five years ago. I asked Jock Young if he had any explanation for corporate crime. He gave me that wild-eyed, glazed stare of a man suddenly possessed by the light of truth (or finally overcome by the magical influence of too much *grand cru* Chablis – two bottles of Les Preuses 1970). After a moment, he yelled 'greed!', and silenced the noise of the incoming train. Before I could recover from this shattering revelation, he was hurtling off down the tracks to Ponder's End, that sociologists' paradise in North London immortalized in Julienne Ford's fairy tale 'Paradigms and Professor Popper's Poppies'.

I had only a dim awareness of corporate crimes, a condition caused, I hasten to add, not by my imbibing excesses. The reason was more mundane. These crimes had been rudely elbowed aside by those practitioners of traditional criminology who seemed obsessed with discovering why powerlessness, in one of its many guises, produced so much serious crime, and how, like good servants of the state, they might design policies for its control and eventual abolition. Their agenda was the swamp my generation waded through to arrive at those sweet-smelling, green pastures called initially the National Deviancy Conference, and later, for reasons only Stan Cohen understands, the National

Deviancy Symposium. Unfortunately the majority of those misbegotten offsprings of Robbins's permissive loins who made this trip in the later 1960s and early 1970s spent most of their energy opposing the criminological establishment on its own ground. With the notable exceptions of Frank Pearce and 'Kit' Carson, they ignored crimes committed by those in positions of corporate power and concentrated on remoulding the powerlessness-crime relationship by pointing accusing fingers at (and up) the police – a group *never* suspected of causing crime by traditional criminologists, who regarded labelling theory as a latter-day heresy.

It was in the context of this neglect that I asked Jock my innocent question. His terse answer, even though it may well be truth boiled down to its sticky essence, failed to satisfy me. There must be more to it than that, I hoped. Chapter 2 is an attempt to prove those hopes justified.

It would be unreasonable to place all the blame on Jock. PC Edwards must also accept a fair share. My arrest by this state bureaucrat nearly ten years ago and her subsequent articulate instructions in the shameless art of appearing beyond reproach, even whilst 'having it off with the family silver', focused my mind on police crime as nothing else had previously. Chapter 3 is the result.

This same state bureaucrat is partly responsible for Chapter 4. After endless rows over Susan Brownmiller's *Against Her Will*, Kubrick's *Clockwork Orange*, and Kesey's *One Flew Over the Cuckoo's Nest*, I decided to write something on rape and sexual assault.

Lesley Neville is another major culprit. Her unpublished autobiography, *I Was a Borstal Tearaway*, caused me to alter my views on the criminal propensities of the 'fairer' sex, or at least led me to stop regarding them as 'fairer', and write Chapter 5 instead.

Chris Hale would have had a lot to say about Chapter 6, as we have co-authored material on unemployment, crime, and imprisonment. But I didn't let him see it in time!

Finally, I would like to thank John Braithwaite, the boys and girls on Middlesex Polytechnic's MA Deviancy course, and John Burton, Director of the School for Conflict Studies, University of Kent, who assures me that the Arabic proverb appearing in the first edition of *Deviance, Society and Reality* (and censored in the second edition) was a mistranslation. It should have read: 'If shit became valuable, the poor would be born with two arsesoles, of which one's product at least would be expropriated by the ruling class.' Whether John is right or not, the sentiments certainly accord with those of this book. People in powerful positions will do, and have done some pretty dreadful things. Unfortunately this is all lost to those who concentrate entirely on crimes committed by the powerless. I hope that this book, in a modest way, redresses the balance. Crimes of the powerful can only be ignored at the risk of enormously increasing our chances of being victimized by them.

Rutherford College

1 Crime, power, and ideological mystification

Murder! Rape! Robbery! Assault! Wounding! Theft! Burglary! Arson! Vandalism! These form the substance of the annual official criminal statistics on indictable offences (or the Crime Index offences in America). Aggregated, they constitute the major part of 'our' crime problem. Or at least, we are told so daily by politicians, police, judges, and journalists who speak to us through the media of newspapers and television. And most of us listen. We don't want to be murdered, raped, robbed, assaulted, or criminally victimized in any other way. Reassured that our political leaders are both aware of the problem's growing dimensions and receptive to our rising anxieties, we wait in optimistic but realistic anticipation for crime to be at least effectively reduced. But apart from the number of police rapidly increasing, their technological and quasi-military capacities shamelessly strengthened, their discretionary powers of apprehension, interrogation, detention, and arrest liberally extended, and new prisons built or old ones extensively refurbished (all with money the government claims the country has not got to maintain existing standards of education, health, unemployment welfare, and social services), nothing much justifies the optimism.

The number of recorded serious crimes marches forever upward. During the decade 1970–80, serious crimes recorded by the police increased for nearly every category: violence against the person rose by 136 per cent, burglary by 44 per cent, robbery by 138 per cent, theft and handling by 54 per cent and fraud and forgery by 18 per cent. These increases were not merely artefacts of an increased population available to commit serious crimes. For even when the changing population size is controlled statistically, crimes continue to rise. Thus in 1950, there were 1,094 per 100,000 population. This rose to 1,742 by 1960, then to 3,221 by 1970, and reached 5,119 by 1980. From 1980 to 1981 they rose a further 10 per cent, to reach an all-time record. Ironically, as 'our' crime problem gets worse, the demand for even more 'law and order' policies increases, even though these are blatantly having no effect on the level of serious crimes. At least not on the level recorded by the police.

The result, so we are told, is that the 'fear of crime' has now been elevated into a national problem. Techniques for avoiding victimization have become a serious preoccupation: more locks on doors and windows, fewer visits after dark to family, friends, and places of entertainment, avoidance of underground and empty train carriages, mace sprays or personal alarm sirens held nervously in coat pockets, a growing unwillingness to be neighbourly or engage in local collective enterprises, furtive suspicious glances at any stranger, and attempts to avoid any encounter except with the most trusted and close friends.

Who are these 'villains' driving us into a state of national agoraphobia? We are told a fairly accurate and terrifying glimpse can be obtained of 'our' Public Enemies by examining the convicted and imprisoned population. For every 100 persons convicted of these serious crimes, 85 are male. Amongst this convicted male population, those aged less than 30 years, and particularly those aged between 15 and 21 years are over-represented. Similarly, the educational non-achievers are over-represented – at the other end of the educational achievement ladder there appear to be hardly any criminals, since only 0.05 per cent of people received into prison have obtained a university degree. The unemployed are currently only (sic) 14 per cent of the available labour force, but they constitute approximately 40 per cent of those convicted. Only 4 per cent of the general population are black, but nearly one-third of the convicted and imprisoned population are black. Urban dwellers, particularly inner-city residents, are over-represented. Thus the typical people criminally victimizing and forcing us to fear each other and fracture our sense of 'community' are young uneducated males, who are often unemployed, live in a working-class impoverished neighbourhood, and frequently belong to an ethnic minority. These villains deserve, so 'law and order' campaigners tell us ceaselessly in their strident moral rhetoric, either short, sharp, shock treatment, including death by hanging or castration by chemotherapy – 'off with their goolies' – or long, endless, self-destroying stretches as non-paying guests in crumbling, insanitary, overcrowded prisons constructed for the redemption of lost Christian souls by our Victorian ancestors. If only these ideas were pursued vigorously and with a vengeance morally justified by the offender's wickedness, then 'our' society would be relatively crime-free and tranquil. So 'law and order' campaigners tell us.

It is tempting to call all this hype – but that would be extreme! 'Conventional' crimes do have victims whose suffering is real; steps should be taken to understand and control these crimes so that fewer and fewer people are victimized. A radical criminology which appears to deny this will be seen as callous and rightly rejected. Furthermore, those crimes so carefully recorded and graphed in official criminal statistics *are* more likely to be committed by young males, living in poor neighbourhoods and so on. A radical criminology which appears to deny this will be seen as naive and rightly rejected. Finally, there are very good grounds for believing that the rising crime wave is real – material conditions for large sections of the community have deteriorated markedly. A radical criminology which remained insensitive of this would be guilty of forgetting its theoretical roots and rightly rejected. So the official portrait of crime and criminals is not entirely without merit or truth.

None the less, before galloping off down the 'law and order' campaign trail, it might be prudent to consider whether murder, rape, robbery, assault, and other crimes focused on by state officials, politicians, the media, and the criminal justice system do constitute the major part of our real crime problem. Maybe they are only *a* crime problem and not *the* crime problem. Maybe what is stuffed into our consciousness as *the* crime problem is in fact an illusion, a trick to deflect our attention away from other, even more serious crimes and victimizing behaviours, which objectively cause the vast bulk of avoidable death, injury, and deprivation.

At the same time, it might be prudent to compare persons who commit other serious but under-emphasized crimes and victimizing behaviours with those who are officially portrayed as 'our' criminal enemies. For if the former, compared to the latter, are indeed quite different types of people, then maybe we should stop looking to our political authorities and criminal justice system for protection from those beneath us in impoverished urban neighbourhoods. Instead maybe we should look up accusingly at our political and judicial 'superiors' for being or for protecting the 'real' culprits.

If we do this, we might also cast a jaundiced eye at the view that serious criminals are 'pathological'. This has been the favourite explanatory imagery of mainstream positivistic criminology. It was, however, an explanation that only remained plausible if crimes were indeed committed by a minority of individuals living in conditions of relative deprivation. For whilst this was true it was obvious, at least to the conservative mind, that 'something must be wrong with them'. However, if we look up rather than down the stratification hierarchy and see serious crimes being committed by the people who are respectable, well-educated, wealthy, and socially privileged then the imagery of pathology seems harder to accept. If these upper- and middle-class criminals are also pathological, then what hope is there for any of us! Wanting to avoid this pessimistic conclusion, we might instead entertain the idea that these powerful persons commit crimes for 'rational' – albeit disreputable – motives which emerge under conditions that render conformity a relatively unrewarding activity. Having rescued the powerful from 'abnormality' we might do the same for the powerless. Maybe they too are rational rather than irrational, morally disreputable rather than organically abnormal, overwhelmed by adversity rather than by wickedness.

If these are the lessons of prudence, then standing back from the official portrait of crime and criminals and looking at it critically might be a very beneficial move towards getting our heads straight.

However, there is an agonizing choice to make between at least two pairs of spectacles we might wear to take this critical look. We could wear the liberal 'scientific' pair, as did many young trendy academics during the 1960s and early 1970s when the stars of interactionism and phenomenology were in the ascendant. Or we might wear the radical 'reflexive' pair, whose lenses have been recently polished to a fine smoothness by those same trendy academics who have now entered a middle-age period of intellectual enlightenment! These spectacles do provide quite different views on the official portrait of crime and criminals.

Liberal 'scientism': partially blind justice

One way of getting a clear perspective on those crimes and criminals causing us most harm, injury, and deprivation is to excavate unreported, unrecorded, and non-prosecuted crimes. This can be achieved by sifting evidence from numerous self-reported crime studies and criminal victimization surveys. This is undoubtedly an important exercise for it leads us to reconsider the *validity* of official criminal statistics and the more extreme pronouncements made directly and uncritically from them.

What lessons are there to be learnt from the results of these surveys?

First, there is much more serious crime being committed than the official police records indicate. The emerging consensus is that one serious crime in three (excluding burglary and car theft) is reported to the police. This knowledge can and does add fuel to the alarmist 'law and order' fire: 'it's even worse than we imagined!' Second, although the official portrait of criminals is not untrue, it is inaccurate. It is more like a distorting mirror; you immediately recognize yourself, but not quite in a flattering shape and form familiar to you. Thus self-report data indicate that serious crimes are disproportionately committed by the young uneducated males amongst whom the unemployed and ethnically oppressed are over-represented, but the contribution they make is less than the official data implies. There are, it appears, more serious crimes being committed by white, respectable, well-educated, slightly older males and females than we are led to believe (Box 1981a: 56–93).

To the liberal 'scientific' mind, there are two problems here of 'slippage', one more slight than the other. Too many people fail to report crimes because they consider the police inefficient; we need to restore police efficiency in order to increase the reportage rate and hence obtain a better more reliable gauge of crime. The second, more important slippage, is that the administration of criminal justice is fine in principle, but is failing slightly in practice. The police pursue policies of *differential deployment* (for example, swamping certain parts of London where the West Indian population is prominent) and *'methodological suspicion'* (that is, routinely suspecting only a limited proportion of the population, particularly those with criminal records or known criminal associates). Coupled with these practices are *plea-bargaining* (negotiating a guilty plea in return for being charged with a less serious offence) and *'judicious' judicial decisions* (which take as much notice of who you are as they do of what you have apparently done). In other words, the police, magistrates, judges, and other court officials have too much discretion. The result is too much 'street-justice', 'charge-dealing', 'plea-bargaining', and 'disparate sentencing'. In these judicial negotiations and compromises, the wealthy, privileged, and powerful are better able to secure favourable outcomes than their less powerful counterparts (Box 1981a: 157–207). This slippage between ideal and practice reveals a slightly disturbing picture. The process of law enforcement, in its broadest possible interpretation, operates in such a way as to *conceal* crimes of the powerful against the powerless, but to *reveal* and *exaggerate* crimes of the powerless against 'everyone'.

Furthermore, because a substantial section of this criminalized population is stigmatized and discriminated against, particularly in the field of employment, its reproduction is secured; many of them, out of resentment, injustice, or desperation, turn to more persistent and even more serious forms of crime. This vicious circle increases the over-representation of the powerless in the highly publicized 'hardened' criminal prisoner population.

The outcome of these processes is that the official portrait of crime and criminals is highly selective, serving to conceal crimes of the powerful and hence shore up their interests, particularly the need to be legitimated through maintaining the appearance of respectability. At the same time, crimes of the powerless are revealed and exaggerated, and this serves the interests of the powerful because it legitimizes their control agencies, such as the police and prison service, being strengthened materially, technologically, and legally, so that their ability to survey, harass, deter, both specifically and generally, actual and potential resisters to political authority is enhanced.

To the liberal 'scientific' mind, a solution of this second and more important slippage would involve a strict limitation on police and judicial discretion and less stigmatization either by decriminalizing some be-haviours, or imposing less incarceration (Schur 1973). The adoption of these policies would narrow the 'official' differential in criminal behaviour between the disreputable poor and the respectable middle-class so that it approximated more closely the actual differences in criminal behaviour – at least criminal behaviour as defined by the state.

Radical 'reflexiveness': artful criminal definitions

Although an enormous amount of carefully buried crime can be un-earthed by this liberal 'scientific' excavation work, we will still be denied an adequate view of those whose crimes and victimizing behaviours cause us most harm, injury, and deprivation.

Through radical 'reflexive' spectacles, all this excavation work occurs so late in the process of constructing crime and criminals that it never gets to the foundations. Those committed to self-report and victimiza-tion surveys do not start off asking the most important question of all: 'what is serious crime?' Instead they take serious crime as a pre- and state-defined phenomenon. But by the time crime categories or defi-nitions have been established, the most important foundation stone of 'our crime problem' has been well and truly buried in cement, beyond the reach of any liberal 'scientific' shovel.

Aware that liberal 'scientists' arrive too late on the scene, radicals resolve to get up earlier in the morning. Instead of merely examining how the law enforcement process in its broadest sense constructs a false image of serious crime and its perpetrators, they suggest we should consider the *social construction of criminal law categories*. This involves not only reflecting on why certain types of behaviours are defined as criminal in some historical periods and not others, but also why a particular criminal law comes to incorporate from relatively homogeneous behaviour patterns only a portion and exclude the remainder, even though each and every instance of this behaviour causes avoidable harm, injury, or deprivation.

Some sociologists have pondered these issues and come to the conclusion that *criminal law categories are ideological constructs* (Sumner 1976). Rather than being a fair reflection of those behaviours objectively causing us collectively the most avoidable suffering, criminal law categories are artful, creative constructs designed to criminalize only some victimizing behaviours, usually those more frequently committed by the relatively powerless, and to exclude others, usually those frequently committed by the powerful against subordinates.

Numerous researchers (Chambliss 1964; Duster 1970; Graham 1976; Gunningham 1974; Hall 1952; Haskins 1960; Hay 1975; Hopkins 1978; McCaghy and Denisoff 1973; Platt 1969; and Thompson 1975) have produced evidence consistent with the view that criminal law categories are ideological reflections of the interests of particular powerful groups. As such, criminal law categories are resources, tools, instruments, designed and then used to criminalize, demoralize, incapacitate, fracture and sometimes eliminate those problem populations perceived by the powerful to be potentially or actually threatening the existing distribution of power, wealth, and privilege. They constitute one, and only one way by which social control over subordinate, but 'resisting', populations is exercised. For once behaviour more typically engaged in by subordinate populations has been incorporated into criminal law, then legally sanctioned punishments can be 'justifiably' imposed.

In a society such as ours, populations more likely to be controlled in part through criminalization,

> 'tend to share a number of social characteristics but most important among these is the fact that their behaviour, personal qualities, and/or position threaten the social relationships of production. . . . In other words, populations become generally eligible for management as deviant when they disturb, hinder, or call into question . . . capitalist modes of appropriating the product of human labour . . . the social conditions under which capitalist production takes place . . . patterns of distribution and consumption . . . the process of socialization for

productive and non-productive roles . . . and . . . the ideology which supports the functioning of capitalist society.'   (Spitzer 1975: 642)

However, this argument needs qualification. It does not maintain that all criminal laws directly express the interests of one particular group, such as the ruling class. Clearly some legislation reflects temporary victories of one interest or allied interest groups over others, and none of these may necessarily be identical or coincide with the interests of the ruling class. Yet the above argument does not demand or predict that every criminal law directly represents the interests of the ruling class. It recognizes that some laws are passed purely as symbolic victories which the dominant class grants to inferior interest groups, basically to keep them quiet; once passed, they need never be efficiently or systematically enforced. It also recognizes that occasionally the ruling class is forced into a tactical retreat by organized subordinate groups, and the resulting shifts in criminal law enshrine a broader spectrum of interests. But these victories are short lived. Powerful groups have ways and means of clawing back the spoils of tactical defeats. In the last instance, definitions of crime reflect the interests of those groups who comprise the ruling class. This is not to assume that these interests are homogeneous and without serious contradictions (Chambliss 1981). Indeed, it is just the space between these contradictions that subordinate groups fill with their demands for legal change.

It might be objected that even though *some* criminal laws are in the interests of the dominant class and that others which are obviously not in these interests are ineffectively enforced, thus making them dead-letter laws, it still remains true that laws proscribing those types of victimizing behaviours of which we are all too aware and which set the nerve-ends of neo-classical/conservative criminologists, such as Wilson (1975) and Morgan (1978) tingling with fear and loathing, *are in all our interests*. None of us wants to be murdered, raped, or robbed; none of us wants our property stolen, smashed, or destroyed, none of us wants our bodies punched, kicked, bitten, or tortured. In that sense, criminal law against murder, rape, arson, robbery, theft, and assault are in all our interests, since in principle we all benefit equally from and are protected by their existence. Without them life would be 'nasty, poor, solitary, brutish, and short'.

This is all true, but it is not all the truth. For some groups of people benefit more than others from these laws. It is not that they are less likely to be murdered, raped, robbed, or assaulted – although the best scientific evidence based on victimization surveys shows this to be true (Hindelang, Gottfredson, and Garofalo 1978) – but that in the criminal law, definitions of murder, rape, robbery, assault, theft, and other serious crimes are so constructed as to exclude many similar, and in important respects, identical acts, and these are just the acts likely to be committed more frequently by powerful individuals.

Thus the criminal law defines only some types of avoidable killing as murder: it excludes, for example, deaths resulting from acts of negligence, such as employers' failure to maintain safe working conditions in factories and mines (Swartz 1975); or deaths resulting from an organization's reluctance to maintain appropriate safety standards (Erickson 1976); or deaths which result from governmental agencies' giving environmental health risks a low priority (Liazos 1972); or deaths resulting from drug manufacturers' failure to conduct adequate research on new chemical compounds before embarking on aggressive marketing campaigns (Silverman and Lee 1974); or deaths from a dangerous drug that was approved by health authorities on the strength of a bribe from a pharmaceutical company (Braithwaite and Geis 1981); or deaths resulting from car manufacturers refusing to recall and repair thousands of known defective vehicles because they calculate that the costs of meeting civil damages will be less (Swigert and Farrell 1981); and in most jurisdictions deaths resulting from drunken or reckless people driving cars with total indifference to the potential cost in terms of human lives are also excluded.

The list of avoidable killings not legally construed as murder even in principle could go on and on. But the point should be clear. We are encouraged to see murder as a particular act involving a very limited range of stereotypical actors, instruments, situations, and motives. Other types of avoidable killing are either defined as a less serious crime than murder, or as matters more appropriate for administrative or civil proceedings, or as events beyond the justifiable boundaries of state interference. In all instances, the perpetrators of these avoidable 'killings' deserve, so we are told, less harsh community responses than would be made to those committing legally defined murder. The majority of people accept this because the state, by excluding these killings from the murder category, has signified its intention that we should not treat them as capital offenders. As the state can muster a galaxy of skilled machiavellian orators to defend its definitions, and has, beyond these velvet tongues, the iron fist of police and military physical violence, it is able to persuade most people easily and convincingly.

It may be just a strange coincidence, as Vonnegut often suggests, that the social characteristics of those persons more likely to commit these types of avoidable killings differ considerably to those possessed by individuals more likely to commit killings legally construed in principle as murder. That the former are more likely to be relatively more powerful, wealthy, and privileged than the latter could be one of nature's accidents. But is it likely?

The criminal law sees only some types of property deprivation as robbery or theft; it excludes, for example, the separation of consumers and part of their money that follows manufacturers' malpractices or advertisers' misrepresentations; it excludes shareholders losing their money because managers behaved in ways which they thought would be to the advantage of shareholders even though the only tangible benefits accrued to the managers (Hopkins 1980b); it excludes the *extra* tax citizens, in this or other countries, have to pay because: (i) corporations and the very wealthy are able to employ financial experts at discovering legal loopholes through which money can be safely transported to tax havens; (ii) Defence Department officials have been bribed to order more expensive weaponry systems or missiles in 'excess' of those 'needed'; (iii) multinational drug companies charge our National Health Services prices which are estimated to be at least £50 millions in excess of alternative supplies. If an employee's hand slips into the governor's pocket and removes any spare cash, that is theft; if the governor puts his hand into employees' pockets and takes their spare cash, i.e. reduces wages, even below the legal minimum, that is the labour market operating reasonably. To end the list prematurely and clarify the point, the law of theft includes, in the words of that anonymous poet particularly loved by teachers of 'A' level economic history, 'the man or woman who steals the goose from off the common, but leaves the greater villain loose who steals the common from the goose'.

The criminal law includes only one type of non-consensual sexual act as rape, namely the insertion of penis in vagina by force or threatened force; it excludes sexual intercourse between husband and wife, no matter how much the latter is beaten by the former to exercise his 'conjugal right'; it excludes most sexual acts achieved by fraud, deceit, or misrepresentation – thus a man may pose as a psychiatrist and prescribe sexual intercourse as therapy to a 'gullible female', because he knows the law will regard this as acceptable seduction rather than rape; it excludes men who use economic, organizational, or social power rather than actual or threatened force to overcome an unwilling but subordinate, and therefore vulnerable female; it excludes the forced insertion of any other instrument, no matter how sharp or dangerous. Thus out of a whole range of 'sexual' acts where the balance of consent versus coercion is at least ambiguous, the criminal law draws a line demarcating those where physical force is used or threatened from those where any other kind of power is utilized to overcome a female's resistance. The outcome is that men who have few resources other than physical ones are more likely to commit legally defined rape, whilst those men who possess a whole range of resources from economic patronage to cultural charm are likely to be viewed by the law as 'real men' practising their primeval arts – and that is something the majesty of the law should leave alone!

The criminal law defines only some types of violence as criminal assault; it excludes verbal assaults that can, and sometimes do, break a person's spirit; it excludes forms of assault whose injuries become apparent years later, such as those resulting from working in a polluted factory environment where the health risk was known to the employer but concealed from the employee (Swartz 1975); it excludes 'compulsory' drug-therapy or electric-shock treatment given to 'mentally disturbed' patients or prisoners who are denied the civilized rights to refuse such beneficial medical help (Mitford 1977; Szasz 1970, 1977a, 1977b); it excludes chemotherapy prescribed to control 'naughty' schoolboys, but includes physically hitting teachers (Box 1981b; Schrag and Divoky 1981).

The criminal law includes and reflects our proper stance against 'murderous' acts of terrorism conducted by people who are usually exploited or oppressed by forces of occupation. But it had no relevance, and its guardians remained mute ten years ago, when bombs, with the United States' and allied governments' blessing, fell like rain on women and children in Cambodia (Shawcross 1979), or when the same governments aid and support other political/military regimes exercising mass terror and partial genocide against a subjugated people (Chomsky and Herman 1979a, 1979b). The criminal law, in other words, condemns the importation of murderous terrorist acts usually against powerful individuals or strategic institutions, but goes all quiet when governments export or support avoidable acts of killing usually against the underdeveloped countries' poor. Of course there are exceptions – the Russian 'invasion' of Afghanistan was a violation of international law and a crime against humanity. It may well have been, but what about Western governments' involvement in Vietnam, Laos, Cambodia, Chile, El Salvador, Nicaragua, Suez, and Northern Ireland? Shouldn't they at least be discussed within the same context of international law and crimes against humanity? And if not, why not?

Thus criminal laws against murder, rape, robbery, and assault do protect us all, but they do not protect us all equally. They do not protect the less powerful from being killed, sexually exploited, deprived of what little property they possess, or physically and psychologically damaged through the greed, apathy, negligence, indifference, and the unaccountability of the relatively more powerful.

Of course, what constitutes murder, rape, robbery, assault, and other forms of serious crime varies over historical periods and between cultural groups, as the changes and contradictions *within* and *between* powerful interest groups, and the shifting alliances of the less powerful bring about slight and not-so-slight tilts of society's power axis (Chambliss 1981). But it is not justifiable to conclude from this that criminal law reflects a value-consensus or even results from the state's neutral refereeing among competing interest groups. It is, however, plausible to view criminal laws as the outcomes of clashes between groups with structurally generated conflicting interests, and to argue that the legislators' intention, or if that is too conspiratorial, then the law's latent function, is to provide the powerful with a resource to reduce further the ability of some groups to resist domination. Needless to stress the point, it is a resource eagerly used to punish and deter actual and potential resisters and thereby help protect the established social order (see Chapter 6).

Nothing but mystification

Unfortunately for those committed to the radical 'reflexive' view, there is nothing but mystification. Most people accept the 'official' view. They are very aware and sensitized to muggers, football hooligans, street vandals, housebreakers, thieves, terrorists, and scroungers. But few are aware and sensitized to crimes committed by *corporate top and middle management* against stockholders, employees, consumers, and the general public (see Chapter 2). Similarly there is only a fog, when it comes to crimes committed by *governments* (Douglas and Johnson 1977), particularly when these victimize Third World countries (Shawcross 1979) or become genocidal (Brown 1971, Horowitz 1977), or by *governmental control agencies* such as the police when they assault or use deadly force unwarrantedly against the public or suspected persons (see Chapter 3), or prison officers (Coggan and Walker 1982; Thomas and Pooley 1980), or special prison hospital staff when they brutalize and torture persons in their protective custody.

Few people are aware how men, who on the whole are more socially, economically, politically, and physically powerful than women, use these resources frequently to *batter* wives and cohabitees (Dobash and Dobash 1981), *sexually harass* their female (usually subordinate) co-workers, or *assault/rape* any woman who happens to be in the way (see Chapter 4). But we are very aware of female shoplifters and prostitutes, and those poor female adolescents who are 'beyond parental control' and in 'need of care and protection', even though this is a gross misrepresentation of female crime and though the relative absence of serious female crime contradicts the orthodox view that crime and powerlessness go hand in hand (see Chapter 5).

Few people become aware of crimes of the powerful or how serious these are, because their attention is glued to the highly publicized social characteristics of the convicted and imprisoned population. It is not directed to the records, files, and occasional publications of those quasi-judicial organizations (such as the Factory Inspectorate in the UK or the Federal Drug Administration in the US) monitoring and regulating corporate and governmental crimes. Because of this, people make the attractive and easy deduction that those behind bars constitute our most serious criminals. As this captive audience is primarily young males amongst whom the unemployed and ethnic minorities are over-represented, it is believed that they, and those like them, constitute our 'public enemies'. Had the results of self-report/victimization surveys and the investigations of quasi-judicial agencies been publicized as much as 'official criminal statistics', and had the radical jaundiced and cynical view of criminal definitions been widely publicized, then the mystification produced by focusing exclusively on the characteristics of the prison population would not be so easily achieved. Instead, there would be a greater awareness of how the social construction of criminal definitions and the criminal justice system operate to bring about this misleading image of serious criminals.

Definitions of serious crime are essentially ideological constructs. They do not refer to those behaviours which objectively and *avoidably* cause us the most harm, injury, and suffering. Instead they refer to only a sub-section of these behaviours, a sub-section which is more likely to be committed by young, poorly-educated males who are often unemployed, live in working-class impoverished neighbourhoods, and frequently belong to an ethnic minority. Crime and criminalization are therefore *social control strategies*. They:

(i) render underprivileged and powerless people more likely to be arrested, convicted, and sentenced to prison, even though the amount of personal damage and injury they cause may be less than the more powerful and privileged cause;

(ii) create the illusion that the 'dangerous' class is primarily located at the bottom of various hierarchies by which we 'measure' each other, such as occupational prestige, income level, housing market location, educational achievement, racial attributes – in this illusion it fuses relative poverty and criminal propensities and sees them both as effects of moral inferiority, thus rendering the 'dangerous' class deserving of both poverty and punishment;

(iii) render invisible the vast amount of avoidable harm, injury, and deprivation imposed on the ordinary population by the state, transnational and other corporations, and thereby remove the effects of these 'crimes' from the causal nexus for explaining 'conventional crimes' committed by ordinary people. The conditions of life for the powerless created by the powerful are simply ignored by those who explain crime as a manifestation of individual pathology or local neighbourhood friendship and cultural patterns – yet in many respects the unrecognized victimization of the powerless by the powerful constitutes a part of those conditions under which the powerless choose to commit crimes;

(iv) elevate the criminal justice into a 'community service' – it is presented as being above politics and dispensing 'justice for all' irrespective of class, race, sex, or religion – this further legitimates the state and those whose interests it wittingly, or otherwise, furthers;

(v) make ordinary people even more dependent upon the state for protection against 'lawlessness' and the rising tidal wave of crime, even though it is the state and its agents who are often directly and indirectly victimizing ordinary people.

Not only does the state with the help and reinforcement of its control agencies, criminologists, and the media conceptualize a particular and partial ideological version of serious crime and who commits it, but it does so by concealing and hence mystifying its own propensity for violence and serious crimes on a much larger scale. Matza captured this sad ironic 'truth' when he wrote:

'In its avid concern for public order and safety, implemented through police force and penal policy, the state is vindicated. By pursuing evil and producing the *appearance* of good, the state reveals its abiding method – the perpetuation of its good name in the face of its own propensity for violence, conquest, and destruction. Guarded by a collective representation in which theft and violence reside in a dangerous class, morally elevated by its correctional quest, the state achieves the legitimacy of its pacific intention and the acceptance of legality – even when it goes to war and massively perpetuates activities it has allegedly banned from the world. But that, the reader may say, is a different matter altogether. So says the state – and that is the final point of the collective representation [i.e. ideological construction – author].'   (Matza 1969: 196)

For too long too many people have been socialized to see crime and criminals through the eyes of the state. There is nothing left, as Matza points out, but mystification. This is clearly revealed in the brick wall of indignation which flattens any suggestion that the crime problem defined by the state is not the only crime problem, or that criminals are not only those processed by the state. There is more to crime and criminals than the state reveals. But most people cannot see it.

2 Corporate crime

'I can be free only to the extent that others are forbidden to profit from their physical, economic, or other superiority to the detriment of my liberty.'
(Émile Durkheim)

Although there have been few studies on public opinion and corporate crime (Cullen *et al.* 1982; Newman 1957; Reed and Reed 1975; Rossi *et al.* 1974; Schrager and Short 1980; Sinden 1980; Wolfgang 1980), they do provide a window on what can best be described as 'collective ignorance'. The one indisputable fact these studies revealed is that the majority of those interviewed were not familiar with the extent of, or damage caused by, corporate crime and amongst the 'knowledgeable' minority, few were able to define it with any precision. Public awareness of corporate crime has certainly increased recently, but none the less there is still more misinformation and mystification about this type of crime than about 'conventional' crime.

The root cause(s) of this collective ignorance is not too difficult to uncover. Corporate crime is rendered invisible by its complex and sophisticated planning and execution, by non-existent or weak law enforcement and prosecution, and by lenient legal and social sanctions which fail to reaffirm or reinforce collective sentiments on moral boundaries. In addition, the type of media to which the majority of people expose themselves under-reports corporate crime, especially in comparison with 'conventional' crimes. Popular television crime series, such as *Kojak, Minder, The Sweeney, Softly, Softly, Starsky and Hutch, Hill Street Blues, Shoestring, The Professionals, The Gentle Touch*, and *Z Cars, never* focus on corporate criminals, and hardly ever refer to a related but different type of upper-world crime, the white-collar criminal. Even when they deal with upper/middle class offenders, as in *Columbo*, it is not because they have committed corporate crimes, but because they have committed the stereotypical conventional crime of murder. A similar ideological one-sidedness holds both for newspapers and films (Chibnall 1977; Cohen and Young 1980; Winick 1978). The majority of people are therefore continually exposed to a portrait of crime in which the background consists of murder, rape, robbery, and theft, and the foreground is full of characters mainly drawn from poor, disorganized, lower-class neighbourhoods. No wonder that corporate crime is not viewed by many people, including most criminologists(!), as a pressing, serious social problem.

Whereas public ignorance of corporate crime is understandable, this latitude should not be extended to those criminologists who argue that our professional efforts should be directed, as they have been traditionally, towards street crimes rather than suite crimes. Foremost amongst these 'neo-classical/conservative' criminologists is James Q. Wilson, whose book *Thinking About Crime* reached the list of American Best Sellers. He considers (1975: xx) 'predatory street crime to be a far more serious matter than consumer fraud, anti-trust violations etc . . . because predatory crime . . . makes difficult or impossible the maintenance of meaningful human communities'.

In two senses, Wilson and other similar-minded authors fail to substantiate their position. First, they fail to discuss *empirically* the relative seriousness of corporate compared with 'conventional' crime. If, objectively, corporate crime is the more serious, in the sense that more people are avoidably killed, maimed, and robbed and that the last of these aggregated far exceeds the value of 'conventional' theft, then that in itself would justify prioritizing its study. Second, the majority of those suffering from corporate crime remain unaware of their victimization – either not knowing it has happened to them or viewing their 'misfortune' as an accident and 'no one's fault'. But the absence of public apprehension over corporate crime does not justify it being ignored by criminologists; rather, it should justify creating a publicity campaign to create an awareness of corporate crime. If the bulk of the community are being criminally victimized in ways they do not understand or realize, surely that too is sufficient reason for prioritizing the study of corporate crime.

A growing awareness of corporate crime

Over forty years ago, Sutherland's (1940, 1945, 1949) contribution to our knowledge and understanding of corporate crime was so significant that it led Mannheim to comment that if there were a Nobel Prize for Criminology, 'Sutherland would have been one of the most deserving' (1965: 470). Sutherland demonstrated that corporate crime was widespread and virtually endemic in contemporary national and transnational corporations. It flowed from a degree of social disorganization within these corporations and also from patterns of differential association amongst its higher-level officials. Its cost, in terms of money lost, was unimaginably enormous. Any criminology which did not devote considerable effort explaining and publicizing corporate crime would, in his view, have failed in its scientific duty.

Although it is now clear that Sutherland's attempt to fit, indeed squash, corporate crime into his theory of differential association has not proved comfortable, and that his concentration on the economic as opposed to the physical and social effects of corporate crime made his study too one-sided, it none the less did, at the time, constitute a rich legacy to bequeath to criminology. Sadly it was a legacy scorned by its putative beneficiaries. With the exception of some work by disciples of Sutherland (Clinard 1952; Cressey 1953; Hartung 1950), the study of corporate crime remained a deserted and neglected area for nearly two decades. And then, following Ralph Nader's (1965) exposure of the car industry's products as being 'Unsafe At Any Speed', the President's Task Force Report on crime (1967), and Watergate's revelation of massive corporate funds being paid illegally to curry political favours and destabilize South American democratic governments, there was a renewed interest in crimes committed in the good name of major corporations.

In his presidential address to the *Society for the Study of Social Problems*, Wheeler (1976) claimed that 'the patterns of illegal activity that lie at the core of large-scale corporate, industrial society . . . have been almost totally neglected'. He partly supported this belief by the fact that of the 3,700 books or articles listed in the two-volume *Criminology Index* (Wolfgang, Figlio, and Thornberry 1975) which reviews theoretical and empirical work in criminology from 1945 to 1972, there were only ninety-two, or about 2.5 per cent, dealing with white-collar or corporate crime. And if the former is subtracted on the grounds that crimes *against* corporations are dissimilar to crimes *for* corporations, then just over 1 per cent of the listed material referred to corporate crime. He urged his audience to attend to this neglect, for the topic was clearly a pressing social problem. In another presidential address, this time to the

Society for the Psychological Study of Social Issues, Stotland (1977) spoke
on the topic of 'white-collar criminals' and argued that although
we were beginning to know something about the people who
commit white-collar and corporate crime, we ought to intensify our
efforts.

Towards the end of the decade, these efforts were clearly being made.
Five books of readings on corporate, governmental, and powerful crimes
have been produced (Geis and Meier 1977; Geis and Stotland 1980;
Ermann and Lundman 1978; Douglas and Johnson 1977; Johnson and
Douglas 1978). There have been research monographs on corporate
crime and law enforcement processes in America (Clinard and Yeager
1980), Australia (Hopkins 1978), Britain (Carson 1981; Carson and
Martin 1974), and Canada (Goff and Reasons 1978). In addition there
has been a detailed examination of corporate behaviour in the North Sea
oilfields (Carson 1981) and transnational pharmaceutical corporations
(Braithwaite 1983). Bequai (1978) has 'summarized the facts' of corporate and white-collar crime, and Conklin (1977), Ermann and Lundman
(1982), and Pearce (1976) have proposed some theoretical understanding.

Finally, just to document the shift in concern about corporate crime,
Clinard and Yeager state that:

> 'Of 28 social problems textbooks published between 1964 and 1978, a
> total of only 110 pages discussed the importance of large corporations
> to society; of these pages only 11 mentioned corporate crime and all
> but one of these pages were contained in two textbooks published in
> 1978. Approximately 96 per cent of all social problems textbooks
> mentioning, generally briefly, either corporations or corporate crime
> were published in 1972 or later.'   (Clinard and Yeager 1980: 13)

This all testifies to a growing recognition of corporate crime as a social
problem, and a gradual, shocking realization that the victimization rate is
higher and causes more suffering than conventional crime. There is also
a growing sense of dismay that attempts to contain and control corporate
crime are largely absent or ineffectual. However, for us to improve our
ability to control corporate crime, it is first necessary to grasp just what it
is we might want to control.

Corporate crime – definition and illustrations

> 'Oh, but you who philosophize disgrace
> and criticize all fears,
> Bury the rags deep in your face

For now's the time for your tears.'
(from 'The Lonesome Death of
Hattie Caroll', Bob Dylan)

It is essential to conceptualize as precisely as possible the nature of corporate crime. Clearly, like many other crimes of the powerful, corporate crime is a 'legitimate racket' – to recall Al Capone's famous phrase – which displays the 'triumph of money over conscience'. But it has to be formulated more precisely if it is not to be confused with other crimes which have the dubious distinction of sharing these aphorismic characteristics. For instance, corporate crime is clearly committed *for* the corporate and not *against* it. Thus, such crimes as embezzlement and other examples of employee theft will not be included in this discussion of corporate crime.

Conklin (1977: 13) suggests the following definition:

> 'Business crime is an illegal act, punishable by a criminal sanction, which is committed by an individual or a corporation in the course of a legitimate occupation or pursuit in the industrial or commercial sector for the purpose of obtaining money or property, avoiding the payment of money or the loss of property, or obtaining business or personal advantage.'

Although Conklin is absolutely right to concentrate on the economic dimension of corporate crime, for ultimately it is always about money, it does obscure the fact that in pursuing economic goals there are *physical* as well as economic impacts, and these are sufficiently important to demand inclusion in any conceptualization. For this reason, Schrager and Short's definition (1977: 409) is worth considering:

> 'Organizational crimes are illegal acts of omission or commission of an individual or a group of individuals in a legitimate formal organization in accordance with the operative goals of the organization which have a serious physical or economic impact on employees, consumers or the general public.'

A number of points contained in this definition need to be spelt out. It clearly does not fall into the easy trap of arguing that for crime to exist there must first be intention. Any discussion of crime must be cognizant of the fact that serious adverse consequences can and often do follow from being indifferent to the outcome of one's actions (or inactions). To avoid considering these consequences on the grounds that they were not intended is not only to be blind to much human suffering, but also to accept the relative positions of *intention* compared with *indifference* on a

points to note about this def

common-sense hierarchy of immorality. In this conventional hierarchy, it is morally worse to intend harm than to be indifferent whether harm results from one's behaviour. But, as Reiman argues (1979: 60–1) this common sense can be turned on its head. If a person intends doing *someone* harm, it cannot be assumed that s/he displays a disdain towards humanity, although it is clearly directed towards the particular intended victim. However, if indifference characterizes the attitude a person has towards the consequences of his/her action, then s/he are indifferent as to who suffers – it could literally be anybody – and this does display disdain for humanity in general. In this sense, the intent to harm someone may be less immoral (or at least no more immoral) than to be indifferent as to whom is harmed. Evil should not be unrecognized merely because it is as banal as indifference; indifference rather than intent may well be the greater cause of avoidable human suffering, particularly in the case of corporate crime. Schrager and Short may not go this far, but they are certainly right to stress that corporate crime should be conceptualized so as to include acts of *omission* as well as the more obvious acts of commission.

Second, they stress that the pursuit of organizational goals is deeply implicated in the cause(s) of corporate crime. But it is important to realize that these goals are not the manifestation of *personal* motives cast adrift from organizational moorings, neither are they disembodied acts committed in some metaphysical sense by corporations. Rather, organizational goals are what they are perceived to be by officials who have been socialized into the organizational 'way of life' and who strive in a highly co-ordinate fashion to bring about collectively their realization. Of course, these strivings to realize organizational goals may become crystallized in standard operational procedures. These confront new employees at all bureaucratic levels as 'solid facts' to be learnt and practised rather than queried and altered. Thus the dead hand of the past presses heavily on the head of the present and gives corporate criminals a genuine sense of irresponsibility because they feel the corporation acting through them as mere passive intermediaries.

Third, although Schrager and Short's definition directs attention to *physical* as well as *economic* consequences of corporate crime, it neglects important victims, namely other corporations and organizations (Vaughan 1980). Through such corporate crimes as bribing foreign and domestic governmental officials, price-fixing, mergers and take-overs, fraudulent advertising, espionage, and patent violation, some competing corporations are forced into bankruptcy, others' capacity to compete is impaired, and still others are robbed of resources vital to maintaining their market position. Of course, these corporate crimes against other organizations ultimately have human victims, such as shareholders, taxpayers, Third World poor, and so on, but none the less it is important to see that corporations sometimes commit crimes against other corporations because this focuses our attention on a vital factor in the cause of such behaviour – namely competition under conditions of scarce or diminishing resources and markets. Schrager and Short's definition therefore needs to be amended with the addition 'general public *and other organizations*'.

Finally, Schrager and Short focus on 'illegal' acts, but they do not stress that this refers to acts punishable by the state regardless of whether they are subsumed under civil, administrative, or criminal law. It is essential however, to make this point strongly. Corporate crime is crime irrespective of whether it is only punishable by an administrative body, or whether it merely violates individuals' civil rights. It might be wondered why much corporate crime is dealt with by administrative agencies rather than criminal courts, but that does not justify excluding corporate acts regulated by administrative agencies from the study of corporate crime.

However, does even this wide definition go far enough? Ought it also to include those forms of deaths, injuries, and economic deprivations which are not as yet covered by criminal, administrative, or civil law, even though they are violations of 'human rights' (Schwendinger and Schwendinger 1975). This clearly raises enormous philosophical and political issues, and may if pushed to an extreme position, risk losing any sympathetic reception for the study and control of corporate crime from those of liberal sensibilities. Consequently this chapter settles on Schrager and Short's amended definition of corporate crime whilst remaining sensitive to those avoidable harmful corporate acts which are excluded. The implications of this will be considered later when the ability of transnational corporations to shape new legislation relating to corporate activities is discussed; this ability clearly enables corporations to prevent some of the avoidable deaths, injuries, and economic deprivation they cause from being included in new administrative regulations or criminal laws.

Before proceeding to estimate the costs of corporate crime, one last distinction needs to be made. In addition to crimes *for* corporations (corporate crimes) and crimes *against* corporations (employee crimes), there are also *criminal corporations*. These are corporations deliberately set up, taken over, or controlled for the explicit and sole purpose of executing criminal activity. An example of this is provided by Hopkins (1980b) in his analysis of an oil corporation which was established and run by a single family. He shows how the family used the corporation to execute a series of financial deals which possibly resulted in shareholders of that and other related companies losing over A$22 millions. A recent study of long-term fraud in the United Kingdom (Levi 1981) also documents how companies are set up with the deliberate intention of using them to obtain goods on credit for which payment is never intended to be made.

Although the crimes of criminal corporations are clearly serious, they should be kept analytically separate from corporate crime. Of course, such separation may not always be easy when dealing with real events. But none the less, it is better to start off with some conceptual purity or relatively homogeneous phenomenon in order first to describe better the extent of that particular type of crime, second to facilitate its sociological understanding, and finally to evaluate the likely effectiveness of possible control/regulation proposals.

CORPORATE CRIME KILLS

Whereas a person involved in the American *Mafia* could say, quite reasonably, 'what's all the fuss about, we only kill each other', the same could not be said in defence of some corporate crimes. When these result in avoidable death, and they do, then it could be anyone who just happens to be there – employees, consumers, ordinary citizens. Thus, in September, 1976, a fire aboard HMS Glasgow, which was at the time undergoing repairs in the Swan Hunter shipyard, resulted in the death of eight workers. The fire was the result of the company failing to provide a proper safe environment for such work (Health and Safety Executive 1980: 15). Following a hoist accident at the power station Littlebrook Dee, Kent, on 1 September, 1978, four people died and five were seriously injured. The cause of this was identified as the company's neglect of safety equipment (Health and Safety Commission 1980: 16). In 1972 at Buffalo Creek, West Virginia, 125 people were killed when a carelessly maintained dam burst (Stern 1976: 3) and at Willow Island, West Virginia, fifty-one people died when a cooling tower collapsed as a result of safety violations (Kennedy 1978). Early in 1979, fifty people lost their lives as a result of an explosion aboard the tanker Betelgeuse whilst it was anchored at Bantry Bay in County Cork. An Inquiry headed by an Irish High Court Judge, Mr Justice Declan Costello firmly placed the responsibility for this on two corporations, Total and Gulf, 'who deliberately decided not to carry out necessary repair work costing a mere £130,000 because they intended to sell the tanker' (*The Observer* 27.7.80: 2). Similar considerations appear to have preyed on the minds of Ford executives during the early 1970s. According to Dowie (1977), this auto-company sold the Pinto model for a period of six years even though they knew from their own test researchers that the product, which had been rushed from design to production in the short period of twenty-five months instead of the planned forty-three, was dangerous. The trouble was the improperly designed fuel tank; this tended to fracture, particularly after rear-end collisions. Dowie claims that between 500 and 900 burn deaths resulted from ensuing explosions. During the period 1969–79 there were, according to the Department of Energy, 106 fatalities on or around installations in the British sector of the North Sea. According to Carson (1981) many of these were avoidable and only occurred because safety standards which applied to onshore industries did not apply to offshore installations. In 1976 twenty-six men died in the Scotia mine, which was unsafe and had been the subject of 652 citing-for-violations of safety regulations (Caudill 1977). And so on . . .

CORPORATE CRIME INJURES

In the early 1960s over 300 consumers suffered adverse side effects from taking the chemical MER/29 which was advertised as medically beneficial to heart sufferers. These 300 suffered from a series of various iatrogenic complaints, including occasional disruption of the reproductive system, loss of hair or a change in its colour and texture, and a variety of eye disorders including the development of cataracts. Ungar (1973) alleges that the test results on which Merrell secured permission from the Federal Drug Administration to market the chemical substance were proven to be 'doctored', thus concealing the extent to which the company knew of the drug's adverse side-effects. But this example of corporate induced injury pales beside one which followed closely afterwards. As a consequence of taking the prescribed drug thalidomide, something like 8,000 pregnant mothers in the United States, Germany, Japan, Britain, Ireland, Sweden, Australia, Canada, Brazil, Italy, and Spain gave birth to monstrously deformed babies. The company which had discovered and later granted licences for the drug, Chemie Grunenthal of Germany, had criminal charges brought against them for deliberately falsifying the test data and concealing the truth about the drug's serious side effects (Sunday Times Insight Team 1979).

Not only are many consumers injured by corporate crime; thousands of employees too suffer from 'accidents' at work (which are in fact not pure accidents but events which spring directly from the conditions of production and are in that sense avoidable) or work-induced diseases, such as asbestosis, lung cancer, and mesothelioma.

CORPORATE CRIME ROBS

For seven years prior to 1961, twenty-nine electrical corporations, including some of the best known names in the country, such as General Electric and Westinghouse, conspired illegally to fix prices on large, mainly government contracts, so as to avoid competition and hence reap enormous illegal profit (Geis 1967; Smith 1961). In July 1977, Revco Drug Stores, one of America's largest discount drug chains, was found guilty of computer-generated double-billing schemes that resulted in the loss of over a half-million dollars in Medicaid funds to the Ohio Department of Public Welfare (Vaughan 1980). A well known Swiss-based pharmaceutical company was suspected by the British government of overcharging the National Health Service for the drug Valium; their agreement to repay £4.5 millions tacitly admitted guilt but not what proportion of their 'extra-legal' profits this sum represented. But these and other financial swindles pale into insignificance when compared to the Equity Funding Scandal (Blundell 1978; Dirks and Gross 1974; Soble and Dallos 1974). The directors and executives of Equity Funding simply made up insurance policies to inflate the company's business and hence improve its share prices. When the whistle was finally blown on the crime by a disgruntled ex-employee, thousands of policy-holders and share-holders simply lost all or a substantial part of their savings or expected pensions, amounting to somewhere between two and three billion dollars.

All the above *examples* of deaths, injuries, and economic losses caused by corporate acts are not the antics of one or two evil, or mentally disturbed, or relatively deprived senior employees. Rather they represent the rational choices of high-ranking employees, acting in the corporation's interests, to *intend* directly to violate the criminal law or governmental regulations, or to be *indifferent* to the outcome of their action or inaction, even though it might result in human lives obliterated, bodies mangled, or life-savings lost.

The physical, economic, and social costs of corporate crime

The physical effects of corporate misbehaviour are difficult to quantify precisely. But if what is sought is merely a gross comparison between the damage of corporate and 'conventional' crimes, then the current level of official information available provides sufficient facts to get the ratio in perspective. Thus workers die of *avoidable* industrial diseases and accidents, and it is sobering to compare these with the conventional crime of homicide. Reiman (1979: 75) estimates that in 1972 the number of persons in the USA dying from occupational hazards (diseases and accidents) was 114,000, whereas only 20,600 died from being shot, cut, beaten, or poisoned, and being recorded as a homicide case. If there were a time clock for murder, it would show one every twenty-six minutes. But as Reiman so graphically points out:

'If a similar crime clock for industrial deaths were constructed . . . and recalling that this clock ticks only for that half of the population that is in the labour force – this clock would show an industrial death about every four and a half minutes! In other words, in the time it takes for one murder on the crime clock, six workers have died "just trying to make a living"!'   (Reiman 1979: 68)

A similarly disturbing picture emerges if we consider the relevant data for Britain. In the table below (*Table 1*), which shows data for the years 1973–79, the combined number of employees dying from fatal accidents or occupational diseases (most of which are avoidable if employing corporations obeyed government regulations and designed safe production schedules or paid for hazard-free work environments) far exceed the number of homicide cases recorded by the police. Furthermore, this comparison becomes even more shocking when it is remembered that the population at risk of being killed at work is *less than half* those who could be 'murdered'. In other words, to obtain an initial fair comparison we would have to multiply the industrial related deaths by at least a factor of two and compare that figure with the number of recorded homicide cases. The result is approximately seven to one!

But even this ratio puts the *best possible* light on the contribution made by employment to the avoidable death toll. For although we can be fairly sure that the recorded homicide figure is reasonably valid, we cannot have the same confidence in the data on occupationally related deaths. The cause of death is frequently ambiguous and pinning it down to occupational environments, which may have been experienced years or even decades ago, is clearly no easy matter. Furthermore, in the processes of socially constructing the cause(s) of death, there are considerable social forces directed towards minimizing the number of deaths certified as occupationally induced.

Since such fatalities are frequently *avoidable*, each one is an indictment of corporate practices, and consequently wherever pressure can be brought to bear, either in the process of recognizing a fatal disease-causing work condition or in the enforcement practices, corporate officials will lean towards favouring those definitions and arrangements which minimize the recording of deaths as arising from occupational hazards. Thus executives have successfully prevented most forms of cancer from being included in the list of occupationally-induced illness, even though the documentation on carcinogenic work environments is substantial (Epstein 1979).

In the endeavour to minimize the contributions work environments make to avoidable fatalities, state officials also play a significant part. They will probably err on the side of caution whenever attempting to unravel the cause of death because recording it as occupationally induced requires the subsequent payment of industrial death benefits. Evidence consistent with this view came to light recently whilst Yorkshire TV was making a documentary on asbestos. It discovered 'that death certificates often do not mention asbestos diseases even when the coroner has conclusive and documented evidence that they were the cause of death. As a consequence, spouses and relatives have been prevented from claiming compensation' (Cutler 1982).

These two forces tend to depress the level of recorded occupationally induced death below a level it would be otherwise. Therefore, to re-echo Reiman: you stand more chance of being killed *avoidably* at work than in any other sphere of your life, including being at home!

But don't feel safe staying at home! The long arm of the corporation's grim reaper is not deterred by such agoraphobic precautions. Consumers may be poisoned in their beds by improperly tested medical drugs, they may be killed over their dinner tables by unhygienically prepared food, they may be blown up to God knows where by the neighbourhood chemical complex exploding, and they may become fatally diseased in their living rooms by industrial pollution. For example, a recent chilling national survey of pollution and its chronic effects on the lives and deaths of American citizens concluded that approximately 9 per cent of all deaths, that is, 140,000 a year, may be attributable to air pollution.

It was because of this shocking rate of avoidable death that the British Society for the Social Responsibility of Science published *Asbestos – Killer Dust* in 1979. In this report, it accused the asbestos industry of deliberately pursuing profit in the face of known dangers, and 'in the light of the damage done to people working in the industry and likely to occur in the future, . . . it is simply incredible' that nothing much is done about it. It concluded that those responsible should be treated like criminals who allow dangerous cars on the road. But it is clear from the Asbestos Advisory Council's latest Report (1980) that this will not happen, so they remain, in Swartz's (1975) chilling words, 'silent killers at work', far more deadly than the phantom killer of the opera. But unfortunately this is not how most people see it. When they think of mass

Table 1   Homicides finally recorded by the police compared with fatal occupational accidents and deaths from occupational diseases, England and Wales, 1973–79

	1 *fatal occupa-* *tional* *accidents*[1]	*2* *deaths from* *occupational* *diseases*[2]	*3* *col. 1 plus* *col. 2*	*4* *deaths finally* *recorded as homi-* *cides by the police*[3]
1973	873	910	1,783	391
1974	786	911	1,697	526
1975	729	957	1,686	444
1976	682	976	1,658	489
1977	614	916	1,530	418
1978	751	866	1,617	472
1979	711	752	1,463	551
total	5,146	6,290	11,436	3,291
adjusted for population at risk (approx)			22,872 7 : 1	

[1] Health and Safety Executive (1980) *Health and Safety Statistics, 1977.* London: HMSO, p. 4 and (1981) *Health and Safety Statistics, 1978/9.* London: HMSO, p. 12
[2] Health and Safety Executive (1980) p. 58 and Health and Safety Executive (1981) p. 63
[3] *Criminal Statistics England and Wales, 1980*, London: HMSO, p. 61 (Murder, Manslaughter, etc.)

murderers, they normally think of one person killing unlawfully a handful of other people. But when many people die from known carcinogenic work-conditions or their employer's refusal to put right unsafe equipment, machinery, or buildings, this is normally seen as a 'disaster', even though their deaths were easily avoidable. In the case of asbestos for example, there has been a voluminous medical literature on its direct link with asbestosis, lung cancer, and mesothelioma. Of course employers can claim unawareness of obscure medical journals. But during a series of lawsuits against Johns-Manville, Pittsburgh Corning, and other asbestos manufacturers, it was revealed that they did know directly from their own scientific researchers whose implicatory findings were suppressed (Ermann and Lundmann 1982: 68–9).

Maybe the only, but significant difference between the two is that corporate crimes 'kill more people than are murdered by acts that come to be listed as criminal homicide in the (American) Uniform Crime Rates' (Geis 1975: 93).

On the occasions when corporate negligence, indifference, or apathy does not result in employees, consumers, or the public being killed, it often leaves them seriously injured or ill. Thus in Britain from 1973 to 1979 there was an annual average of 330,000 non-fatal accidents at work. The vast bulk of these were not caused by employees' carelessness or stupidity but by the conditions under which they are obliged to work. These put pressure on employees to take risks – even violating the corporation's own safety standards. But in this contradiction between productivity and safety, between speed and conformity to regulations, which does the corporation prioritize? A clear answer is given in Carson's (1981) analysis of the other price paid for North Sea oil. He claims that when oil companies were faced with the contradictory demand for speedy exploration and extraction and the requirements of safety they, with successive British governments' blessing, chose speed. Consequently most accidents, and there were nearly 500 of them during the 1970s, were not the result of employee thoughtlessness but emerged directly out of the contradictory demands made upon the workforce. Also during the period 1973–79, there was an annual average of nearly 14,000 persons diagnosed as suffering from an occupationally induced disease. The number of persons injured or made ill at work far exceeds the number against whom indictable crimes of violence, including rape and indecent assault, were committed. Thus in 1977 over 340,000 persons at work in the UK suffered through accidents and occupationally-induced ill health compared with 93,500 persons victimized by indictable crimes of violence. If we multiply the former figure by a factor of two to obtain a roughly comparable population at risk size, we arrive at a ratio of seven to one in favour (*sic*) of work-induced avoidable suffering. The magnitude of this ratio, rather than the exact validity of the aggregate figures on which it is based, ought to be stressed, for it reveals just how much more objective damage is caused to persons at work than members of the public experience through 'conventional' criminal violence.

But even these comparisons understate the excessive amount of corporate-induced death and suffering because they omit any reference to consumers *physically* harmed by the sale of improperly researched substances, dangerous or poisonous products, and so on, or citizens physically harmed through industrial air pollution. According to the American National Commission on Product Safety (1971: 1) approximately 20 millions out of a total population of over 250 million are seriously injured annually by consumer products, with 110,000 resulting in permanent disability and 30,000 resulting in death. And according to the American National Cancer Institute, one of the major causes of lung cancer is 'neighbourhood air pollution from industrial sources of inorganic arsenic' (Reiman 1979: 78). Other types of cancer were also found to be higher in geographical areas where chemical plants were situated.

So if consumer and citizen avoidable death and injury were added to workers avoidably killed and injured, then the ratio between corporate criminal violence and 'conventional' criminal violence would clearly put the former in an extremely unfavourable light. Indeed, it would be seen as a major source of avoidable and illegal human suffering. This conclusion should not be seen to reflect callous indifference to individuals who have suffered miserably or fatally at the hands of persons committing 'conventional' crimes; their agony is real and should never be ignored. But neither should we enable this sympathy to blind us to the greater truth that more persons suffer, many fatally, from corporate crime than 'conventional' crime. If we are to prioritize the study and publicization of one, surely it should be that which, in objective terms, causes more human suffering rather than the other which is *perceived* by the public to be the more serious even though they are clearly wrong.

In *Pretty Boy Floyd*, Woody Guthrie caught poetically the awesome and terrifying instrument through which corporate officials economically harm others. He wrote:

> 'Now as through this world I ramble,
>   I see lots of funny men,
> Some rob you with a six gun,
>   And some with a fountain pen.'

This irony was not lost on a US judge. 'In our complex society', he said, 'the accountant's certificate and the lawyer's opinion can be instruments for inflicting pecuniary loss more potent than the chisel or crowbar' (Morgenthau 1969: 17).

Robbing others, directly or indirectly, is a major form of corporate criminal activity. Price fixing (Geis 1967; Smith 1961) and illegal monopoly pricing (Klass 1975) both mean that customers pay more than they would under competitive conditions; bribing corrupt officials (Braithwaite 1979b; Jacoby, Nehemlis, and Ells 1977) may mean reducing competitors' profit margins or even driving them into bankruptcy; illegal mergers and take-overs and other shady financial manoeuvres may result in many shareholders being defrauded (Hopkins 1980b); misleading advertising as well as trimming production costs may result in customers buying goods whose quality fails totally to match manufacturers' glossy claims, thus leaving a swindled consumer population (Moffit 1976); corporate tax evasion and avoidance may mean more average taxes paid by individual members of the public (Vanick 1977).

Given the relative invisibility of these crimes, even to those victimized, the fact that they are infrequently reported to or detected by relevant authorities, the absence of any centralized data-collecting agency, and the inconsistent publication of those that are collected, it is impossible to quantify with any accuracy just how serious corporate crime is in economic terms. Furthermore, the figures involved are so astronomic as to be literally incomprehensible. The public understands more easily what it means for an old lady to have five pounds snatched from her purse than to grasp the financial significance of 25 million customers paying one penny more for orange juice diluted beyond the level permitted by law. The public tend to focus more on the one penny than on the quarter of a million illegal profit and conclude that the incident is insignificant. But it is not.

There have been attempts to estimate the economic cost of corporate crimes and render these in a meaningful fashion (Bequai 1978: 1; Clinard 1978: 83–102; Conklin 1977: 2–8; Geis 1975: 95–7; Hills 1971: 167–68; McCaghy 1976: 205; President's Task Force Report 1967: 47–51; Stotland 1977: 180–82). Although authors have arrived at different figures, thus reflecting the inherent difficulty and speculative nature of the task involved, they have been unanimous in one conclusion: persons are deprived of far more money by corporate crimes than they are by ordinary economic crimes, such as robbery, theft, larceny, and auto-theft. Conklin (1977: 4) estimates that in 1977 these four offences in the USA accounted for between $3–4 billions compared with the annual loss of around $40 billions resulting from various white-collar crime, of which consumer fraud, illegal competition, and deceptive practices account for at least half. Johnson and Douglas (1978: 151) point out that the Equity Funding scandal, 'perhaps one of the largest securities and investment frauds ever perpetuated on the American public, . . . involved more losses than the total losses of *all* street crime in the US for one year'. In a similar vein, Geis (1978: 281) writes that 'the heavy electrical equipment price-fixing conspiracy alone involved theft from the American people of more money than was stolen in all of the country's robberies, burglaries, and larcenies during the years in which the price fixing occurred'.

Whether we are consumers or citizens, we stand more chance of being robbed by persons who roam corporate suites than we do by those who roam public streets. Furthermore, *in the aggregate* we stand to be robbed of far more by these fine gentlemen acting in the good name of their corporation than by the common rogues apparently acting from some morally worthless motive.

Finally, there are the social consequences of corporate crime compared with 'conventional' crime. A number of writers have recently argued very strongly that the *latter* is more corrosive to social life. Thus Wilson writes:

> 'Predatory crime does not merely victimize individuals, it impedes and, in the extreme case, even prevents the formation and maintenance of community. By disrupting the delicate nexus of ties, formal and informal, by which we are linked with our neighbours, crime atomizes society and makes of its members mere individual calculators estimating their own advantage, especially their own chances for survival amidst their fellows. Common undertakings become difficult except for those motivated by a shared desire for protection.'
>
> (Wilson 1975: 21)

And echoing this sentiment, a British criminologist claims:

> 'If the cities are to be saved as centres of a civilized urban life, and not plunged into gutted and fearful waste-lands . . . delinquency will have to be tackled as a problem with high priority – perhaps as *the* urban problem. City life cannot exist without security in its open spaces, some unarmed trust and reciprocity. In Britain . . . there is a mass exodus of skilled workers and middle class groups from the metropolis and other inner cities . . . these areas are left with heavily welfare-dependent populations; the old, the sick, the handicapped, the uneducated, the dull, the retarded, and the unskilled. What is not realized . . . is that although the movement from the cities has many other long-term causes, delinquency has now ceased to be merely a symptom of urban breakdown (if it ever was) . . . and has become a major contributor to it.'
>
> (Morgan 1978: 21)

Furthermore, she argues that unless some inroad is made now into reducing or containing the problem of street crime, the loss of community will spread outwards, like a cancerous growth, to desirable middle-class areas in the city.

At an abstract level, these arguments are probably true. Beyond historically determined levels of societal tolerance, crime is dysfunctional to social life. But the issue is, on which type of crime ought we to be concentrating? Surely the deleterious consequences street crime has on our sense of community pale beside the way in which corporate crime fractures the economic and political system. Thus Conklin, reiterating the President's Commission on Law Enforcement and Administration of Justice, writes that:

'such offences "are the most threatening of all – not just because they are so expensive, but because of their corrosive effect on the moral standards by which American business is conducted". Business crimes undermine public faith in the business system because such crime is integrated with "the structure of legitimate business". Such crime reduces willingness to engage in commercial transactions. Stock manipulations and frauds undermine the capitalist system, which requires public investment for capital. The discovery of fraud through adulteration and mislabelling of grain which is shipped abroad has created distrust among foreign businessmen who purchase grain from American companies.'   (Conklin 1977: 7)

Writing on another type of corporate crime, Braithwaite argues that:

'Bribery and corruption by large corporations are most serious forms of crime because of their inegalitarian consequences. When a governmental official in a Third World country recommends (under the influence of a bribe) that his country purchase the more expensive but less adequate of two types of aircraft, then the extra millions of dollars will be found from the taxes sweated out of the country's impoverished citizens. For a mass consumer product, the million dollar bribe to the civil servant will be passed on in higher places to the consuming public. While it is conceivable that bribes can be used to secure the sale of a better and cheaper product, the more general effect is to shift the balance of business away from the most efficient producer and in favour of the most corrupt producer. The whole purpose of business-government bribes is after all, the inegalitarian purpose of enticing governments to act against the public interest and in the interests of the transnational. Every act of political corruption rewards corruptibility in politics and exacerbates the social selection into public office of those who are most adeptly corrupt. To the extent that politics and government administration become more corrupt, then to that extent will men and women of high principle find entry into politics repugnant. *Transnational corporate corruption is therefore perhaps the most pernicious form of crime in the world today because it involves robbing the poor to feed the rich, and brings into political power rulers and administrators who in general will put self-interest ahead of the public interest, and transnational corporation interest ahead of national interest.*'
                    (Braithwaite 1979b: 126)

Whether one agrees with the sentiments expressed by Wilson and Morgan on the one hand or the President's Commission and Braithwaite on the other is not a matter of blind prejudice, but of weighing carefully the relevant evidence. From the evidence presented above – and this is merely illustrative of the evidence available – it should be clear that corporate crime ought to be a prioritized concern because it is the more serious. This concern should focus first on understanding 'how it is possible' for corporate crime to be endemic in our 'law and order' society, and second, and hopefully flowing from this understanding, 'how can it be contained or regulated?'

But before proceeding, a caveat needs to be made. Prioritizing corporate crime has to be set in context. It has been neglected relative to the study of conventional/street crime. To argue now for its prioritization means no more than demanding as much attention be given to it as there is to street crimes. There is no concealed value judgement here that street crimes are less of a social problem, particularly if the degree of fear and apprehension experienced by the majority of citizens is considered. Citizens in inner-city areas are desperately worried and rightly so, about street crime. That terrain, so proudly occupied by the radical Right's law and order campaigners, has to be won back, and Ian Taylor's (1982) recent attempt, following earlier sorties of Platt (1978) represents the appropriate move from the Left. But whilst the law and order debate ebbs and flows over the political terrain, there is a strategic need to establish a second front where radical criminology takes on corporate crimes and crimes of other powerful institutions and privileged people.

Explaining corporate crime

> 'The greatest evil is not now done in those sordid "dens of crime" that Dickens loved to paint. It is not done even in concentration camps and labour camps. In those we see its final result. But it is conceived and ordered (moved, seconded, carried and minuted) in clean, carpeted, warmed and well-lighted offices, by quiet men with white collars and cut fingernails, and smooth-shaven cheeks who do not need to raise their voices. Hence, naturally enough, my symbol for Hell is something like . . . the offices of a thoroughly nasty business concern.'
>
> (C. S. Lewis, *The Screwtape Letters and Screwtape Purposes*)

ORGANIZATIONS ARE CRIMINOGENIC

Merton's (1938) attempt to explain crime as a response to anomie – the disjuncture between cultural goals of success and legitimate opportunity structures through which success might be realized – has been reproduced over 110 times, a fact which in itself testifies to the importance of this analysis. Because of, rather than despite its fame, it has been subjected to a prolonged critical attention (Clinard 1964; Lemert 1967; Taylor, Walton, and Young 1973; Thio 1975). Among the various criticisms of Merton's analysis one is particularly relevant to any discussion of corporate crime. Anomie only offers a plausible account of deviant motivation *if* the cultural goal of success is as unidimensional as Merton suggests and *if* the pursuit of this goal is prevalent amongst those with blocked legitimate opportunities. Many critics point to empirical evidence which fails to support these conditional clauses. They argue that industrialized societies are characterized by a plurality of cultural goals and these vary systematically among individuals in different strata and many individuals in the lower strata have limited and realistic ambitions. This makes the simple characterization in Merton's analysis unacceptable, *at least as a motivational account of why lower-class persons might commit crimes.*

This criticism would not be valid if anomie analysis were applied to corporate crime. For the one characteristic organization theorists (Blau and Scott 1962; Etzioni 1961; Parsons 1963) agree on is that corporations, like all organizations, are primarily orientated towards the achievement of a particular goal – profit – at least in the long run. In the short run, other goals, such as growth through acquisition or increased market share may be emphasized. Diversification, particularly into potentially competing industries might become a preferred short-term stratagem. For instance, the American oil industry has fairly recently expanded into the solar, sea, and wind energy industries so that in the long run competition between alternative forms of energy can be regulated. Finally, vertical expansion so that suppliers can be controlled may also be a short-run goal. But in the final instance, these short-run goals are pursued with a green glinted eye focused on long-run profitability.

This defining characteristic – it is a goal-seeking entity – makes a corporation inherently criminogenic, for it necessarily operates in an uncertain and unpredictable environment such that its purely legitimate opportunities for goal achievement are sometimes limited and constrained. Consequently, executives investigate alternative means, including law avoidance, evasion, and violation and pursue them if they are evaluated as superior to other available strictly legitimate alternatives.

Environmental uncertainties for a corporation are so numerous as to defy classification, but none the less, there are five important sources of problems which potentially interfere with a corporation's ability to achieve its goal(s) easily without bending, evading, or breaking legal regulations. These sources are:

Competitors – technological breakthroughs; price structure; marketing techniques; mergers; new or expanding markets;

Governments – extending regulations to cover more corporate activities either through new laws or tougher enforcement of existing laws;

Employees – any collusive activity, but especially those joining trade unions pursuing 'militant' wage settlements and making 'radical' demands on altering conditions of work/employment;

Consumers – especially when demand for product is elastic and consequently fickle, or when 'consumerism' is prevalent and making highly visible any dubious corporate practice;

Public – especially through a growing 'environmentalist' sensitivity to conserving fresh air, clean countryside, and natural resources.

The contradictions between corporate goal-achieving behaviour and each of these environmental uncertainties creates a strong strain towards innovative behaviour which can stretch over the spectrum law abiding – law avoiding – law evading – law breaking. Examples of the last possibility can be associated with each of these environmental uncertainties. Thus:

Competitors – espionage, arson, patent copying; bribery and corruption to influence those in new or expanding markets, such as government officials in developing economies (Braithwaite 1979b; Jacoby, Nehemlis, and Ells 1977); price-fixing to squeeze out new competitors or to rationalize competition (Fuller 1962; Geis 1967; Smith 1961); mergers or take-overs in violation of anti-monopoly legislation (Snider 1978).

Governments – tax evasion through to avoidance especially for transnational corporations (Vanick 1977); illegal campaign funds to politicians in return for promises (Chambliss 1978); bribing state officials in return for later lucrative employment; fraudulent information to prevent, influence, or repeal legislation (Schrag and Divorky 1981: 94–127; Sunday Times Insight Team 1979: 90–116; Ungar 1972); exporting illegal behaviour to another state where it is not illegal (Braithwaite 1979b); fraudulent billing of government body (Klass 1975; Vaughan 1980).

Employees – pay less than legal minimum wage; non-recognition and harassment of trade unions (Krisberg 1975: 44; Pearce 1976: 97–100; Weiss 1978); refusal to make work conditions safe or properly inspected/maintained (Ashford 1976; Swartz 1975).

Consumers – fraudulent advertising, misleading sales behaviour; false labelling of products (Rothschild and Thorne 1976; Schrag 1971; Moffit 1976); manufacture and distribution of untested and dangerous products (Dowie 1977; Vandivier 1972; Sunday Times Insight Team 1979); exportation of products which are safe and healthy in one cultural environment but poisonous in another (Muller 1974;

Chetley 1979); selling adulterated goods; selling goods at 'over-inflated prices' (Monopolies and Mergers Commission 1980).

Public – pollution of air and land; depletion of scarce resources; increased tax bill (because of corporate tax avoidance schemes); refusal to make safe areas of contact between corporation and public (Stern 1976); bribery and corruption to undermine the democratic process (Braithwaite 1979b; Ermann and Lundman 1982: 106–26).

From the above argument a simple hypothesis can be inferred: *when these environmental uncertainties increase so the strain towards corporate criminal activity will increase*. Of course other factors will need to intervene to transform this motivational strain into actual behaviour; that they frequently do intervene can be judged from the following research.

Staw and Szwajkowski attempted to test the following hypothesis: 'when the organization is located within a scarce environment, one method of coping with intra- and extra-organizational demands may be to perform activities which are legally questionable . . . the more scarce the environment of a business organization, the more likely it will engage in activities which are considered unfair market practices or restraints of trade' (1975: 346–47). Their dependent variable constituted 105 large companies (drawn from the 500 largest firms in the US) which during the period 1968–72 were involved in trade litigation for committing, or having being accused of committing, one or more of the following: price discrimination, tying arrangements, refusal to deal, exclusive dealing, franchise violation, price fixing, foreclosure of entry, reciprocity, allocation of markets, monopoly, conspiracy, and illegal mergers and acquisitions. Their independent variable consisted of the firm's financial performance, particularly return on equity and return on sales compared with the remaining non-litigated top 500 firms. The results of their analysis strengthens their belief that 'environmental scarcity does appear to be related to a range of trade violations' (Staw and Szwajkowski 1975: 353). It appears therefore that these types of corporate crime serve not only to reduce environment uncertainty but point to *resource procurement* (i.e. grabbing more) as a particularly important organizational source of motivation to commit these crimes.

BRINGING CUNNING PEOPLE IN TO DO THE DIRTY WORK

'The Lilliputians look upon fraud as a greater crime than theft, and therefore seldom fail to punish it with death; for they allege that care and vigilance, with a very common understanding, may preserve a man's goods from theft, but honesty has no defence against superior cunning.'   (from Jonathan Swift's *Gulliver's Travels*)

Although corporate crime represents an attempt to resolve some contradictions between pursuing a limited number of organizational goals and environmental constraints, it is an attempt initiated and implemented by *individuals*. Organizations *per se* do not plan, think, or act; there are human agents eagerly willing to accomplish these in its good name. Consequently, whilst corporate crime cannot be understood without grasping the fact that it stems from contradictions between a corporation's goal(s) and its environment, that understanding remains one-sided if individuals are left out of the analysis. Traditionally, individuals have been the central feature of attempts to understand corporate crime, but unfortunately for criminology, it was their pathological characteristics which were advanced as the cause of their deviations. Consequently, the unity between organizational demands and officials' behaviour was fractured and until this was healed, understanding corporate crime remained crippled.

As the vast bulk of corporate crime is initiated (if not always implemented) by high-ranking officials, two processes need to be considered: (i) whether factors associated with upward mobility in corporations are inherently criminogenic; and (ii) whether the social-psychological consequences of success within a corporation are criminogenic.

Stotland (1977) drew a portrait of the executive's motives for being prepared to go along with corporate crime. He argued that these were: a desire to secure career advancement or at least not prejudice career chances; a willingness to push matters in order to measure his own cleverness and particularly dexterity at getting around the rules; to experience the satisfaction which comes from having the power that goes both with high corporate status and criminally victimizing other organizations or persons; a need to maintain his position within the peer group or family network. However this sketch hardly rises above a 'Dallas'-type description and Stotland failed to provide any empirical grounding for his arguments. Furthermore, it offered only a static picture of the corporate executive and fails to visualize him as caught in and conditioned by organizational processes of career advancement.

To move beyond this inadequate description, Gross (1978) argued that we should analyse the social characteristics of corporate criminals first by visualizing what qualities these *organizational positions* demand, and second by considering whether younger corporate officials who preen themselves to fit this image are more likely to succeed in their career. In other words, we should examine in detail the career mobility patterns within and between corporations, for those who succeed are more likely to have just those qualities which corporate crime requires.

Gross examined over one dozen research projects on corporate career mobility and was able to discern some 'distinctive features' of those who attain 'top positions'. They had fought their way to the top, often against strong competition – their ambition, and not their meekness, enabled them to inherit the heavenly positions of top management. They were not so much intelligent as shrewd – their organizational sense enabled them to sniff out the golden chance and grasp it firmly, it enabled them to strain forward rather than stand back waiting passively to be asked. They had the moral flexibility to meet shifting organizational demands and still enjoy the sleep of the just – their ability to relativize other moral imperatives whilst constantly prioritizing the pursuit of organizational goals did not make them necessarily immoral, but it did facilitate a moral flexibility others denied themselves. Nothing succeeded so much as success for the organization. Putting these distinctive features together, Gross concluded that:

> 'the men at the top of organizations will tend to be ambitious, shrewd and possessed of a non-demanding moral code. Their ambition will not be merely personal, for they will have discovered that their own goals are best pursued through assisting the organization to attain its goals. While this is less true, or even untrue at the bottom of the organization, those at the top share directly in the benefits of organizational goal achievement, such as seeing their stock values go up, deferred compensation, and fringe benefits . . . . Further, being at or near the top, these persons are those most strongly identified with the goals of the organization . . . they believe in the organization, they want to attain its goals, they profit personally from such goal attainment. So they will try hard to help the organization attain those goals. Finally, if the organization must engage in illegal activities to attain its goals, men with a non-demanding moral code will have the least compunctions about engaging in such behaviour. Not only that, as men of power, pillars of the community, they are most likely to believe that they can get away with it without getting caught. Besides, they are shrewd.'
>
> (Gross 1978: 71)

Not only does the promotion system mean that people who rise to the top are likely to have just those personal characteristics it takes to commit corporate crime, but these are also reinforced by the psychological consequences of success itself, for these too free a person from the moral bind of conventional values. That sociologists have been partially blind to this possible contributory cause of corporate crime springs ironically from the central position Merton's famous essay 'Social Structure and Anomie' (1957) played in forming criminological consciousness. In this, he explored the effect of anomie – the disjuncture between cultural goals and the availability of legitimate means to achieve these goals – as a possible source of crime. He argued that since crime, as officially recorded, was greatest amongst the working class, it followed that anomie too must be greatest in that social stratum. This analysis obscured Durkheim's original formulation (1898) in which anomie was conceptualized as normlessness, as a condition of moral deregulation. This led him to focus on the top social stratum as the primary location of anomie, for it was power and not poverty that facilitated too easily the personal achievement of socially inculcated cultural ambitions. Furthermore, once achieved, these targets no longer constrained individuals' aspirations or behaviour; instead, successful individuals experienced a release from moral and social binds. In a condition of pure individuation, the successful experience the sensation that anything and everything is possible. Looking over the abyss of infinite possibility, they find it easy to slip into endless striving and pursuit of whatever is, at that moment, desired. As Durkheim, comparing poverty and wealth, put it:

'Poverty protects against . . . (subjective deprivation) because it is a restraint in itself. No matter how one acts, desires have to depend upon resources to some extent; actual possessions are partly the criterion of those aspired to. So the less one has the less he is tempted to extend the range of his needs indefinitely. Lack of power, compelling moderation, accustoms men to it . . . . Wealth, on the other hand, by the power it bestows, deceives us into believing that we depend on ourselves only. Reducing the resistance we encounter from objects, it suggests the possibility of unlimited success against them. The less limited one feels, the more intolerable all limitation appears.'

(Durkheim 1951: 254)

In Simon and Gagnon's further analysis of the 'anomie of affluence', they construct a typology of possible responses to the too easy achievement of cultural goals. One major response, of particular relevance to understanding how executives can initiate and implement corporate crime, is called the 'conforming deviant'. They described this response as closely resembling Durkheim's original view on anomie and its consequences. They write:

'Having acquired the means of gratification, such persons must explore the dimensions of pleasure in search of modes of gratification; given the overdetermined character of their pursuit of the unreachable, their quest for new experiences begins to consume them. Reinforcing this quest for the extraordinary, which by definition should bring them quickly to the margins of deviance, is the fact . . . that one of the frequent rewards of achievement is an immunity to many of the sanctions that constrain and punish the less successful. Wealth insures a protective primary group as well as differentially protective social responses.' (Simon and Gagnon 1977: 372)

It seems reasonable to infer from the above that numerous corporate executives, having already responded to the situational demands necessary for career mobility within an organization by displaying sufficient degrees of competitive ambition, shrewdness, and moral flexibility will experience a further development of these characteristics when they have to respond to the relatively unaccountable and unconstrained power of being at or near the top of a large national, but especially transnational corporation. They are then in a high state of preparedness to commit corporate crime should they perceive it as being necessary 'for the good of the company'.

There is no intention in these arguments to give any sustenance to the view that corporate officials have been so successfully socialized into the 'way of life' that they cannot see what they are doing or that the organizational constraints upon them were so tight as to be 'coercive' and therefore excusing. A number of American studies, including Denzin (1977) on the liquor industry, Farberman (1975) and Leonard and Weber (1970) on car manufacturers and retailers, Geis (1967) on the heavy electrical equipment industry, and Blundell (1978) on an insurance company have all reported evidence supporting the view that higher officials create conditions under which their subordinates find it hard to refuse co-operation in illegal activities. There exists according to these studies a 'metaphysical pathos of "Godfatherism"' (Needleman and Needleman 1979: 518). According to this view top corporate officials make their organizational inferiors 'offers they can't refuse'.

It would be an easily acceptable explanation, if only it were entirely true. But the fact is, the data in these studies cannot be turned into generalizations, for they relate only to industries with high levels of vertical integration and economic concentration, involving an oligopolistic control over product supply frequently accompanied by a franchise relationship between manufacturer and seller. Consequently, there is no evidence that this 'Godfatherism', or as Needleman and Needleman (1979: 518) prefer to call it, 'crime-coercive system' exists in other industries operating under other forms of competition. Furthermore, even within the narrow spectrum of industries covered by the above studies there was considerable evidence (Farberman 1975: 447) of persons being prepared to refuse the offer and accept the consequences, which were not always as severe as the Godfather analogy suggests. Thus rather than adopting the language of coercion and hence drawing parallels between corporate officials and, say, soldiers at the front in World War I compelled to go over the top at dawn to meet the German machine-gun bullets or be shot as 'deserters', it might be more realistic to argue that corporate officials are frequently placed in a position where they are required to choose between impairing their career chances or being a loyal organizational person. That the latter seems to be chosen overwhelmingly testifies not to the existence of coercion, but to careful selection procedures for placing persons in corporate positions coupled with successful methods of persuading them that their interests and the corporation's interests happily coincide – or at least, that that is the most sensible, pragmatic way of looking at it.

As the corporate lawyer put it, when asked why he went along with producing completely bogus insurance policies as part of the Equity Funding Scandal: 'I didn't think anything of it; it was something the company needed done, that's all' (Blundell 1978: 171). Or as a laboratory supervisor, who was asked to go along with the manufacture of 'doctored' data so as to secure a contract deadline put it (Vandivier 1972: 22):

'I've been an engineer for a long time, and I've always believed that ethics and integrity were every bit as important as theorems and formulas, and never once has anything happened to change my beliefs. Now this . . . . Hell, I've got two sons I've got to put through school and I just . . .'

Another co-conspirator, reflecting on a similar dilemma, said (Vandivier 1973: 24):

'At 42, with seven children, I had decided that the Goodrich Company would probably be my 'home' for the rest of my working life. The job paid well, it was pleasant and challenging, and the future looked reasonably bright. My wife and I had bought a home and we were ready to settle down into a comfortable middle-aged, middle-class rut. If I refused to take part in the . . . fraud, I would have to either resign or be fired.'

A former sales manager looking back on the time he had to juggle with the moral and immoral balls of corporate demands said that:

'One faces a decision, I guess at such times, about how far to go with company instructions, and since the spirit of such meetings only appeared to be correcting a horrible price level situation, that there was not an attempt to actually damage customers, charge excessive prices, there was no personal gain in it for me, the company did not

seem actually to be defrauding, corporate statements can evidence the
fact that there have been poor profits during all these years . . . . So I
guess morally it did not seem quite so bad as might be inferred by the
definition of the activity itself.'   (Geis, in Geis and Meier 1977: 123)

Finally, Judge J. Cullen Cancy, prior to imposing a sentence on the
Heavy Electric Industry conspirators, caught nicely their contradiction:

> 'They were torn between conscience and an approved corporate
> policy, with the rewarding objective of promotion, comfortable secur-
> ity, and large salaries. They were the organization, or company man;
> the conformist who goes along with his superiors and finds balm for
> his conscience in additional comforts and security of his place in the
> corporate set-up.'   (Geis, in Geis and Meier 1977: 125)

Executives who commit corporate crime are not coerced into it, they
do not necessarily have to go along with the advice or instructions of
superiors. They are men who rationally weigh up the advantage of
conformity to criminal demands or staying on the path of righteousness;
for the most part they choose the former simply because it does not weigh
on their conscience and because it seems more likely to secure economic
and career advancement within the corporation. Their basic motive is no
mystery, 'they want nothing more than we all want – money, power,
consideration – in a word success; but they are in a hurry and are not
particular as to their means' (Ross 1907: 46).

FROM CORPORATE MOTIVES AND WILLING PERSONNEL TO CORPORATE CRIME: WHAT STANDS IN THE WAY?

> 'The most blameworthy acts are so often absolved by success that the
> boundary between what is permitted and what is prohibited, what is
> just and what is unjust, has nothing fixed about it, but seems suscepti-
> ble to almost arbitrary change by individuals.'   (Émile Durkheim)

So far, the explanation of corporate crime has concentrated on the *specific*
long-term goal-orientated feature of corporations and the personnel
who might become suited knights ambitiously pursuing the Holy Grail of
profits, and who would, if necessary, be willing to initiate and execute
crimes for the good of the corporation. Given the power of large,
particularly transnational corporations whose capital resources often
outstrip the Gross National Product of some industrialized countries,
there is every likelihood of success, both in business and in crime. None
the less there is a need to consider three countervailing social control

forces, which appear to have some effect on persons contemplating 'conventional' crimes, to see if they act as brakes on persons contemplating corporate crime. These are: (i) does the criminal justice system or other state and societal forms of regulation *deter* corporate crime? (ii) are there sufficient moral or cultural impediments in the way of corporate crime? and (iii) are the structural opportunities for corporate crime sufficiently limited?

DETERRENCE

> 'The thief who is in prison is not necessarily more dishonest than his fellows at large, but mostly one who, through ignorance or stupidity steals in a way that is not customary. He snatches a loaf from the baker's counter and is promptly run into gaol. Another man snatches bread from the table of hundreds of widows and orphans and similar credulous souls who do not know the ways of company promoters; and, as likely as not, he is run into Parliament.'
>
> (George Bernard Shaw)

Given the environmental problems facing corporations and the preparedness of executives and officials unhindered by moral or ethical constraints to find 'rational' solutions, an operative criterion frequently forces itself into their consciousness – 'will it pay' (and in whispered voices) 'even though it is technically illegal?' Since power has the capacity to sanctify crimes, almost in strict proportion to their enormity, corporate officials frequently discover themselves in the enviable situation of being able to conclude that 'it will'.

To understand how this is possible, we need to consider how laws against corporate activities are enforced and the social meaning of sanctions imposed by typical violators. In particular it is revealing to consider two principles in deterrence theory which are considered to inhibit 'conventional' crime – these are 'the certainty of being caught' and 'the severity of the punishment'. For the irony is, in a society like ours apparently dedicated to 'law and order' and having a penal policy based largely on deterrent principles, it appears that corporate crime somehow gets left out of the arena of legal and social control.

The certainty of (not) being caught

For the most part corporate crimes are not/do not fall under the jurisdiction of the police, but under special regulatory bodies. In America, there are the Occupational Safety and Health Administration, the Food and Drug Administration, Fair Employment Practices Commission, Securities and Exchange Commission, the Environmental Protection Agency. In the UK, there are numerous inspectorates, commissions, and government departments, including inspectorates of factories, mines and quarries, explosives, railway, agriculture, alkali and clean air, and Scottish industrial, and commissions, such as monopolies and mergers, and such departments as energy, and trade and industry.

There are four important points to make about these special agencies.

(i) Although they all have powers either to initiate or recommend criminal prosecution, they are primarily designed to be *regulatory* bodies whose main weapon against corporate misbehaviour is administrative, i.e. (occasional) inspection coupled with (polite) correspondence.

(ii) The resources they command make them no match for national and transnational corporations. This was made very clear by Her Majesty's Factory Inspectorate, which in the *Manufacturing and Service Industry Report 1978*, wrote:

> 'The Factory Inspectorate . . . works against a background of increasing commitments and slender resources. There is a limit to what a force of some 900 inspectors in the field (700 general inspectors and 200 specialists) can do in practice. The Inspectorate is responsible for some 18,000,000 people at work scattered through some 500,000 or 600,000 different workplaces . . . . It is obvious that an Inspectorate of its present size in relation to its responsibility cannot hope to achieve either all it would like or all the public would like it to do.'
>
> (Health and Safety Executive 1980: vi–vii)

When these scarce resources are compared with those devoted to 'conventional' crime it is quite staggering. There are at present in Britain something like 120,000 police and although some of these are in the Fraud Squad, they represent an exceedingly small per cent of the force, and in any case, the majority of their work consists of monitoring and prosecuting white collar rather than corporate criminals. The British government in 1980 felt that the problem of social security fraud was large enough to justify introducing 1,000 *new* inspectors; yet it is hard to see how this problem exceeds that of the health, safety, and welfare of the workforce for whom there are only 900 inspectors. What it does reflect is the willingness of the British government to increase the chances of criminalizing poor, oppressed, and sometimes inadequate individuals whilst leaving the rich corporate executive free to operate within and outside the law.

(iii) The resources these agencies have available to pursue corporate crime through the courts are inadequate in comparison with those available to large national and transnational corporations. Braithwaite (1979b: 130) believes that, 'government lawyers, who must in many ways be all-rounders, cannot compete with the corporation lawyer who spends his whole life finding out all there is to know about a narrowly delimited area of "legal loop-holes"'. This belief is firmly backed up by the experience of the West German government when in 1965 it attempted to bring criminal charges against nine Chemie Grunenthal executives who were indicted for causing bodily harm and involuntary manslaughter in connection with the drug thalidomide. Corporate lawyers managed to delay the case coming to court for two years and then they prolonged the proceedings for a further two years. When Grunenthal finally decided to make civil compensation to the satisfaction of suffering parents and children, the federal government's prosecution lost the bit between its teeth and permitted the hearing to be suspended indefinitely. So none of the executives was ever convicted.

Another example comes from Britain. The Bingham Report (1978) on oil sanctions-busting during the decade following Southern Rhodesia's unilateral declaration of independence contained a twelve-page (unpublished to the public) appendix, entitled *Evidence of Criminal Offences*. This listed the names of oil company directors who may have committed offences. It also contained the view that an oil company in Mozambique might be vulnerable to prosecution – this company, despite its name, is London-registered, with British directors, and was directly covered by sanctions legislation. However, despite this evidence, prosecution would have been political suicide since the defendants might have argued that civil servants and certain government ministers knew of the oil sanctions-busting arrangements and therefore the company considered their actions, although technically illegal, were informally condoned by governmental officials. That the Director of Public Prosecutions did not press for prosecution suggests that this line of defence might have been effective, or might have resulted in the prosecution net catching even larger, embarrassed fish. The police were also involved in capturing the oil-sanctions busters but Martin Bailey (1978), writing in *The Times*, reported that 'Scotland Yard's investigation into (this) major case of corporate law-breaking was surprisingly modest. James Smith, a chief superintendent, had the assistance of only one other detective'.

(iv) These regulatory agencies are increasingly faced with transnational adversaries who are capable of shifting their main base of operation – or if that is too drastic, their illegal activities at least – to other countries where laws against such behaviour do not exist, or if they do, where enforcement is even more lax. The exportation of corporate crime is certainly big business (Braithwaite 1981a; Chetley 1979; Muller 1974) not only for the corporations concerned but also for local political and governmental leaders. This simple manoeuvre puts these corporations beyond the regulatory influence of agencies whose powers are purely national. Furthermore, one country's legal system often constitutes an impediment to another country's attempts to gather information necessary to pursue a domestic case against a transnational corporation. Thus Switzerland's Privacy Laws provide a naturally safe haven for transnational corporations who want to keep their financial dealings closed (Klass 1975). Establishing guilt in a corruption case, for example, particularly before the US Corrupt Practices Act, 1977, would be extremely difficult if not impossible. As Jacoby, Nehemlis, and Ells convincingly argue:

'In order to obtain judicially admissible evidence, US investigators would have to obtain proof that (i) a payment was intended for a foreign official, (ii) it was made with a corrupt intent, and (iii) it was made for a prohibited purpose. Collecting such evidence would necessitate the co-operation of foreign governments. Whether (they) would allow US investigators to implicate one of their own nationals under US law is doubtful .... Moreover, a US citizen accused of foreign bribery would be denied due process of law under the US constitution unless he could produce foreign witnesses and documents in his own defence. These essential components of a fair defence would not be available to a defendant, as they are beyond the compulsory judicial process of US federal courts.'

(Jacoby, Nehemlis, and Ells 1977: 218)

Corporate executives contemplating the possibility of being required to commit corporate crimes know that they face a regulatory agency which for the most part will be unable to detect what is going on, and in the minority of cases when it does, it will have no heart and few resources to pursue the matter into the criminal courts. This enforcement structure does little to deter corporate crime.

The (lack of) severe punishment

Deterrence theorists (Zimring and Hawkins 1973: 174) point out that formal sanctions, particularly if they are not severe, will only deter if there are negative social sanctions to reinforce them. Assuming this to reflect common-sense rationality, it follows that there are three types of sanctions which prey on the minds of thoughtful officials contemplating the commission of corporate crime: (i) legal sanctions, and especially 'will I be sent to prison?'; (ii) occupational sanctions and especially 'will my job be lost or my promotional chances endangered?'; (iii) social sanctions – 'will I be rejected by family, friends, and acquaintances and required to resign from the country club?' For the most part, the evidence from corporate officials who have been sanctioned is that for *this type of crime*, criminalization and stigmatization are not fearful consequences likely to occur. The corporate calculator has little to fear; and he is correct in not being deterred for the costs incurred by corporate crime are indeed small.

Studies on the enforcement of laws prohibiting certain corporate activities in America (McCormick 1977; Seymour 1973), Canada (Goff and Reasons 1978; Snider 1978), and England (Carson 1970) all suggest that even in that minority of cases where criminalization occurs, the legal sanctions imposed fail to act as a deterrent because they are trifling fines rather than imprisonment and normally are directed at smaller, relatively less victimizing, corporations.

McCormick (1977) analysed the nature of anti-trust enforcement in the US from 1890 through to 1969. This eighty-year period reveals very clearly how laws against corporations are (not) enforced and consequently how executives are (not) deterred. The US authorities instigated 1,551 cases, but of these only 45 per cent were prosecuted as criminal; the majority were dealt with as civil matters even though little difference could be found in the types of anti-trust behaviour these corporations committed. Of those prosecuted criminally, about 80 per cent were convicted, the majority of these entering pleas of *nolo contendere*, which means they refused to defend themselves. This in effect constitutes a plea bargain because the court is tacitly prepared to impose a modest sentence in return for its time, energy, and resources not being devoted to the expensive business of proving corporate guilt. In fact, not one business person was imprisoned for violation of the Sherman Anti-Trust Act 1890 until the 1961 Heavy Electrical Conspiracy trial – other persons had been imprisoned under this act but they were trade union officials! Furthermore, of the twenty-eight executives found guilty in 1961, only seven were sent to prison, and then the maximum length of sentence was thirty days which was, of course, substantially reduced by remission. Since then, imprisoning corporate officials has become less novel but by no means universal. During the fourteen years following the Electrical conspiracy verdict, a further thirty-eight corporate executives out of nearly 800 convicted have been imprisoned for violations of the anti-trust laws. The next most famous conspiracy, the Folding-Carton case in 1976, resulted in 36 per cent of those convicted being jailed – the heaviest sentence being fifteen days (Clinard and Yeager 1980: 281). Such sentences are hardly likely to deter other executives, particularly when evidence (to be considered below) shows that few people think any the worse of them.

The most frequent legal sanction imposed against corporations and their executives are fines. These can be in the form of a regulatory agency fine, which is comparable to a fixed-fine imposed on traffic offenders, and a criminal fine imposed by the court. The former are trifling and would be too insignificant to have any impact on corporate crime (Clinard *et al.* 1979: 143). The latter can be, and have been *absolutely* large. Thus in the Electrical conspiracy, General Electric was fined $437,000. But when this and fines imposed on others as well as those firms involved in the Folding-Carton industry conspiracy are calculated againt the gross revenues and then standardized as a fine imposed on a person earning $15,000 annually, it is clear that they are *relatively* minuscule. Ermann and Lundman (1982: 148) show that the heaviest fine in 1961 was the equivalent of $12.30 and in 1976 it was $1.80!

Just as a theatregoer is prepared to add the possible cost of illegal parking to the costs of his/her evening's entertainment, or a city businessperson is prepared to add to the costs of a tax-deductable lunch, so a corporation regards fines as 'reasonable licence fees' (Dershowitz 1961: 285) for engaging in illegal conduct. Aptly summing up this situation, Green (1972: 96) said that 'while some court imposed fines achieve compensation and others create deterrence, anti-trust fines have the distinction of doing neither'.

Carson (1970) analysed the Factory Inspectorate files on a randomly selected sample of two hundred firms in one district of south-east England covering the years 1961 to 1966. During this period, the inspectorate recorded over 3,800 offences and *every firm had at least one violation recorded against it*. The vast bulk of these acts involved insecure or improperly adjusted fencing of dangerous machinery, inadequate precautions against fire and explosion, as well as failure to inspect equipment and maintain healthy work conditions. These offences cannot be regarded as trivial because sometimes they result in an employee's or innocent bystander's death, serious injury, or permanently impaired health. Yet despite the potential and actual harmful consequences of the failure to comply with factory regulations, the pattern of enforcement does not deter. The inspectorate had six major methods of responding to a prima facie case of violation. These were: no formal action, notification of matters requiring attention, indirect threat of prosecution, direct threat of prosecution, and prosecution. Only 1.5 per cent of the actual enforcement decisions constituted prosecution, and of these cases all pleaded guilty and were fined on average only £50. The major response of the inspectorate was to write a letter stating what was wrong, and how and when it might be improved. Imagine the outcry if the police were to send this type of letter to an adolescent they had reason to believe had violated the law:

Dear G. E. Rald,

We should like to take this opportunity to inform you that on 12th March this year you were seen entering empty handed into the private premises of Ms P. C. Edwards of Convent St., Folkstone and leaving shortly afterwards with your hands full.

In our opinion, this constitutes a violation of the Theft Act 1968 subsection 32 (c) and we would be grateful if you would consider the following advice: please stop going down Convent St. and entering houses without the owners' permission.

We should warn you that next March 12th another police constable will be on foot duty in Convent St., and should he notice a repetition of your behaviour, we shall have to consider the possibility of taking even more stringent action than we have on this occasion.

Not only is this mild rebuke the typical response made by the inspectorate, but it is even the usual response to firms detected three or more times; for these, the rate of prosecution was still only 3.5 per cent!

Naturally this enforcement pattern could be justified by the inspectorate who see their primary function not as a kind of industrial police force, but more of a pastoral mission rounding up wayward factory owners and showing them the light and contentment to be gained from compliance with current standards of safety, health, and welfare required by law. However, this pastoral mission is not only up against hardened heathens, but it also considers that some ought not even to be read the lesson. For the inspectorate tended to initiate a prosecution only against firms who had 'unsatisfactory attitudes'; others whose violations were seen to stem from adverse economic circumstances, or from some other extenuating condition were not prosecuted. In other words, many executives in firms experiencing economic difficulties and who know from experience that the inspectorate mainly imposes administrative sanctions will calculate that their best interests lie in not conforming to factory health, safety, and welfare regulations; instead they will gather their excuses and get on with the violations.

These above studies and many others all support the view that there is no general deterrent in the typical sanctions imposed on corporations and their offending executives. Polite advisory letters, relatively minuscule fines, and short prison sentences leave corporations licenced to continue and leave us, as Dylan advised, with heads buried deep in our rags.

But there is one final possible regulatory factor – civil damages. Surely corporations will not deviate easily when they realize just how high civil damages can be? The evidence here too is not particularly encouraging for those who consider corporations are regulated by deterrence. In the 1976 Folding-Carton conspiracy, *International Paper* had to pay $27 millions in class-action treble damage settlements. But against their gross revenues and then standardized for a person earning $15,000 per annum this represented only $96. On the same calculation the highest settlement came to $675 paid by *Federal Paper*. Such civil action settlements, whilst absolutely large are again relatively insignificant. Indeed, in the trial of Ford Motor Company in Indiana, 1978, it became evident according to Swigert and Farrell, that:

> 'the manufacturer had known that the fuel tank on its subcompact Pinto was defectively designed and had consciously decided to proceed with production in spite of the potential hazards. The decision, the grand jury found, was predicted on a cost-benefit analysis. Officials at Ford allegedly predicted the number of severe burn injuries and deaths that would result from the defect, and estimated that the cost of repairing the car would exceed anticipated court settlements.'   (Swigert and Farrell 1981: 166)

Even if the typical criminal sanction holds out little hope as a general deterrent, does it act as a specific deterrent? Are those who have to pay fines deterred in future? It is difficult to see why they would be deterred any more than fined traffic-offenders are deterred; they can calculate rationally the cost of future fines and build that into any contemplation of irregular and illegal behaviour. However, there is a study which tends to go against this common sense reasoning. In an attempt to consider the specific deterrent function of sanctions imposed under consumer protection legislation in Australia, Hopkins (1980a) asks: 'do sanctions applied to corporate offenders prevent or reduce the likelihood of recidivism?' Reminding us that Sutherland's answer was definitely not, Hopkins points out with insight that this negative answer was only possible because Sutherland conflated individual and corporate crime, thus reducing large rambling enterprises with thousands of employees to a single entity. If any one of these employees committed a corporate crime, then this was added to any previous crime committed by any other employee, no matter how distantly related to the organizational site of previous offences. This, said Sutherland, constituted recidivism. Clearly this was an unsatisfactory procedure severely reducing the acceptability of his answer. Hopkins argued that much of this type of corporate crime (violation of consumer laws) could be viewed as a breakdown in communication or organizational procedures, and he attempted to see if, as a result of being fined, these companies made any effort to locate the flawed chain of information and correct it. In other words, did they, as a result of being fined, take steps to prevent the reoccurrence of this behaviour? His conclusions were:

> 'Of the 15 companies in which offences were attributable to organizational defects, nine made significant changes designed to reduce the likelihood of recidivism. Two made minor changes which, while forestalling the possibility of an exact repetition of the offence in question, failed to rectify the general weakness which the offence had uncovered. Two companies made no changes at all, and for two, no information was available. Where organizational defects were involved therefore, the prosecution can be said to have led to significant organizational improvements in at least 60 per cent of cases.'
>
> (Hopkins 1980a: 210)

From the available evidence, it seems fair to conclude that the typical legal sanction against corporate crime does not act as a general deterrent – others are not put off merely because some corporations and their executives have been fined, particularly when the fines are comparatively small and tax-deductable – and the evidence, such as it is, suggests that a specific deterrent function may operate, but only to deter corporations from recommitting the *same* offence. The one study on which this latter conclusion is based cannot be generalized to demonstrate that there is a specific deterrent effect for all other corporate offences, and in any case, it should be treated very cautiously, not only because a single study can often be shown later to have missed the general condition, but also because it flies in the face of empirically grounded deterrence theory. Thus as Andeneas argues:

> 'A trusted cashier committing embezzlement, a minister who evades payment of his taxes, a teacher making sexual advances towards minors and a civil servant who accepts bribes have a *fear of detection which is more closely linked with the dread of public scandal and subsequent social ruin than with apprehensions of legal punishment.*'
>
> (Andeneas 1966: 964)

There are no sharp judicial teeth or public claws to arouse a fear of detection in corporate executives. An occasional court appearance can become enshrined as mere ritual ceremony totally encapsulating a particular moment of time which can be easily forgotten. The evidence is, in the case of corporate crime, that nothing much happens by way of public scandal and social ruin. The majority of executives found guilty of corporate crime not only retain their jobs or have others found for them, but also find that funds to cover their fines are somehow made available. For some, the crime may even pay: thus in the Goodrich disc-brake scandal of the late 1960s, when the company attempted to foist a defective brake-disc system on to a customer who happened to be too clever to be deceived, two of the main executives involved were later promoted (Vandivier 1972: 33). Many companies in the Heavy Electrical Equipment conspiracy did not dismiss 'guilty executives' (for they had merely been doing their job) but even those who did, did not do so with the intention of ruining them. Indeed, all the dismissed executives were soon re-employed, sometimes in positions with higher salaries than their previous position! This is of course, in marked contrast to the typical experience of persons found guilty of 'conventional' crimes (Martin and Webster 1971).

Not only are there few adverse occupational consequences, but there is very little social scandal. Those few cases which are prosecuted fail to arouse media-indignation, except when it expresses disapproval for the way executives are very occasionally over-sanctioned! And amongst neighbours, an executive found guilty of corporate crime continues to be regarded as 'upright and steadfast; indeed, they will probably see him as solid and substantial a citizen as they themselves are' (Geis 1978: 283). In any case, amongst such a community there is a strong ethic directed towards making money but a great disapproval of it being stolen directly, as in the case of larceny, burglary, or robbery. Thus, since the executive's way of making money for the corporation is not viewed as either immoral or criminal, his neighbours are hardly likely to discriminate against him; after all, there but for the grace of the enforcement agencies . . .

Because corporate crimes are hardly likely to be described as heinous in the media, few consciences are outraged and scandalized; consequently, the ingredients which deterrent theorists argue are necessary to achieve a specific deterrent effect do not typically exist. In these circumstances, executives feel free to commit corporate crimes. It also means that other executives calculating the odds will most likely decide that their jobs, their friendship network, and their club affiliations will not be put at risk. As any good control theorist (Box 1981a; Hirschi 1969; Johnson 1979) knows, even if people have a high stake in conformity, this will not act as a brake on their criminal behaviour if they perceive – quite rightly in the case of executives contemplating corporate crime – that this stake will not be put at risk by undertaking such a shady but profitable enterprise.

IDEOLOGICAL SUPPORTS: STRUCTURAL IMMORALITIES,
NEUTRALIZATIONS, AND CORPORATE SELF-IMAGE

> 'Criminaloids move in an atmosphere of friendly approval . . . and this
> can still smart any conscience with the balm of good fellowship and
> adulation.'   (Edward Ross, *Sin and Society*)

Corporate officials are able to transform motives which make corporate
crime possible into actual behaviour because they operate in a *subculture
of 'structural immoralities'* (Mills 1956: 138). This is conceptually similar
but not identical to the phenomena described by Matza (1964: 33–68) as
the *subculture of delinquency*: both consist of 'precepts and customs that
are delicately balanced between convention and crime'; both 'posit
objectives that may be attained through (crime) but also other means';
both 'allow (crime) but it is not demanded or necessarily considered the
preferred path'; and both consist of 'norms and sentiments' which are
'beliefs that function as the extenuating conditions under which (crime)
is permissible'. Thus, these subcultures respectively enable corporate
officials and lower-class adolescent males to commit crimes without too
many pangs of conscience; through their sanitizing prism, each subculture softens criminal acts so that they assume the appearance
of 'not really' being against the law, or it transforms them into acts required by a morality higher than that enshrined in a parochial criminal
law.

There are however, two main major crucial differences between these
subcultures. Whereas lower-class juvenile delinquents find themselves
confronting a legal system which has literally declared war against them,
upper-class corporate officials find a legal system which is either at, or on
their side; for the most part it is unwilling and if not, unable even to
guarantee compensation for the victims of corporate crime let alone to
contain and control the crime itself. Second, corporate officials are
comparatively more committed to conventional values and a respectable
self-identity than typical lower-class male adolescents. Consequently,
they have an even greater need to neutralize the moral bind of the law and
thus protect their respectability and self-identity from the signs of
discreditability implicit in corporate crimes.

It is not difficult for corporate officials to cover themselves in 'purity'
even when they are breaking the law because the 'structural immorality'
of their corporate environment provides a library of verbal technique for
neutralizing the moral bind of laws against corporate behaviour.

First, officials can *deny responsibility*. They do this, not by pleading
momentary insanity, as Matza (1964: 69–100) says delinquents frequently do, but by pleading 'ignorance', 'accident', or 'acting under

orders'. Laws attempting to regulate corporate activity tend to be excessively vague, consist of ambiguous definitions, and subject to subtle but significant shifts in meanings; or at least, that is how they can be interpreted, particularly by those desiring to violate them. As Merton (1957: 141) sees some corporate misbehaviour, 'it is not easy to say whether it is an instance of praiseworthy salesmanship or a penitentiary offence'. In these circumstances, it is convenient for corporate officials to pull the cloak of honest ignorance over their heads and proceed under its darkness to stumble blindly and unwittingly over the thin line between what is condoned and what is condemned.

Claiming that whatever happened was an 'accident' is another means of denying intent. Of course, this is not entirely implausible. None of the fatal accidents or occupational diseases mentioned earlier were the result of any corporate officials intending to kill or mutilate hundreds of employees, customers, or civilians. Their primary motive was 'for the good of the company': that meant creating more efficiency in the productive process, cutting costs, not making unnecessary repairs, and so on, all with an eye on improving the corporate's profitable position. They did not intend to harm anyone; the consequences might be unfortunate, but accidental and irrelevant for establishing whether or not the act was criminal. Thus by prioritizing *intention* and relegating consequences as *accidents* – conveniently turning a blind eye to strict liability – corporate officials can proceed to commit corporate crimes because they do not perceive them as such in the first place.

A third means of avoiding responsibility consists of shifting the blame to even higher officials. This may be achieved by engaging in what Matza (1969:93) refers to as 'natural reduction', that is, reducing oneself – the subject – into a thing-like object incapable of transcending circumstances, which in this particular mundane instance means viewing oneself as incapable of disobeying orders from high places. Thus one conspirator in the 1961 Great Heavy Electrical Industry conspiracy said: 'We understand this was what the company wanted us to do', and another reported that, 'It (the instruction) came to me from my superior . . . but my impression was that it came to him from higher up'. And a lawyer involved in the Equity Funding Scandal of the mid-1970s said: 'It was like someone asking you to help move a sofa from here to there. I didn't think anything of it; *it was something the company needed done, that's all*' (Blundell 1978: 171).

A second technique of neutralization available to corporate officials is to *deny the victim*. When the 'victim' is, say, a government agency such as the Inland Revenue (UK) or Medicare (US), or another vast transnational organization, or when it is millions of individuals deprived of trivial amounts of property, or when whole countries or even continents are 'victimized' as in the case of bribery and corruption of Third World governments or legal officials, or the exportation of products whose consumption is only really safe in a western cultural environment (Chetley 1979), then it is possible for the corporate official to convince himself that there is *no real person suffering*, and therefore there is no real criminal victim. This is plausible because in our common-sense construction crimes involve real people as victims; many corporate crimes, because they fall on impersonal organizations or distant countries, fail to match this common-sense stereotype, and therefore can be viewed as non-criminal. It is a very convenient stereotype!

A third technique is for corporate officials to *condemn the condemners*; they can deny the legitimacy of the law which regulates their behaviour as well as the competence of those attempting to enforce 'unnecessary' law. The law, they can argue to themselves, should have no business regulating the behaviour of corporations, particularly in a *free-enterprise* system; the state, to quote a fashionable political phrase, 'should get off our backs'. 'If', argues Conklin (1977: 94), 'businessmen feel ideologically deprived by government regulation because they think that the law is unfair and unduly restrictive of the economic forces to which they have a strong commitment, they may violate the law'. The law can not only be condemned for being 'unnecessary' but also because those who formulate and publicly defend it are 'hypocrites'. Clearly those firms who engaged in oil-sanctions busting on the South African continent after Southern Rhodesia had illegally declared unilateral independence were able to 'neutralize' their own and subsequent misbehaviour in this way. They knew that the government which had passed the order prohibiting the supply of oil to Southern Rhodesia was sufficiently realistic to know it could not be enforced. But what must the hypocritical collusion of government officials in this illegal activity have done to the way corporate officials regard laws against corporate behaviour more generally? Clearly, it could not have enhanced it; why obey a legal system in which senior officials publicly pose as against one thing but privately collude in its occurrence – not only ought they to be condemned as hypocrites but their laws ought also to be disregarded as mere propaganda concealing the lack of will to control corporate behaviour.

Fourth, corporate officials may be able to *appeal to higher loyalty* and by that technique deny the moral bind of the law. This can take at least three forms. Officials could accept responsibility for their behaviour but argue that in being willingly *loyal* to the corporation they were obeying a superior moral imperative. They could also argue that in general there is frequently a difference between morality and legalism and that the former has a greater claim on their allegiance. As one executive in the Great Electrical conspiracy stated:

> 'One faces a decision, I guess, at such times, about how far to go with company instructions, and since the spirit of such meetings only appeared to be correcting a horrible price level situation, that there was not an attempt to damage customers, charge excessive prices, there was no personal gain in it for me, the company did not seem actually to be defrauding . . . *morally* it did not seem quite so bad as might be inferred by the definition of the activity itself.'
>
> (Geis, in Geis and Meier 1977: 123)

And another said:

> 'Sure such collusion was illegal, but it wasn't unethical. It wasn't any more unethical than if the companies had a summit conference the way Russia and the West meet. Those competitors' meetings were just attended by a group of distressed individuals who wanted to know where they were going.'   (Smith 1969: 888)

Finally, officials can claim that business ethics are morally superior to mere formal legalism. Thus free enterprise – the pursuit of fair profit, the generator of wealth and employment, the backbone on which social welfare is possible – can be viewed, at least by corporate officials, as *the primary ethic for and of an industrial society*, and conformity to this neutralizes any obedience to the law merely because it happens to be the law. This can be felt particularly strongly by corporate officials if the law attempts to interfere with free enterprise. Thus by referring to such values as '*our* country's values', business men appeal to a higher loyalty than obedience to the law and thereby free themselves from its moral constraint.

By the use of these techniques of neutralization, which are themselves embedded in the 'structural immorality' of corporations, executives are able to violate the law without feeling guilt or denting their respectable self-image. Furthermore, this final piece of identity cosmetic can be enhanced by the official portrait of crime as being *essentially* a lower-class phenomenon. Since murder, assault, and theft are committed by working-class men, corporate executives see their own virtue reflected in the guilt of those beneath them. Thus corporate officials are both mystified as to their own crime, and misdirected as to the distribution of crime in general. Both mystification and misdirection preserve the appearance of corporate respectability and help keep invisible, to themselves and others, the underlying ugly reality of corporate crime.

OPPORTUNITY

> 'You got criminals in high places,
> And law-breakers making the rules.'
>
> (Bob Dylan)

The third major structural feature facilitating corporate crime is opportunity. There are at least three dimensions to this: the relationship between corporate and enforcement agencies; the nature of laws against corporate activities; and, probably *the greatest of them all*, the power of corporations to intervene in the process by which corporate behaviour becomes incorporated in criminal law.

Obviously the lenient system of law enforcement constitutes a kind of opportunity structure denied to those subjected to higher rates of prosecution and the imposition of severe sanctions. But the fact that corporate activities are not subject to high levels of surveillance compared to, say, lower-class adolescents whenever the 'Special Patrol Group' (UK) swoop down on ethnically mixed neighbourhoods, and that they are not confronted by regulatory agencies with sufficient resources to maintain an adequate level of surveillance through frequent inspection, also constitutes a greater opportunity structure conducive to corporate crime. Corporate officials can further reduce the surveillance on them by simply shifting resources, records, money, and personnel between national boundaries thus rendering their behaviour virtually disentangleable even to the most persistent regulatory agency. Finally, the sweet exchange of personnel from agency to corporation (and vica versa) and the extent to which some agency officials are amenable to getting their hands grubby with filthy lucre again make the executive suite a relatively safe place for planning illegal behaviour – there might even be some people present who are supposed to be enforcing the law!

A second dimension to the corporate illegal opportunity structure consists of the nature of criminal law itself and the legal requirement of intent which still dominates corporate crimes.

Criminal laws aimed at regulating corporate activities tend to refer to a specific rather than a general class of behaviour. For example, as tax avoidance schemes are dreamt up by corporate accountants and lawyers or financial entrepreneurs, so the law attempts to encapsulate them by making that specific tax avoidance scheme illegal. But of course, given the superior cunning of these corporate gentlemen, they are always able to discover another scheme, and still another scheme, and so on. Until a tax avoidance clause is incorporated into law which would require corporate officials to establish the legality of any avoidance scheme, there will always be a wide-open prairie of opportunity for gouging back profits from the exchequer, leaving ordinary tax-payers to 'foot the bill'.

Criminal laws against corporate behaviour again facilitate crime because they focus purely on the regulation broken and not on the consequences of that broken regulation. Thus the company responsible for the hoist accident at Littlebrook Dee power station were not prosecuted for the fact that five men died, but for the fact that the machinery was not properly maintained or inspected. For this, they were fined £5,000. In conventional crime there is no such similar fracture; a person is charged with the consequences of his/her action; if someone dies as a consequence of being stabbed, the assailant is more likely to be charged with a homicide offence rather than 'carrying an offensive weapon'. The point of this fracture between regulation broken and its consequences is that it facilitates corporate crime; executives need only concern themselves with the likelihood of being leniently punished for breaking regulations, whilst ignoring its consequences for the law does not concern itself with the consequences either.

Most laws against corporate criminal behaviour require that *intention* be proved before guilt can be established. Not only is this virtually impossible (and improbable) in cases of injury – fatal or otherwise – to employees or the public, but in cases of financial irregularities it is always open for the suspect(s) to plead that it was not his intention to defraud shareholders, indeed even though he engaged in what appears to be financially irregular practices, his intention all along had been to improve shareholders' financial interests, but unfortunately due to unforeseeable circumstances, matters went sour. It was just this kind of argument that two company directors put forward when they were prosecuted in New South Wales in 1979 for apparently causing shareholders to lose more than A$22 millions (Hopkins 1980b).

Although some of these opportunity structures – provided ironically, by the legal system itself – could be blocked, it is unlikely that they would be. Clearly, business interests would be against any general proscription and particularly against strict liability, since then it 'would not be possible to know with any degree of certainty whether a proposed course of action was legal' (Hopkins 1980b: 427) and that would deprive corporate executives of an essential precondition for entering or staying in the market, namely *predictability*.

Important as these two above opportunity structures are for facilitating corporate crime, *the greatest opportunity lies in their ability to prevent their actions from becoming subject to criminal sanctions in the first place*. Their ability persistently to cause avoidable harm, injury, and suffering is because they prevent much of this becoming incorporated into laws against corporate behaviour. Whether or not the avoidable harm, injury, and suffering should then be called 'crime' is a point legal theorists then dance on for ever; but a 'crime' by any other name causes at least just as much pain and grief.

To understand why the criminal (and administrative) law is so narrow in its encroachment on corporate activity, we need to consider those moments in history when the state does create laws apparently against the interests of business and financial élites. For these not only reveal something about the nature of criminal law and hence crime itself, but also how corporations are able to channel some of their resources into a concerted attempt to prevent their socially injurious behaviours from being criminalized.

Graham's (1972) analysis of the social processes leading to the US Comprehensive *(sic)* Drug Abuse Prevention and Control Act, 1970, considers how, through tough lobbying tactics and calling on good connections – especially in the House of Representatives – the pharmaceutical manufacturers were able to limit the discussion of amphetamine abuse so that it focused on that small minority of persons who inject it. The vast bulk of users – housewives, businessmen, students, physicians, truck drivers, and athletes – many of whom obtain their pills through legitimate channels, represented a considerably profitable market provided it could be kept clear of federal control. To this end, Hoffman-La Roche, who annually reaped profits during the late 1960s of about $40 million, was prepared to exert effective pressure on the legislature. Senator Dodd, who had attempted to bring more amphetamine use under control, argued that Hoffman-La Roche 'paid a Washington law firm three times the annual budget of the Senate subcommittee staff to assure that their drugs would remain uncontrolled' (Graham 1972: 22). And Senator Eagleton, who had successfully brought in a reclassification amendment so that amphetamine would be more tightly controlled, stated, when he saw the amendment subsequently overturned: 'when the chips are down, the power of the drug companies was simply more compelling than any appeal to the public welfare' (p. 53). The outcome is that an industry which has skilfully managed to convert a chemical with meagre medical justification and considerable potential for harm (Grinspoon and Hedblom 1975) into a legitimate drug, remained free from federal control to go on manufacturing, distributing, and advertising it. The industry's corporate leaders must have laughed demonically to themselves when they saw the full weight of the law coming down on people manufacturing and distributing comparatively harmless drugs, such as marijuana. Legitimate drug rackets are after all not only lucrative – there's gold in them there pills (Klass 1975) – but they also provide the occasion for seeing oneself – if you are involved in them – as sharper, shrewder, and more powerful than those ending up the wrong side of the law.

Shover (1980) examined the clash of interests in the run up to the US Surface Mining Control and Reclamation Act, 1977. He revealed that although this appeared to be an instance favouring a pluralist conception of law-making, i.e. law representing a compromise between the interests of numerous groups, it was in fact a law which basically reflected the interests of the coal industry and those dependent upon it – manufacturers of heavy equipment and the electric utilities, who consume nearly 80 per cent of domestically mined coal. It appeared that when this alliance of powerful forces realized that some legalistic gloss over their environmental vandalism was necessary or desirable, not because they wanted it but because the public were increasingly becoming aware of pollution, they actively encouraged the legislature to formulate a bill which created the illusion of controlling corporations. In fact it provided the industry with more control over its environment by making conflicts over environmental damage an administrative problem whose outcome could be predicted by corporate executives. It thus gained for the coal industry what all organizations strive for, namely rational control of the environment through being better able to predict its fluctuations.

Similar processes, reflecting the ability of corporations to prevent their socially and economically injurious behaviour being criminalized operate also in Britain. Thus Gunningham considered the clash of interests between 'in the red corner' the National Smoke abatement Society, the Conservation Society of Britain, Friends of the Earth, and other groups for the non-pollution of the environment and in the 'blue corner':

> 'capitalists with strong economic interests in maintaining the status quo. These were involved because in a capitalist market economy, the organization of economic activity has historically been based on numerous fragmented units, each seeking to operate as profitably as possible, whilst paying only the costs which it is impossible to avoid. Thus the dilemma of the polluting industry is that controlling pollution is expensive, but adds nothing to the value of the goods produced, and is bad business for any firm whose main concern is to maintain profitability in a competitive situation.'   (Gunningham 1974: 39)

The outcomes of these conflicting interests are enshrined in the Clean Air Acts of 1956 and 1968 and the Deposit of Poisonous Wastes Act 1972. Under these acts, the Alkali and Clean Air Inspectorate was responsible for ensuring that the emission of *some* pollution from industry was no more than 'practicably reasonable', a level so ambiguous and vague and capable of numerous interpretations by corporate lawyers that the actual amount of pollution was frequently allowed to rise above a level found tolerable by local residents. Thus in 1971, United Carbon Black Ltd of Swansea was forced to spend money on improving its air emissions because local residents had formed a strong pressure group. Similarly, the Imperial Smelting Corporation (a Rio Tinto Zinc subsidiary) at Avonmouth was discovered by scientists working at Bristol University to be 'poisoning' local agricultural land as well as inhabitants. Again, after a period of closure, this company improved its pollution control. The point is, in both these cases the Alkali Inspectorate had been satisfied that the pollution control by these corporations was 'practicably reasonable'. Furthermore, this should not be too surprising. Under the acts, corporations are required to measure their own pollution level and report this to the inspectorate. Clearly such a self-monitoring system is wide open to abuse, particularly amongst those who have a clear but maybe not clean motive for doing so.

Gunningham concluded that the acts only reflected the types of control which were economically convenient to industry, and that 'since strict enforcement of more severe legislation would attack the very root of capitalism . . . then any compromise between alternative policies and views is always struck within an area which does not threaten these interests' (Gunningham 1974: 83).

A further example of how the interests of the powerful are enshrined in legislation which has the appearance of opposing them is provided by Carson's (1974, 1980) analysis of the Factory Regulation Act, 1833. He suggests that although manufacturers had an instrumental influence in supporting this act – it helped to rationalize and make predictable the conduct of competitors – they also saw it as having a symbolic dimension, which if anything, was predominant in their minds. Carson suggested that:

'The Act of 1833 publicly affirmed that the precepts of common humanity were not so alien to the logic of industrial capitalism that checks could only by imposed from without. In this way it facilitated public representation of the relationship between the state, capital, and an emerging working class as one of pre-eminent moral stature.'   (Carson 1974: 137)

However, the achievement of this symbolic significance could be attained with minimum constraint upon factory owners' autonomy and an ineffectual enforcement. Thus in the process of passing the 1833 Act, 'a tide which might have run much more strongly in the direction of the "criminalization" of the offending employer was effectively stemmed' (p. 138).

mountain of victimized employees, consumers, taxpayers, shareholders, and the public continues to grow. Would it really be justifiable to turn away from such carnage and pillage? Maybe liberal reformism is something to be contemplated today, even by those waiting patiently for the revolution tomorrow.

Although there are some grounds for not expecting too much from slight changes in the system, there are, none the less, other grounds for believing that *something* good can be achieved, at least in *principle*. If hundreds of corporation-caused deaths can be prevented, if thousands of occupational diseases and injuries can be avoided, and if millions of pounds stolen by corporations can be saved, then these would be no bad achievements. The question is, however, can these be realized in practice?

The history of attempts to control and regulate corporate crimes does not give much cause for optimism, and indeed the idea of it reduces radicals to knowing laughter. For it is quite clear that despite innovative legislation, the proliferation of enforcement agencies, the relatively new use of imprisonment for corporate offenders, and absolutely (but not relatively) large fines for offending corporations, there has not been a substantial brake on corporate crime. In many ways, it has been a huge, cynical black-comedy – although the victims are not laughing.

But there are some silver linings peering over the edges of this dark cloud of history.

First, in North America at least, there is a growing awareness of corporate crime, although not necessarily the extent of it. Throughout the 1970s attitudes have shifted. Undoubtedly the best illustration of this can be obtained by comparing the research of Rossi *et al.* (1974) with that of Cullen, Golden, and Cullen (1982). The latter study, which was conducted in Macomb, Illinois, discovered that during the period 1972 (when Rossi carried out his research in Baltimore) to 1979, 'the seriousness rating of white-collar crime . . . increased both absolutely and to a greater extent than any other category', and more important, increases in seriousness ratings were pronounced in two categories of corporate crime, particularly 'violence' (resulting in death or injury) and 'price-fixing'. The authors suggest that these changes may reflect the publicity surrounding the Ford Pinto car scandal, and the various price-fixing conspiracy trials including the Folding-Carton industry trial in 1976. This research is not isolated. Further confirmation that public attitudes towards corporate crime are hardening and becoming more punitive have come from other American studies (McCleary *et al.* 1981; Sinden 1980; Wolfgang 1980; Yoder 1979). The last author commented 'increasing numbers of Americans have become aware that crime exists in the suites of many corporations just as surely as it exists in the streets of their cities and suburbs'.

Where this awareness of corporate crime has been expressed electorally, corporate victims have benefited. Thus in 1970 a new prosecuting attorney was elected in King County, Washington (Seattle and environs), partly on a platform of increasing consumer fraud and general white-collar prosecution. Stotland and associates analysed the effects of subsequent increases in prosection and enforcement and concluded that 'a tendency toward an upward rise of home repair fraud was reduced by convictions . . . however, the increased sanctions did not appear to have completely reversed the upward movement of home repair fraud' (1980: 262).

Clearly a major problem in controlling corporate crime is raising victim and public consciousness to a level where the community desires and supports a policy of more active and effective state control and regulation. This could be (and has been) achieved not only by investigative journalism and television documentaries, which do appear to have influenced the general level of awareness amongst American citizens to such an extent that Spiro Agnew referred to it as the 'post-Watergate' morality. However, more still is needed. Raising victim consciousness could also be achieved by incorporating it as a function explicitly pursued by controlling and regulating agencies. Intense and widespread publicization of corporate crime could produce a greater public sensitivity and this in turn, could become the catalyst out of which stronger and tougher enforcement programmes blossom.

The second hopeful sign is that the state and its criminal justice system (broadly conceived to include criminal, administrative, and civil law) has shown itself receptive to arguments that corporate crime victims deserve protection and that corporate criminals deserve sanctioning, particularly when those arguments have been well orchestrated, empirically supported, and contain implicit electoral threats. The criminal justice system projects itself above social conflicts and expects to be recognized as fair and just because it is guided by universal principles that transcend sectional interests. But there are contradictions between these principles and judicial practice, and these can be exploited advantageously for corporate victims. A forceful demonstration that the law is failing to realize its own professed principles may have the beneficial effect of shaming it into action. For example, it claims allegiance to equality before the law, yet it systematically flouts this by treating corporate offenders and offending corporations leniently. It also claims our allegiance because it offers to protect our lives, limbs, and property, although it does little to protect us from predatory corporations.

Pushing the state and its legal institutions to act consistently with their own principles at least brings out the contradictions between what they say they are doing and what they are actually doing. Publicizing this may undermine their legitimacy, an outcome they would want to avoid. In response, they may close the gap, if only slightly, between principles and practices.

The final glimmer comes from recent attempts to develop novel strategies for controlling corporate crime. These turn out to be old ideas – worn-out and discredited as solutions to conventional criminals – reinvigorated by appearing in new bottles. If employees, consumers, and other corporate victims had their awareness sharpened and supported by trade unionism, consumerism, and environmentalism, and if the state and legal institutions could be shamed into closing the gap between lofty principles and tawdry practices, then some of these old ideas could be put into effective operation.

ENTERPRISING IDEAS FOR SANCTIONING DEVIANT ENTERPRISES

There seems to be agreement that corporate criminals can be deterred because their crimes are essentially *instrumental*, being outcomes of a fine balance between perceived costs and rewards, and they have no *emotional commitment* to them, whereas they do have a very high *stake in conformity and respectability*. Similarly, corporations are very much in the business of projecting a favourable image of themselves and their products, so that business might flourish. Consequently, it appears that in principle at least, both corporations and their officials could be deterred, unlike their conventional counterparts. But how?

The history of penal practice is replete with particular sanctions falling into disuse. *Positive repentance* is one such practice. There was a period when deviants were publicly humiliated and self-confessions, accompanied with displays of repentance, were deemed necessary rungs in the ladder towards social reintegration. This practice could be revived and applied to corporations (Fisse 1971). When they behave illegally, they could be required to pay for publicizing their own failures, negligence, indifference, apathy, and greed, and also the names, photographs, and misdeeds of each corporate offender. These adverts need not follow the insipid SMOKING CAN BE DANGEROUS FOR YOUR HEALTH recipe. Instead, they could be imaginative products of creative advertising agencies, paid for by the offender(s), to persuade employees, consumers, and the general public to be cautious in the future of this corporation and its officials.

The idea of positive repentance for corporations has already been implemented in some American states, but the results have not been too impressive, largely because the logic of the sanction has not been followed through. Thus the Federal Trade Commission instructed STP, a marketer of oil additives and other automotive products, to correct false, misleading, and fraudulent advertising claims, or face criminal prosecution. The corporation chose the former; the agency fined it $500,000 and instructed it to spend a further $200,000 in corrective advertising. However, STP placed these adverts in such outlets as *Business Week*, *Harvard Business Review*, *National Geographic*, and *Time Business Edition*, whereas the original misleading advertisements appeared in such consumer-orientated journals as *Auto News*, *Car and Driver*, *Hot Rod*, *Motor Age* and *Playboy* (Ermann and Lundman 1982: 140). So those less likely to buy the products knew what these could and could not achieve, whilst potential consumers remained misguided by the original advertisements.

However, although this example reflects the failure of the Federal Trade Commission to think the sanction of positive repentance through to its logical conclusion, it also demonstrates just how powerful this sanction could be, had it been accompanied by just one further instruction – 'publish the repenting adverts in the original outlets'. That STP deliberately chose to place the correct information in obscure papers read by financial enthusiasts rather than motor enthusiasts (the two populations may overlap, but not by much) indicates just how much of a deterrent positive repentance could be if properly executed.

When Philip Schrag (1971) became director of the New York Department of Consumer Affairs, he soon realized that companies could easily delay criminal prosecution cases, so he moved from a 'judicial model' of control to a 'direct action' model. This included threats and use of adverse publicity, revocation of licences, writing directly to consumers to warn them of company practices, and exerting pressure on reputable financial institutions and suppliers to withdraw support of the targeted company. In his view, this produced better results because the companies wished to avoid their respectability being tarnished.

There are, however, two major problems with a policy of imposing positive repentance directly, or in Schrag's case, indirectly. First, the company may refuse or not be deterred. Second, the regulatory agency may in response be able to impose a fine, but this would normally be small and ineffectual. This leaves criminal prosecution as the only viable option. But this would be a tiresome choice to make unless conviction were probable. However, under the present arrangements for prosecuting corporations, convictions are very infrequent.

One of the major stumbling blocks in the criminal prosecution of corporations and their officials is that costs to the state become excessive as the case is stretched out for endless months and sometimes years. According to Braithwaite (1981b) there are numerous reasons why smart lawyers are able to accomplish this form of economic deterrence. For example:

the complexity of the law enables them to discover loopholes and multiple meanings in the vague and often ambiguous wording of corporate law(s) – the pursuit of each interpretation is a further delay in the case reaching a conclusion;

the complexity of company records, which are not only subject to mysterious, (but relief-bringing) disappearances down the corporation vortex, but when occasionally discovered are often so specialized and riddled with technical jargon that the average jurist finds them unintelligible – naturally corporate lawyers render them intelligible in ways which favour their clients;

the complexity of corporate structures, which often consist of so many subsidiaries and specialized divisions, within and beyond national boundaries, that unknotting the tangled thread of responsibility becomes difficult, if not impossible, thus making the view that 'no one was to blame' easy to accept;

the complexity of science, which renders forging a direct causal link between corporate practice and the death, injury, or economic loss of employees, consumers, and the general public, very difficult to prove 'beyond a reasonable doubt', particularly when those 'experts' called in to testify to the relationship add so many qualifications and possibilities that almost everything appears possible but nothing certain.

All the above suggests that serious consideration should be given to abandoning judicial practices which protect the accused from arbitrary or unjust conviction, or which ensure they receive the benefit of the doubt, and exploring alternative judicial principles more relevant to prosecuting (and convicting) corporations and their officials (Friedman 1979). For example, regulatory agencies should be strengthened, particularly in their legal departments, so that it would be possible to nurture a pool of state lawyers sufficiently specialized and experienced to be a fair match for corporate lawyers. The 'right to trial by jury' could also be abandoned. Instead, trials could be heard by a panel of judges or juries especially selected for their ability to understand the complexities of cases against corporations. The 'limited' intrusion of 'strict liability' into criminal law could be expanded to cover more and more corporate behaviour so that the issue of responsibility and intention becomes subsidiary to the more pressing need to compensate victims and make the offending corporation foot the bill. Finally, maybe the 'balance of probabilities' should be substituted for 'beyond reasonable doubt'. Achieving the latter is so difficult that attempts to put corporations and their officials down the hole they belong in are often stymied.

Whilst each of these may be attractive, they do raise a vexing question: would their acceptance represent an indefensible system of dual justice, one providing fewer rights to the accused and thus increasing the chances of conviction? It would be too easy to say 'Yes, and not before time either.' Clearly it would be difficult to justify a dual system of justice if it led to certain types of people being more easily convicted, for the whole concept of the rule of law was to tip the balance of power away from the accusing state to the accused individual because it was rightly felt a too one-sided contest without such protection. But would the same objection have such weight if one judicial system applied to *individuals* and the other to *corporations* (and other organizations)?

This question is crucial, for the essence of corporate crime is not the behaviour of individuals, but the 'behaviour' of corporations. It is, in other words, endemic *within* the corporation's standard operating procedure (Hopkins 1980a), or is inherent *within* the nature of relationships between corporations and their environment in a world capitalist economy (Barnett 1981), or *within* the asymmetric power relationship between transnational corporations and national state regulatory agencies (Braithwaite 1979b, 1981a). Prosecuting individual corporate executives, particularly where some have the dubious 'responsibility for going to jail' (Braithwaite 1981b: 35) in exchange for premature elevation to a high salaried but non-responsible position, is simply missing the point. *In order to be effective, the level of intervention to regulate corporate crime has to be organizational rather than individual.* But it was not with this intervention level in mind that the rule of law and various protective judicial principles were formulated. To grant these rights and judicial privileges to corporations (and other organizations) is simply to give them additional resources for a judicial battle in which many, particularly the transnationals, are already more than a fair match for national state regulatory agencies. Indeed, it would be unjustified (and plain silly) to strengthen corporate power further by granting them judicial privileges originally formulated to protect relatively powerless individuals.

If it is agreed that to regulate corporate crime the level of intervention should be organizational (although individual offenders should be prosecuted in tandem) and different judicial principles to increase the state's chances of securing conviction should be instituted, then what? Ironically, it is just at the organizational level that ideas of deterrence, inca-pacitation, rehabilitation, and restitution to the community and the offended gain this season's attractive fashionable glow.

First, there is the issue of *fines*. Their paltry and insignificant level has already been considered. Clearly there is scope here for change. Fines could at least be raised to a level comparable *pro rata* to a parking fine! But there is a limit to achieving justice through this judicial sanction. If fines were so high that corporations went bankrupt, innocent employees, consumers, and dependents would suffer. It would be wrong to make them pay the price of justice – although this might nudge us into remembering that innocent wives and children and other dependents are made to suffer when the state imprisons thousands of working-class men for crimes which are often insignificant compared with corporate crimes. Clearly a balance has to be located between a reasonable fine and one that cripples. Given the rational nature of corporate crime, a higher level of fines than is imposed currently would probably deter some potential offenders. But relying on this instrument is crude, lacks imagination, and does not achieve other goals desirable in the control and regulation of corporate crime (Stone 1975).

To prevent offenders repeating their misbehaviour, we no longer hang murderers, castrate rapists, or cut off thieves' hands. Instead, we commit these and other offenders to varying terms of imprisonment. This incapacitates them temporarily; whilst imprisoned they cannot victimize the public, although they do continue to victimize other prisoners, sometimes at a rate that exceeds community crime levels. Indeed, according to Marvin Wolfgang (Braithwaite 1981b: 15) the chances of being a victim of homicide in the US are five times as high for white males inside prison than for those outside. The chances of being raped are also high (Brownmiller 1975: 257–67; Davis 1970).

Corporate executives could be incapacitated by imprisonment; whilst inside they could not be victimizing employees, consumers, share-holders, or the general public. In addition, the fear of imprisonment may instil the fear of rape into young, smooth, neat, corporate executives – as it did in the case of certain Watergate conspirators – and lead to a dramatic and welcome improvement in their behaviour. There is there-fore some hope that imprisoning executives might, through incapacita-tion and deterrence, bring down the incidence of corporate crime. But this must be a cautious and overly optimistic conclusion. If corporations merely promoted or recruited new personnel to replace the faint-hearted or imprisoned, then frightening and removing executives to prison may have only a minimal impact on corporate crime.

There is however, a way round this: 'imprison' all or part of the offending corporation. By nationalizing for a specific period – length depending upon the expected time needed for rehabilitation and the severity of the offence – and placing public-appointed directors to the board with a duty to inform the public and advise the remaining corporate directors, the chances of recidivating could be reduced considerably. Since no more is claimed for the incapacitation effect on conventional criminals, it appears reasonable to recommend it for offending corporations. However, within the political climate of industrialized capitalistic societies, such 'socialist' penal sanctions might well be viewed as draconian and ideologically repugnant. There are though two other measures which would achieve the same limited objective and which appear more liberal in comparison with nationalizing (imprisoning) offending corporations.

The courts could impose a *probation order*. This would not mean that an executive reports once a week to a local probation office to affirm that all is well back in the corporate suite. It would mean that courts appoint teams of probation officers, drawn from a pool of accountants, lawyers, engineers, mechanics, chemists, physicists, management scientists, and so on, and selected to meet the requirements of each situation. The purpose of the 'new' probation-order team would be to monitor standard operating procedures, research programme strategies, communications networks, command structures, and any other structural factors which might be linked to the corporation's previous misbehaviour and then make recommendations which the company could not refuse to implement without the risk of revoking the probation licence and returning to court for resentencing.

Of course this liberal reform would mean a dramatic increase in the cost of the probation service. Not only would their number have to be increased but they would also need to undergo years of specialized training for which they would expect a commensurate reward. The attractiveness of this reform though is that it need not add to public expenditure. Whereas conventional criminals lack the wherewithal to pay for being placed on probation, no such inability is true for corporations. Consequently, the costs of strengthening and extending the probation service could be defrayed by charging a fee to the offending corporation. This would be sufficient to guarantee that the public were not indirectly paying for the corporation's rehabilitation.

Another possibility is that the court could impose a *community service order*. Under this a corporation could be required to, say, build a new hospital, or pay for a motorway, school, nursery, or library. In this way badly needed public resources, which cannot be easily paid for, could be met by those corporations whose financial reserves are sufficient for a proportion to be ploughed back into the community from which they were originally largely reaped. An alternative form might be for the corporation to sell a proportion of its products at strictly cost price to those sections of the community who are under-privileged and in need of these occasional subsidies.

Finally, the court could act directly in the interests of the victims and instruct the corporation to *compensate* them. This would avoid civil actions, which are often defeated because individual victims, even when they decide to act co-operatively, are rarely a match for corporations who decide it is better to be prudent than just. For example, in early 1983 MP Jack Ashley was attempting to secure the passage of a Private Member's Bill through parliament which would require pharmaceutical companies to establish a 'no blame compensation fund'. This would enable victims to claim damages without facing the difficult task of proving corporate negligence before receiving any compensation. The immediate cause of this putative legislation is the possibility that nearly 70 arthritic sufferers have died and nearly 4,000 have been injured as a result of taking the drug Opren. As yet, the manufacturer has not paid civil damages because negligence has not been proven in court.

The selective imposition of fines, probation orders, community service orders, and compensation orders, particularly when coupled with 'positive repentance' for the corporation and occasional imprisonment (not for merely thirty days) for executives would undoubtedly achieve the penal aims of deterrence, incapacitation, rehabilitation, and restitution better than the present system of token fines and infrequent short imprisonment sentences. But for these to be achieved, a substantial proportion of offending corporations must first be caught. To ensure a steady supply of corporations who could be prosecuted, other liberal reforms need to be considered.

An obvious major difference between corporate and conventional crime is that the former's victims often remain unaware. This has considerable implications for regulating and controlling corporate crime. Police work with conventional crime is primarily *reactive*; it responds to victim-complaints. If the regulatory agency relied on victim-complaints for corporate crime, then it might never find itself in business. Relying, as they do, on irregular, inadequate, notified, and often superficial inspections, or on data provided by the corporations themselves renders state regulatory agencies and the police (where they are relevant, as in say the fraud squad) very defective in their ability to locate corporate crime.

Since a low rate of detection is a major encouragement to corporate crime, it might be necessary to pursue *proactive* policies such as deploying state spies and informers, entrapping corporate offenders, and strongly encouraging 'whistle-blowing' or 'grassing'. It could be argued that since these are indefensible when applied, as they are currently, to conventional criminals, they ought not to be extended to corporate criminals. But this argument needs considering. It is easy to capture a large number of conventional criminals without needing to spy, entrap, or encourage 'grassing'; this is not true of corporate criminals who are extremely difficult to detect. In many of the conventional crimes for which offenders receive imprisonment, there are no real victims. For example, nearly one-quarter of people in prison are there because they were unable to pay their fine, others are there because of 'consenting' sex below the age of consent, drug addiction, being drunk and disorderly, or begging abroad. With corporate crime however, there are always victims and they are frequently numerous. For their sakes, and the sakes of others who follow, more efficient means of apprehending offending corporations are desirable. Finally, people who 'grass' on conventional criminals constantly risk physical and sometimes fatal retribution, whereas corporate 'informers' are dismissed and risk prolonged unemployment and career fracture. The state is better able to protect the corporate 'grass' because he (or she) could be guaranteed a job for life as a reward for information leading to conviction for a serious corporate crime.

BUT WOULD THESE IDEAS BE EFFECTIVE?

In the film *Hospital* George C. Scott plays the administrator attempting to impose some order on the chaos of misadventure, accidents, and disasters passing themselves off as medical care. In a moment of weary despair, he turns to a colleague and says, 'It's like pissing into the wind!' There are reasons for believing that if the above liberal reforms were implemented, they might not significantly reduce the volume of corporate crime. This is not, as Young (1981: 328) asserts, because they are 'well calculated to be ineffective', but rather because they have not been framed with a crucial issue in mind – how far can a national state regulatory agency effect the operations of a transnational corporation, particularly when its parental state is one of the two world imperialist powers?

The history of corporate legislation enforcement is a history of penalizing the small fish whilst letting the big ones escape. For example, Snider examined the enforcement of the Canadian Combine Investigation Act, 1889, which makes it 'illegal to conspire or arrange with another person to limit unduly the facilities to manufacture any article, or to prevent or lessen unduly competition in the manufacture or production of any article and to thereby increase the price' (1978: 147). This is an indictable offence which carries a two years' prison sentence. During the period 1961–73, the Department of Consumer and Corporate Affairs was more likely to take out an enforcement order against a company that did *not* dominate the market, and was therefore in no position to affect the market price than one that did have such power! Snider argues that the presence of dominant companies 'seems to make the government prosecutors more wary, probably because such companies always have the most skilled battery of lawyers who will pursue each case to the Supreme Court if possible' (1978: 154). Goff and Reasons, after analysing the period 1952–72, came to the same conclusion: 'the Combines Branch has centred its attentions upon the investigations, prosecutions, and conviction of small- medium-sized companies and corporations, leaving the very largest corporations free to engage in their monopolistic practices' (1978: 86).

An analysis of enforcement practices in the US during the mid 1970s reached a similar conclusion:

'the amount of fine bears no systematic relation to the size of the firm. In fact, of all fines imposed in 1975 and 1976, the medium fine . . . for large firms ($1,000) was smaller than that for medium-size corporations . . . . In addition, smaller fines were used in proportionately more cases involving the largest corporations: for these firms, 86 per cent of all fines were $5,000 or less, while only 6.5 per cent were over $45,000. The corresponding percentages for medium-sized corporates were 68 per cent and 18 per cent respectively and for smaller firms 54 and 38.5 per cent respectively.'

(Clinard and Yeager 1980: 126)

If the enforcement practices were strengthened and a more determined effort were now made to capture the big corporations, there would probably be a rude surprise. Bigger fish might indeed be caught, but in the meantime they have grown into killer sharks with teeth big enough to bite through any net we might attempt to throw over them. National corporations have become transnational corporations, and the concentration at the top of major world industries has become even more concentrated in the hands of transnationals.

The internationalization and concentration of capital would not be material to the control and regulation of corporate crime if transnationals were well behaved. But the sad fact is, *they are the worst offenders*. This emerged clearly from the recent, and as yet, most comprehensive survey of corporate crime in the US. Clinard and Yeager's study involved:

'a systematic analysis of federal administrative, civil and criminal actions either initiated or completed by 25 federal agencies . . . against the 477 largest publicly owned manufacturing corporations in the US during 1975 and 1976. In addition, a more limited study was made of the 105 largest wholesale, retail, and service corporations.'

(Clinard and Yeager 1980: 110–11)

However, even this study was restricted in its ability to portray the extent and incidence of corporation crime. It was not able to cover financial, banking, and commercial corporations. Neither was it able to cover all complaints made by employees, consumers, and the public. Instead, it confined itself to *actions initiated against corporations* (which is the equivalent to arrest/prosecution) and *actions completed* (which is the equivalent to conviction). Consequently, the study probably covered 'only the tip of the iceberg of total violations, but they do constitute an index of illegal behaviour by the large corporations' (Clinard and Yeager 1980: 111).

Clinard and Yeager discovered that violations were far more likely to be committed by large corporations. Thus, if the corporations in their study were divided into three groups depending on the size of their annual sales, then they calculated that those with sales over $1 billion constituted 42 per cent of all corporations but committed nearly three-quarters of not only all violations but all serious violations, whereas those small firms with sales with less than half a billion dollars constituted nearly one-third of firms analysed but only committed less than 10 per cent of all violations. Not only were the largest firms the most criminal, but those corporations that dominated 'the oil, pharmaceutical and motor vehicle industries were the most likely to violate the law.' (Clinard and Yeager 1980: 119). Relative to what their size warranted and depending on which type of offence was examined, the oil-refining industry committed crimes at a rate five to nine times higher than would be expected, the motor industry three to seven times, and the pharmaceutical industry was four to six times as criminal as would be predicted.

When it is realized that of the fifteen largest corporations in the world in 1978, three were car manufacturers, eight were oil companies, and one was in chemicals, it can be appreciated that the largest corporations within the most concentrated sections of international capital formation are committing more than their share of law violations. Furthermore, these giant corporations possess such wealth and power that they not only affect our lives, limbs, health, and property from the forceps to the grave, but they also bend the political democratic process in such a way that their interests are often prioritized over those of the electorate, consumers, employees, and shareholders. The outcome is that national states, which exist to prevent life being poor, nasty, short, brutal, and solitary, are a match for the unreasonable person who commits conventional crimes, but 'are no match for the resources and size of . . . great corporations: General Motors could buy Delaware . . . if DuPont were willing to sell it' (Nader and Green 1973: 79).

In the final analysis, it may be that national states and their control agencies are relatively autonomous of a particular social class, and that in that sense could, under the right circumstances, become an instrument, at least for a specific and limited objective, of any particular class or alliance of classes or pressure groups. Under their temporary influence, the state could introduce some or all of the liberal reforms outlined above. These would undoubtedly deter smaller corporations and bring down the incidence of corporate crime, particularly amongst the relatively smaller national-bound corporations, and even those larger corporations whose capital equipment is relatively fixed and who need the local more specialized work force. If capital transfer to other countries was also made illegal or tightly controlled, this would also help to prevent corporations evading the law by exporting those behaviours which would be illegal in one country to another where they are not. However, even these barriers would not prevent forever a corporation determined to maximize its interests. Neither would a sovereign state's government necessarily want to oppose transnational corporations, for the former often find themselves in the unenviable position of needing the latter more than the latter need them.

A clear example of this is provided by Carson (1981) in his analysis of the other price of Britain's oil. He argues that in order to extract Britain's oil reserves fast – a policy objective pursued dogmatically by all governments over the last fifteen years – it was necessary to depend upon the transnational oil companies. They agreed to extract oil quickly, but argued they would not be able to do so if hindered by trifling safety regulations that applied to on-shore industries. To disarm reluctant government ministers, the transnationals pointed out that there were other vast reserves in South America, Mexico, and Alaska, and that rather than find themselves restricted with petty regulations they would prefer to spend vast amounts on exploratory research elsewhere. British governments had no strength to resist these arguments, and as a consequence the North Sea Oil installations, working literally at breakneck speed unfettered by safety regulations comparable to those operating on-shore, had a fatality rate eleven times greater than the construction industry, nine times higher than mining, and six times greater than quarrying. Carson concludes, after carefully researching the individual incidents which constituted this high rate of fatality (as well as those involving serious injuries) that the majority could have been avoided if the 'political economy of speed' had not been allowed to supercede the 'political economy of employees' lives and limbs'.

With the internationalization of capital and the concentration of power in the hands of fewer and fewer transnational corporations, national law violation may well become old fashioned. These giant corporations may simply opt for law evasion. That is, they may choose to export, say, plants emitting too much (illegal) pollution, or manufacturing processes where the labour costs are legally maintained at a 'high' level, or products banned for safety reasons, to other countries where pollution laws, legal wage levels, and product safety regulations are all less stringent. The exportation of 'corporate crime' will normally be to Third World countries which, because they are more dependent upon capital, have fewer resources to check manufacturer's claims or police corporate activities, and because their officials are more susceptible to corruption are less likely to circumvent corporate behaviour. This is a depressing conclusion for liberal reformers. National states simply may not possess the will or power to 'knock the stuffing' out of the worst corporate offenders. Maybe persuasion, based upon appeals to ethical considerations and the flickering embers of nationalism are the only tools left to crack corporate crime. But they will not succeed where the law has failed.

If there is no preparedness to see extensive nationalization of the worst offending corporations and if there is no political or national will to place public officials on the boards of directors to guarantee that 'our' interests are given as much consideration as those of the corporation, then clearly the will to control corporations has atrophied in the withering light of pragmatism. Maybe smaller corporations can be deterred, but any attempt to constrain seriously the large transnational corporations will ultimately affect us adversely where it hurts most – in our economic performance. So better to become subservient than to waste our energies attempting to bring the worst criminal organizations to justice.

But if that is the depressing conclusion, then it has implications for our treatment of conventional criminals. In 1981, there were nearly 85,000 males and 4,000 females received into prison under sentence in England and Wales. Of these 20,000 males and 1,100 females (nearly 25 per cent and about 30 per cent respectively) were imprisoned for defaulting on fine payments. Can it be justified to send to prison people too poor to pay fines – and there are more such persons during times of economic crisis – not only when the original crime of which they were convicted did not warrant a prison sentence, but when their crime is trivial in the extreme in comparison with corporate crimes which we lack the political will to tackle directly by socialist remedies? By the same logic, can it be right to send people to prison because they have been found guilty of drunken-ness, vagrancy, offences related to prostitution, and drug offences (of whom there were nearly 900 men and 100 women in 1981)? Maybe such considerations will also mellow our attitude towards the imprisonment of nearly 9,000 men and 500 women (representing nearly 25 and 45 per cent respectively of all those sentenced to immediate imprisonment) for theft, handling stolen goods, fraud, and forgery, when the amounts of value involved are nothing in comparison with the millions stolen by offending corporations on whom our criminal justice system has given up. If there is no way of implementing justice for the largest and worst offending corporations then it is surely unjust to pursue with such ruthless and cruel tenacity the majority of those eventually condemned to prison. By all means punish those committing violence against us, but when we fail to punish those practising minor acts of genocide, let us be merciful on those committing comparatively minor acts of violence. If that is too hard to stomach, then the political will should be discovered or constructed so that our government will pursue vigorously and ruthlessly all those, including transnational corporations, who violate laws, particu-larly those designed to protect our lives and limbs. If the price of achieving justice for offending corporations is a more socialized mode of production, that may be a price worth paying if our lives, limbs, and property are protected from predatory transnational corporations.

3 Police crime

A minority of people, most of whom are relatively powerless, directly experience an 'unacceptable face of police work'. This 'ugly face' is carefully concealed from the majority of respectable citizens, who instead are presented with a media-projected image of the police which is both partial and idealized (Chibnall 1977; Christensen, Schmidt, and Henderson 1982; Hurd 1979). In this image, the police are dramatically portrayed as waging war on our behalf against such dangerous criminals as muggers, armed robbers, thieves, murderers, terrorists, and an assortment of psychopaths.

Not only does this image obscure the wider political and necessarily repressive function the police fulfil – about which more later – but it also mystifies the extent and nature of police crime against particular segments of the public. It performs this mystification not by denying the existence of police crime – that manoeuvre would simply lack credibility – but by transforming its meaning. Instead of portraying police crimes, like any other crime, as wrong and indefensible, it justifies them within the context of police work; 'bending the rules', as it is euphemistically described, enables officers to solve a particular contradiction between enforcing the law, which requires they 'get their man', and relying on a criminal justice system which respects the rights of the accused to such an extent that the guilty are often found innocent. Thus when officers are portrayed, as they are, for example in *The Sweeney*, employing physical violence, blackmail, bending the Judges' Rules, breaking in and removing 'villains' personal effects, or planting evidence on 'villains' who are 'due for some', they are not invariably seen as criminal. Instead their behaviour is rendered as 'good and necessary police work' because it effectively administers and achieves justice (albeit it rough) and thereby protects us from those criminals who pose a real threat to the community.

Only those police crimes capable of being mystifyingly transformed into 'acceptable rule-bending but necessary police work' are featured regularly in popular television series. The public are sensitized to officers solving the *Dirty Harry Problem*, as Klockers (1980) calls it, because the criminal justice system is presented as a slow, bureaucratic machine which possibly provides too many protective civil rights to criminals – a theme publicized by Robert Mark (1973) when he was Commissioner of the Metropolitan Police – and because criminals are described as increasingly sophisticated and protected by bent lawyers who find technical loopholes through which the guilty escape.

Those police crimes which cannot be transformed into this cozy comforting image, such as corruption and gratuitous violence – particularly against ethnic minorities, the economically marginalized, and political radicals – are either denied, or when that is impossible, put down to the antics of an odd, disturbed, or greedy person. Sergeant Challenor represents a notable example of this latter strategy. In the mid 1960s, he was allowed, discreetly and conveniently to retire prematurely after it was alleged that he had systematically planted bricks in innocent demonstrators' pockets as evidence that they intended using them against the police! This one 'bad apple', and numerous other examples throughout the 1970s is the nearest the media has come to portraying police crime. It is never presented as something endemic and inherent in the nature of police work.

What police crimes?

In this chapter we will not be concerned with crimes police officers commit as individuals. Like all members of the public, they occasionally and episodically break the law. The focus here will be on law violations by police in their capacity as police officers. In particular various forms of *brutality* such as killing or 'beating-up' suspects or bystanders, 'rioting' (Stark 1972) and arresting, threatening, intimidating, and blackmailing innocent citizens, and *corruption*, such as accepting bribes for not enforcing the law, fabricating or forgetting evidence, covertly (or even overtly) planning or executing crimes, directly (as part of the deal) or indirectly (by concealing the extent of the value concerned) acquiring part (or all) of the proceeds. Brutality and corruption by their very nature are not actions performed by officers acting in isolation from peers; they are essentially acts which can only be carried out (and concealed) with the active, or at least passive support of peers and the connivance of superiors.

It is very difficult in the present law and order climate even to mention police violence and corruption without being accused of adopting an hysterical and anti-police stance. The Home Office, the Police Federation, and other establishment supporters immediately issue denials or reiterate the 'bad apple' theme. The police, we are told constantly, are doing a commendable job against dedicated and unscrupulous people out to undermine the fabric of a decent democratic society. Any suggestion that violence and corruption are endemic in police work is officially viewed as 'gross exaggeration'.

Of course, it is hard to meet this accusation successfully because the evidence needed to prove widespread police violence and corruption is often shielded by official secrets or official anal retentiveness. Yet it is our duty to try because in a democratic society citizens are expected to criticize those in positions of power, particularly those who are not closely accountable for how that power is exercised. Fortunately there is sufficient evidence, often bearing official credentials, to give even the most doubtful pause for thought.

POLICE BRUTALITY

By the very nature of their work, police officers are likely to confront 'dangerous, violent criminals' who directly threaten their lives. Like every other citizen, officers have the right to protect themselves, even if in the extreme it means causing another's death. Unfortunately, the disturbing fact about police-caused homicides is that the deceased often fails to resemble this stereotype. Without the excuse of justifiable self-defence, there emerges the haunting spectre of police murdering or illegally killing civilians. This nightmarish image has been brought into sharp focus recently by a disturbing number of notorious cases – Liddle Towers in 1976, Blair Peach and James Kelly in 1979, James McGeown in 1980, Colin Roach and James Davey in 1983, each of whom died after coming into physical contact with the police. (A number of notorious cases also occurred in prison, for example, Richard 'Cartoon' Campbell and Barry Prosser in 1980, Winston Rose in 1981, Terry Smerdon and Jim Heather-Hayes in 1982, and Oliver Clairmonte in 1983.) In each of these 'sudden' deaths in police (and prison) custody, a number of people have suspected murder or at least manslaughter – suspicions which have not diminished even though the Director of Public Prosecutions Office has refused to prosecute a single police officer in connection with these and nearly thirty other cases referred to it since 1970. This official passivity is even more surprising considering that in many instances coroner's courts returned verdicts of 'misadventure', 'accidental death', 'suicide', or 'unlawful killing'.

Fortunately, the indignation of families and friends, sympathetically reported by investigative and conscientious journalists, and supported by diligent MPs, has kept the issue of police-caused homicide alive. Indeed, as a result of persistent questioning in the House of Commons, the Home Affairs Select Committee was asked to examine the procedures by which deaths in police custody were investigated. Responding positively, this Committee prized open a box of 'official secrets' just enough for the curious to glimpse some unpleasant truths (1980).

What emerged is that underneath the tip of these highly publicized cases lurks an iceberg of suspicious deaths. In England and Wales from 1970 to 1979 there were 274 deaths in police custody – there were unfortunately no comparative data for Scotland or Northern Ireland (see *Table 2*). Whilst no reasonable person would argue that all these were the result of police malfeasance, there undoubtedly exists a number of deaths, like those of McGeown and Kelly, where their causes remain shrouded by festering ambiguity. This ambiguity does not only stretch to those twenty-three cases where no inquest was held, or those further sixteen cases in which an 'open verdict' was returned. It also reaches those where 'natural causes' (sixty-six), 'death by misadventure' (sixty-eight) and 'accidental death' (forty-six) verdicts were recorded, for there is a growing disquiet concerning the very procedures and processes by which these categories are constructed in coroners' courts where an adversary process is not mandatory. This means that witnesses and documents are not always examined, and even when they are, the examination may not be as thorough, exhaustive, and subject to cross-questioning as it might be in a court of law.

There has also emerged alarming evidence on the growing number of deaths in police custody. From a low of eight in 1970, these rose to a peak of forty-eight by 1978. Even more disturbing, the number of such deaths which were officially categorized as 'misadventure' and 'accidental' increased disproportionately. Whereas in 1970 these constituted only 25 per cent (two out of eight) of the verdicts on deaths in police custody, they constituted 50 per cent (sixteen out of thirty-two) of the verdicts in 1980.

All this would be bad enough, but 'reality' is probably worse! In the

Table 2 Deaths in police custody 1970–79: England and Wales: by cause of death

year	total no. of deaths in custody	inquest held verdict: death due to –					circumstances not established		
		natural causes	mis-adventure	accidental death	suicide	other verdicts	open verdict	no verdict given	no inquest held
1970	8	4	1	1	1	—	1	—	—
1971	19	4	4	2	6	2	—	—	1
1972	19	5	3	6	3	—	2	—	—
1973	21	8	3	4	3	—	1	—	2
1974	27	8	6	3	3	2	2	—	3
1975	42	8	16	7	3	2	1	1	4
1976	23	5	5	1	7	—	3	1	1
1977	35	8	10	6	5	1	—	2	3
1978	48	8	10	10	8	2	4	—	6
1979	32	8	10	6	2	1	2	—	3
	274	66	68	46	41	10	16	4	23

Reprinted from: Home Affairs Committee (1980) *Deaths in Custody*. London: HMSO, p. 120.

first place there is a glaring omission in the above data. It refers only to persons killed whilst *in* police custody. There are many deaths which result *after* release from custody or after contact with the police which never became custody, but which are none the less causally linked with events occurring during that custody or encounter. Thus both Liddle Towers, who died after being released from custody, and Blair Peach, who died, according to the evidence of many eye-witnesses, after being hit by police whilst he was leaving a legal demonstration against the National Front, are not included in the official total of 274 deaths in police custody. It would be unsafe and naive to assume that these were the only two cases not accounted for in the 274 deaths in custody. Consequently, the 'real' number of unjustifiable police-caused homicides in England and Wales remains unknown, partly because the total number of police-caused homicides remain unknown. However, it is surely higher than the number of officers convicted of murder or manslaughter, which is none!

Second, if data on police-caused homicides were complete – which they are not – and they were broken down by 'victim' social character- istics – which they are not – then it might be seen that the 'target' population is not random, but is drawn from the economically margin- alized, politically radical, and ethnically oppressed. The warrant for this assertion is that evidence of this kind is available for the North American continent, and there is no reason to believe that the situation there differs dramatically from that in England and Wales. Of course, the total number of civilians killed pro rata is much higher simply because the weaponry of the American police is that much deadlier. But the actual victimization *pattern* should not differ greatly from that in England and Wales because the social structures, i.e. economic and ethnic inequali- ties are not that dissimilar.

In the United States of America, 'in a typical year of the late 1960s and early 1970s, there are at least 300 – and perhaps as many as 600 – citi- zens killed by the police. In other words, those figures mean that between 2 and 4 per cent of all homicides each year resulted from police shootings' (Binder and Scharf 1982: 3). This assertion approximates closely to that of Sherman and Langworthy (1979: 553) who concluded after carefully analysing all major sources of data, 'the police may be responsible for 3.6 per cent of all homicides – about one out of every twenty-eight'. As in England and Wales, the number of police-caused homicides in the US has also increased throughout the late 1960s and early 1970s at a rate faster than the increase in police personnel (Takagi 1974; Harring *et al.* 1977). But the one data area available for America though not England and Wales is the incidence of these killings on racial minorities. In a number of reports, it has been revealed that negroes are much more likely than whites to be killed by the police. The editors of *Crime and Social Justice* (1977) claimed that for the years 1950–72 the rate of police-caused homicides of negroes was between ten and thirteen times greater than of whites. Employing a different data source, Kobler (1975) came to a similar conclusion although he did not express his results in rates per 100,000 population. He scanned newspaper reports of police-caused homicide and concluded that only 43 per cent involved white victims although whites represent an overwhelming proportion of the total population. In his study of seven cities, Milton (1977) found that 79 per cent of police shooting victims were black, although only 39 per cent of the population in these urban areas were black. Harding and Fahey (1973) examined data for one city and came up with respective percentages of 75 and 33. And, to labour the point, other authors (Burnham 1973; Fyfe 1978, 1982; Meyer 1980; Robin 1963) have all reported large discrepancies between the expected rate of black-victimization of police killing and the actual proportion of blacks in the population at risk. Of course, some of this over-representation in the population 'executed without justice' may be explained by the greater involvement of negroes in violent crimes in which guns are employed. However, the evidence is that even when this and other factors are taken into account, negroes are still more likely than whites to be killed by the police, particularly in those cities where regulations relating to police use of deadly force are not stringent and refer to vague criteria, such as 'under certain specified conditions' which are never specified! (Fyfe 1982: 718)

The crucial issue in police-caused homicides is 'what proportion are unjustifiable?' This is impossible to gauge accurately by examining official data because it is commonly recognized that suspected officers, with the collusion of their peers and supervisors, cover up or destroy incriminating evidence. It is also argued that coroners' courts, criminal courts, and the attached legal-medico professionals afford a protective shield which justice finds virtually impenetrable (Binder and Scharf 1982; Fyfe 1981; Kobler 1975; Sherman and Langworthy 1979). There are many instances where the evidence against the police seems over-whelming (Takagi 1974), but calculating the contribution these instances make to the totality of police-caused homicides is not easy. One attempt has been made by Kobler (1975). After analysing a nationwide newsclipping service on police killings, he concluded that '30 per cent (of victims) were either involved in no criminal activity or in a misdemeanour such as a traffic violation. An additional 27 per cent were engaged in property crimes, including auto-theft'. Fyfe analysed police shooting at *property* offenders in Memphis for the years 1969–75; he reported a 'black death rate . . . *while unarmed and non assaultive* (5.4 per 100,000) that is eighteen times higher than the comparable white rate (0.3)' (1982: 720). It hardly seems justifiable to kill citizens who decided to avoid arrest – as the police often allege – when their crime, had they been brought to justice, would not have earned even a prison sentence. Surely in these circumstances, officers' lives were not threatened to such an extent that fatal force was either required or justified.

What seems certain from the above is that the police, both in the US and the UK are using deadly force more frequently (and with more effect) than they were a decade ago, and that the unfortunate recipients of this are more likely to come from the ethnically oppressed (and probably the economically underprivileged as well). Furthermore, and being as cautious as possible, in at least a quarter of these, deadly force was probably not justified.

Police-caused homicides, and within that category unjustified killings, are intricately linked with, and an ultimate expression of police brutality against citizens. In North America, the rate of police-caused homicides may be greater than in Britain merely because the police there are armed – although that is now changing and British police are increasingly equipped with weapons they have been trained to use (*State Research Bulletin* No. 25, 1981). None the less, police can kill citizens in many ways, so that an exclusive focus on guns and their discharge is misleading. Any brutal assault, executed with truncheons or other blunt instruments, or involving boots, knees, heads, or fists, can and sometimes does result in a citizen being killed or severely injured. It is therefore vital to get some grip on the incidence of police brutality so that the extent of police violence against the person can be gauged.

One method of doing this is to examine complaints citizens make against the police for allegedly assaulting them. In England and Wales this is numerically the largest category of complaint against the police; for example, out of a total of 16,789 allegations in 1979, 3,178 (19%) were for assault. Furthermore, and again underlining the increased resort to violence, the number of such complaints have risen dramatically; thus in 1970 there were only 1,093, which means that allegations of assault have risen nearly 300 per cent over the last decade. This apparent dramatic rise in police crime cannot be explained away by the sheer increase in police personnel; this has risen from 92,844 in 1970 to 116,000 in 1980, which constitutes only a 25 per cent increase. In other words, complaints of assault have risen much faster than the number of police against whom such allegations can be made.

The incidence of police brutality can be put into perspective by comparing it with recorded indictable offences alleging assault and/or wounding. Taking 1970 as a base year, and calculating the rate of assault by considering the population at risk, i.e. those aged 15 to 65, and calculating the rate of police assault by considering the total number of police available to commit this, we discover (see *Table 3*) that the rates in England and Wales are very similar. Comparing columns 3 and 6 we see that throughout the 1970s both rates were roughly between 2 and 3 per 1,000 population. It is also clear that as the public have become more violent, so have the police; taking 1970 as the base year (=100) the public increased their rate of assault/woundings to 243 compared with a rise to 280 for the police. If, as the police frequently allege, the increase in recorded crimes of violence is proof that our society is becoming more and more dangerous and in need of a more determined and strengthened police force, then by the same logic, the increase in recorded allegations of police brutality is proof that the police are becoming more violent and that we need better institutionalized methods of deterrence and accountability.

There is also evidence that the proportion of complaints which allege police brutality has increased. Thus Stevens and Willis (1981: 9) show that allegations of assault by the Metropolitan police increased from 16.9 per cent of all complaints in 1970 to 20.9 per cent in 1979.

Finally, the victims of these assaults, as any conflict theorist (Chambliss and Seidman 1971; Collins 1975; Quinney 1974; Turk 1969, 1981) would predict, are likely to come from those ethnic minorities and economically marginalized groups who are already underprivileged. Consistent with this prediction, Stevens and Willis show that nearly one-quarter of complaints alleging police brutality are made by black or Asian citizens whereas they only constitute something like 6 per cent of the total population.

Not all citizens who consider they have been assaulted by the police are likely to lodge a complaint; consequently official data on complaints, like that on reported crime, are likely to be a gross under-estimation. One way around this problem would be to conduct a 'victimization' survey.

An attempt to accomplish this has recently been conducted by a Home Office research team (Tuck and Southgate 1981). They interviewed a sample of 568 West Indians and 255 whites living in Hulme, Moss Side, Lloyd Street, Rusholme, and Alexandra Park wards of the Greater Manchester police district in 1980. They reported that about 6 per cent of the population felt they had at some time had grounds for complaining, and between 2 and 3 per cent had experienced this sensation during the last year. Of those occurring within the last year, 21 per cent involved

Table 3 Increases in recorded indictable assault/wounding offences compared with increases in recorded complaints against the police for assault, England and Wales 1970–80

year	1 number of assault/wounding offences recorded[1]	2 per cent +/– 1970 = 100	3 rate per 1,000 adult population[2]	column 4 per cent +/– 1970 = 100	5 number of complaints against the police for assault[3]	6 per cent +/– 1970 = 100	7 rate per 1,000 police officers[4]	8 per cent +/– 1970 = 100
1970	39,266	100	1.26	100	1,093	100	1.2	100
1974	61,878	158	2.01	159	1,982	181	2.1	175
1977	80,609	205	2.59	205	2,888	264	2.9	242
1980	95,601	243	3.03	240	3,067	280	2.6	217

Notes
[1] Criminal Statistics, England and Wales, 1970, 1974, 1977, 1980 (London: HMSO)
[2] based on population aged 15–64
[3] Director of Public Prosecutions and Police Complaints Board, Report 1981
[4] Annual Statistical Abstracts for relevant years

allegations of assault. If this data source were sufficiently large and representative, it could serve as a basis for generalizing to the adult population of England and Wales; on that calculation, it would mean that each year something like 150,000 people out of a total 31 million aged 14–65 feel that they have been assaulted by the police recently. This is a startling and disturbing figure although it must be taken cautiously because the basis for its calculation is not entirely satisfactory.

Another study, this time in three American cities (Reiss 1971), used observers of police-public encounters to record instances where they considered the police had employed excessive physical force. In 3,826 such encounters they observed brutality 37 times. Since some encounters involved more than one citizen, the rate of assault was actually 5.9 per every 1,000 white citizens involved and 2.8 per 1,000 black citizens, and if the target population were limited to those the police considered 'suspects' then the comparable rates were respectively 41 and 23. Reiss concluded that 'if one accepts these estimates of the undue force against suspects, then there should be little doubt that in major metropolitan areas the sort of behaviour commonly called "police brutality" is far from rare' (Reiss 1971: 74). The higher rate of assault against whites is surprising, although without further details on the class position and employment status of the whites involved in these encounters it is impossible to disentangle the ethnic and the economic factors at work in these instances of police brutality.

What is clear from the above evidence is that police brutality is not an isolated incident but is a regular and frequent occurrence in police work. It qualifies for inclusion as a major crime problem because so many citizens are victimized and because the misuse of state power which involves the death (murder) or serious injury (assault) of citizens constitutes a crucial issue for our democratic political system.

Finally, unlike corporate crime, the victims, their friends, relatives, and neighbours are *aware* of this crime of domination. It is experienced by them subjectively as a part of their everyday harsh reality. Many young black males in British inner-city areas are now reluctant to drive their own car because they know the police will stop them, and if there is the slightest affront, real or imagined, to authority, a physical altercation or a trip to the station with the possibility of being charged – for crimes committed? – is a likely outcome. Curiously, this element of 'street crime' is ignored by campaigners for law and order; yet it is clear that relations between the police and economically marginalized populations – particularly Britons of West Indian extraction – are so bad that the resultant police violence constitutes a major element in street crime

(Humphrey 1972; Kettle and Hodges 1982: 64–97; Lambert 1972; Lea and Young 1982b; Scraton 1982).

POLICE CORRUPTION

According to McMullan (1961) 'A public official is corrupt if he accepts money or moneys worth for doing something which he is under a duty to do anyway, that he is under a duty not to do, or to exercise a legitimate discretion for improper reasons.' An even briefer definition is provided by Manning and Redfinder (1977) who suggest that 'corruption . . . refers to departures from correct procedures in exchange for goods, services, or money'.

Police forces everywhere and whenever they have existed have been poisoned by a well of corruption (Sherman 1974). The disease has varied in chronicity and acuteness, but its cure remains illusive, despite the recent 'discovery' of democratic forms of public accountability. Its current manifestations, both in Britain and North America, where public accountability is allegedly strict, demonstrates this failure. One contributory factor to the continued existence of police corruption is its relative invisibility, which in turn reflects a vital difference between the victim of police brutality and the 'victim' of police corruption.

The victims of police brutality are likely to feel aggrieved, indignant, and physically hurt. For these reasons, they are more likely than the 'victims' of police corruption to report the crime to officials or researchers. Consequently, as was documented above, there is quantitative evidence of police brutality. Police corruption, however, is not so easily discovered and is certainly less amenable to quantification.

It is sometimes 'victim'-initiated. For example, owners of licensed premises, parking lots, pornographic shops, homosexual bars, and other businesses where legal requirements and their regulation are unpredictable and uncertain, might actively seek out police officers to negotiate the exchange of money or goods in return for 'environmental tranquillity'. In this way, the costs (and hence profits) can be better forecast.

Similarly, persons engaged in lucrative criminal activities might suggest to officers courses of action other than law enforcement; this might well succeed because the profits from illegal enterprises, especially those involving the supply of heavily demanded services such as drugs, pornographic material, sex, gambling, and loans at higher than legal interest rates are large enough to divert considerable sums to officials in return for protection and still leave sufficient for the operators to live comfortably.

Finally, persons caught in minor criminal activity, such as parking illegally or exceeding speed limits, or being drunk in charge of a motor vehicle might attempt to avoid being booked and risking licence-endorsement by offering officers small inducements not to enforce the law.

On other occasions, the police initiate the corruptor-corruptee relationship but the former enters it appreciating the mutual benefits it involves.

Only rarely, as the police slip into extortion and protection rackets, is there a genuine 'victim'. For example, Chambliss (1978) documents the case of a restaurant's new owner being forced to pay the police – and through them the local organized crime cabal – in exchange for health, fire, and alcohol licence authorities relaxing the frequency and severity of their inspections and penalties.

Because the 'victims' of police corruption are more willingly, indeed eagerly involved than the victims of police brutality, it is relatively harder to quantify because those involved are less likely to report it. What would be the point of informing officers, as you handed them a stuffed manilla envelope, that 'this is corruption, PC Edwards!' Consequently, corruption penetrates the public consciousness rarely, like a missed heart-beat in an otherwise perfectly functioning body. This shock to the system occurs irregularly and with differing severity. Probably the most disturbing in England and Wales were the activities of Sergeant Goddard in Mayfair fifty years ago, or the so-called Brighton Conspiracy in 1957 which ended in a detective inspector being jailed for five years and a detective sergeant for three – whilst the rest of the gang avoided conviction – (Judge 1972), the Metropolitan drug squad and obscene publications squad corruption scandals of the early 1970s (Cox *et al.* 1977), and the investigation into corruption in the Metropolitan and City of London criminal investigation departments which was established in 1978 and was still proceeding (slowly) in 1983 (see below).

No general quantitative picture emerges from these episodic investigations because they are fundamentally concerned to gather sufficient evidence to mount a prosecution. The standard required to do this successfully is different from that necessary to document the existence and extensiveness of police corruption. Thus the Knapp Commission into police corruption in New York published a report which was not concerned with culpable individuals but with illuminating the problem. They concluded:

'We found corruption to be widespread . . . . In the five plainclothes divisions where our investigation was concentrated we found a strikingly standardized pattern of corruption. Plainclothesmen, participating in what is known in police parlance as a 'pad', collected regular bi-weekly or monthly payments amounting to as much as $3,500 from each of the gambling establishments in the area under their jurisdiction, and divided the take in equal shares. The monthly share per man . . . ranged from $300 and $400 in midtown Manhattan to $1,500 in Harlem. When supervisors were involved they received a share and half. . . . Evidence before us led us to the conclusion that the same pattern existed in the remaining divisions we did not investigate . . . . Corruption in narcotics enforcement lacked the organization of gambling pads, but individual payments . . . were commonly received and could be staggering in amount. . . . Corruption among detectives assigned to general investigative duties also took the form of shakedowns of individual targets of opportunity. Although these scores were not in the huge amounts found in narcotics, they not infrequently came to several thousand dollars . . . . Of course not all policemen are corrupt . . . an appreciable number do not engage in corrupt activities.'

That final note of cautious damnation by faint praise reached a kernel truth of corruption when it continued:

'(but) even those who themselves engage in no corrupt activities are involved in the sense that they take no steps to prevent what they know or suspect to be going on about them.'   (Knapp Commission 1973)

Explaining police crime

A fully social theory of police crime requires relating the micro factors of opportunities, career socialization, determinants of career advancement, occupational subculture, and (lack of) deterrence to the macro processes of social control in an unequal society where the problem of legitimacy has not been resolved successfully. Incorporating a macro dimension is necessary because whilst the micro processes are relevant to developing an understanding of 'why do they do it', they do not illuminate 'why they are allowed to do it'. This is important because 'being allowed to do something' frequently becomes part of the reason why one goes ahead and does it. This latter issue, the issue of 'licence' can only be grasped by situating the police in a broader, historically informed frame, namely viewing them as an agency for, and deriving benefit from, supporting, and reproducing forms of domination, and suppressing, fracturing, and demoralizing forms of resistance.

GETTING THAT WAY

Like corporate criminals, deviant police are not pathological villains. Despite the widely held belief that the force attracts authoritarians who hide and execute their lust for brutality behind a badge, there is no methodologically sound evidence that recruits intend doing police work in that fashion. Again like corporate criminals, deviant police get that way largely because of occupational experiences and socialization, particularly as these are mediated through the attitudes, beliefs, and values of police peers who warn recruits, in a friendly but informed fashion: 'don't be a sucker', 'everyone's doing it, so don't you be a fool', 'there's no other way of getting the job done efficiently, and the public wants the job done', 'if you're not with us, you're against us and we're against you'.

From the officers' perspective, police work is dangerous, socially isolating, and contains problems of authority which not only undermine efficiency, but frequently poison police-public encounters. The police regard themselves as front-line troops against certain types of violent criminals, terrorists, militant dissenters, and industrial agitators; they also view themselves as 'guardians of public morality' (Box 1981a: 171–77), although they realize that over many moral issues, particularly prostitution, homosexuality, abortion, pornography, alcohol and other drug consumption, there exist heated, volatile disagreements; finally they are often called in to dampen volcanic flare-ups between domestic couples. During the numerous occasions officers are engaged in these tasks, they perceive themselves to be highly visible targets for physical, and possibly fatal, aggression, which they have to face heroically – a theme well explored in the film triology, *New Centurions, Blue Knights*, and *Choirboys* (Reiner 1978).

The accumulation of experiences in which these dangers are present (and manifest) leads many officers to construct an image of the potential 'symbolic assailant' (Skolnick 1966: 45–8). The police not only treat very cautiously those citizens who resemble this 'symbolic assailant', but frequently engage in first-strike defensive behaviour against them. Naturally, the 'symbolic assailant' is likely to be a pastiche of class, sex, and racial ingredients, in which economically marginalized, ethnically oppressed males figure prominently. Whilst this may offer a rough and ready guide to lurking street dangers, it is likely to distort reality and consequently involve many citizens who although, from the officer's perspective, look 'dangerous and offensive', are in fact passive, innocent, and law-abiding. When these individuals are the recipients of police first-strike defensive behaviour, they perceive it, not unreasonably, to be an instance of police brutality.

Yet the police are likely to believe that unless they defend themselves in this manner, nobody else will offer protection. They know, again from occupational experiences and peer-group socialization, that many of the public who witness police in difficulties belong to that large section of the community under surveillance, harassed, and apprehended by the police. From this quarter, the police realistically expect little direct assistance; indeed, verbal encouragement for 'villains' often accompanies these altercations.

The police also believe that the criminal law offers them scant protection because it fails miserably to punish actual, or deter potential, assailants. Having consistently and actively campaigned in favour of capital punishment, at least for murderers of police officers, and feeling fortified by public support, the police have looked on astonished as successive parliaments over the last two decades have refused to reintroduce hanging. This has only fostered a belief that the police must protect themselves actively and hence deter potential assailants, a belief shored up by their experience of how the judiciary typically deals with citizens who assault the police. For example, a police sergeant interviewed by Baldwin and Kinsey said:

> 'But then you've got the other situation where they start to cut up rough. And whenever they start cutting up in this station – in any station – they're lost. If they take a swing at a cop it's fatal. That's the only time when it's a dead cert; and the idea is don't treat them gentle.
>
> The only reason is that if he does it and gets away with hitting a policeman, he goes up to court and gets fined £25 at £3 a week. That's no deterrent to stop him hitting a copper. The only deterrent is to hit him back fucking harder than he hit you and to let him know it's not just one – there's two and a half thousand of us that'll keep on hitting him.'   (Baldwin and Kinsey 1982: 50)

Social isolation does not prevent the police viewing themselves as active partners in an alliance with the 'respectable' public; it merely prevents them testing such a conception! The police have come to consider that the law fails to protect this section of the public and that their duty is to fill this breach. When the rights of the accused provide large loopholes for bent solicitors to get their clients off, when the police are put in velvet gloves and prevented from obtaining the information they need to secure a deserved conviction, when the courts refuse to impose sentences commensurate with the public's view (as mediated by the police), *then* the time has come for the police to step in and protect the public by making certain that the evidence is forthcoming, that persons who are 'due for some' are 'fitted-up', and that instant street (albeit rough) justice is administered. In a remarkable passage, Sir Robert Mark manages to reflect, without apparent criticism, each of these aims. He writes:

> 'I can remember a very successful, fairly senior detective in Manchester, who, when dealing with hardened criminals, had his own version of the Judge's Rules. It consisted of greeting the prisoner with the blunt enquiry, "Will you talk or be tanned?" If the reply was in the negative, sometimes colourfully so, the prisoner was removed smartly to the lavatory, where he was upended and his head jammed down the bowl. It usually took two to hold him, whilst a third repeatedly pulled the chain until a waggling of the feet indicated a more compliant attitude. He then signed a form headed by the usual caution against self-incrimination.'   (Mark 1978: 55–6)

The police also pick up on the fears and anxieties of those living in inner-city areas who are victimized by 'street crime', particularly mugging and robbery, committed, so it is alleged, mainly by a racial and culturally 'alien' minority. Whatever the truth of these beliefs – and they are the subject of a current heated debate in Britain (Bridges and Gilroy 1982; Gilroy 1982; Lea and Young 1982a) – they are real in their consequences. The police justify 'hard' policing not only because that is what the victimized, terrified inner-city, and decent working-class citizens want, but also because the law, under the malignant influence of soft liberalism, has virtually abandoned protecting the innocent in favour of 'treating' the villain. Cloaked in a vigilante garb, the police give 'sus' laws a hard and sometimes racist twist (Institute of Race Relations 1979). They take 'law and order', which originally meant the application of law rather than arbitrary justice to help maintain order, and transform it into the imposition of order (perceived through a conservative lens) by the application (legal or otherwise) of law (as interpreted by the police). In this topsy-turvy world, the police's conception of justice often becomes experienced by citizens as brutality.

A further weakening of officers' bond to the strict application of Judge's Rules or norms of proper and professional conduct is caused by the excessive amount of over-criminalization. Laws against activities that large sections of the public want, and are prepared to pay for, not only bring citizens and police into fractious encounters, but also lead to a public view of the police as hypocrites. At the same time that police are attempting, albeit in an haphazard fashion, to enforce laws against immorality, they are themselves frequently seen to be violating these laws: they are not averse to drinking alcohol after licensing hours, or viewing pornographic material, or hiring prostitutes – indeed the very qualities of being a good officer resemble those of being a 'masculine character'.

Attempting to enforce these laws leads not only to injustice, because they cannot be enforced consistently across the gamut of offenders, but it also alienates some officers themselves from the law. When they come to see the law as hypocritical, because the lawmakers are not themselves averse to engaging in the very activities they have apparently banned from the world for the rest of us, then some officers lose any sense of commitment to enforcing it and instead follow their political leaders into those 'naughty but nice' banned activities. This does not stop merely as passive participation but often takes the form of entrepreneurial activity (Cox, Shirley, and Short 1977).

When officers view the law as hypocritical and they combine this with their conviction that it is also inefficient and ineffectual, then they might decide to distance themselves from proper professional conduct norms and act instead in accord with their own sense of 'fairness'. Sir Robert Mark believes that many officers become personally involved in criminal cases because they know the 'truth'. Because of this, (1977: 67) 'All are under occasional temptation to bend the rules to convict those whom they believe to be guilty, if only because convention has always inhibited them from saying how badly they think these rules work'.

Not only do these views of the law enable police to bend the rules, they also enable them to justify corruption. When they realize citizens are making enormous amounts of money out of breaking laws against morality and organized crime and that the law is too inefficient and ineffectual to stop them, some officers undoubtedly ask 'why shouldn't I?' For many, there is no persuasive answer to prevent them. Again Sir Robert Mark located an 'unjust' justice system in the causal nexus of police corruption. He argued:

> 'a few may sometimes be tempted . . . to exploit the system for personal gain. A detective who finds general acceptance of a system which protects the wrongdoer can come to think that if crime seems to pay for everyone else, why not for him? The next step may be to demand money for not opposing bail, for not preferring charges, for omitting serious charges, for a share in the stolen property and so on.'   (Mark 1977: 67)

At any police Christmas Carol Service one might expect to hear them heartily singing the Beatles song 'With a little help from my friends'. For without such friendly assistance, neither brutality nor corruption would be possible. The very structure of police work is likely to create just this mutual support. Officers know their work is dangerous and that they cannot rely on the public or the law for protection; naturally they turn to each other. Work hours are irregular and 'anti-social'; for their social life officers primarily socialize with each other. In many communities, the police are viewed as 'an army of occupation'; in response officers turn inwards for friendship and support from colleagues. Most officers seek promotion and enhanced career prospects; they soon realize that 'loyalty' and 'being one of the boys' are vital ingredients in this occupational quest. But 'loyalty' and 'being one of the boys' easily turns into 'honour' – a sense that we are all comrades in the same boat and *secrecy* is a vital weapon for keeping it afloat (Stoddard 1968).

The consequences of 'secrecy' for police crime are obvious; if comrades are willing to support or help fabricate alibis, or are willing to 'turn a blind eye' to brutality and corruption, then these criminal acts are facilitated because they are rendered invisible and impenetrable to any investigation. Furthermore, an unwillingness to go along with this code soon leads an officer into isolation within the force, transferral to unsuitable and unpleasant work, and pressures to resign. These themes were well explored in two recent films, *Serpico* and *Fort Apache, New York*. In both, the 'liberal heroes' (played respectively by Al Pacino and Paul Newman) defy the informal police code of secrecy and instead attempt to expose police corruption and brutality. Both end up under irresistible pressure to leave the force. The problem of police crime remained untouched in an essentially protective and facilitative environment. Thus the very informal police culture, which itself arises reasonably out of the contingencies and contradictions of police work, becomes itself caught up in the causal nexus of police crime.

The police occupy the narrow waste-ground between 'convention' and 'deviance'; here they are tempted by provocation and opportunity to step over to the wrong side. Occupational experiences, peer-group socialization, and a growing sense of isolation, suspicion, and cynicism, prepare them to abandon subservience to the law; insults from sections of the public and an informed awareness that crime pays whilst the criminal justice system has gone soft provide the final straws. But even here, at the existential moment when provocation and opportunity coincide, when it looks too easy and rewarding to slip over the invitational edge into deviancy, they could still be deterred.

WHAT'S TO STOP THEM?

It is a commonplace cynical view that whatever opportunities individuals have for committing crimes and however tempting the rewards, resistance will occur if there exists a strong possibility of being caught and punished. Only those with nothing to lose or who live on the razor edge of desperation commit crimes recklessly. But when crimes can be committed without running high risks of apprehension, or if caught severe punishment, then their tempting rewards become irresistible, particularly to the morally pragmatic. This simple observation, a touchstone of deterrance theory, has relevance for understanding police misbehaviour.

A 'magical cloak of immunity' seems to stretch protectively over individual police and police collectivities. The institutionalized checks on their behaviour – the procedures for investigating public complaints against the police and the provisions for rendering the police publicly accountable – are largely ineffective. The occasional special attempts to remedy these deficiences by establishing an official investigation, such as that carried out in 1971 by Her Majesty's Inspector of Constabulary (Crime), Frank Williamson, into the alleged corruption inside the London CID and the attempt by Operation Countryman from 1978 to 1982 to clean up alleged corruption in the Metropolitan Robbery Squad can be thwarted by non-cooperation and blocked by reticent senior officers so successfully that few culprits will be brought to justice. Indeed, one sad irony of these investigations is that the officers conducting them are often reduced to objects of ridicule and derision, who give up in disgust and sometimes retire early.

Complaints against the police

The present procedure for handling complaints against the police (in the UK) was established by the Police Act 1976, which modified the Police Act 1964. Once a member of the public (or another officer) lodges a complaint and shows determination to proceed, the incident is officially recorded and then investigated by a senior officer, usually from another force. Where possible criminal changes are involved, the completed file is sent to the Director of Public Prosecutions (DPP) who then decides if there is sufficient evidence to make conviction more than 51 per cent certain, bearing in mind the reluctance of juries to find police officers guilty. In other non-criminal complaint cases, the local deputy chief constable decides on the basis of evidence whether to bring disciplinary charges. If he decides against taking such action, then the file is referred to the Police Complaints Board, which is the 1976 Act's innovatory attempt to introduce an independent element into the proceedings. This board can ask for further information or even additional investigation, and can ultimately order the deputy chief constable to bring disciplinary charges.

There is an extraordinary consensus over the need to reform these existing procedures. Not only does this view command the agreement of such obvious bodies as the National Council for Civil Liberties, Justice, and The Runnymede Trust, but even the Police Complaints Board, the Police Federation, Police Superintendents' Association, the Home Office, the House of Commons Home Affairs Select Committee (1982), Lord Scarman (1982), and the present Home Secretary all consider that the present system must be improved. Beyond this however, they disagree. The reasons for reform and the shape these might take are the subject for a bitter and continuing debate. But one shortcoming in the present arrangements does seem clear – they are simply not effective. Very few police accused of violating the law in the course of their duty are eventually convicted. Because of this, the majority of citizens have no faith in the justice of a system which allows the accused to investigate themselves and leaves police lawlessness relatively unchecked. Consequently, most police-public encounters involving illegal or irregular police behaviour do not even get reported; the victims turn away, convinced justice would be denied them.

According to a recent Home Office Research Unit survey (Tuck and Southgate 1981) of 568 West Indians and 255 whites living in Manchester in October 1980, as many as 2 to 3 per cent had directly experienced an incident during the last year which gave them grounds for believing that the police had behaved illegally towards them. Yet none of them made a formal complaint to the police! Most firmly believed that 'nothing would be done' and that it would all be a 'waste of time'. This cynical view is not merely held by 'ill-informed and ignorant' citizens, nor by the so-called anti-police elements. According to a report in *The Guardian* (6.8.81: 2) a number of solicitors with direct practical experience of the system in operation thought it was 'hopeless' largely because none of their clients, even those with apparently water-tight cases against the police, had their allegations upheld.

Given the lack of public confidence, it is not surprising that nearly one-half of those who do make some effort to complain formally withdraw their accusation(s) even before it is investigated (Police Complaints Board 1980: 23). There are numerous possible reasons for this. Sometimes because they 'cool down' and regard their accusations as trivial or not worth the effort of pursuing, sometimes because they are satisfied by the police receiving the complaint that the matter will be dealt with informally, and sometimes because they are persuaded not to continue. But one further reason has become very important recently. Stevens and Willis point out that:

'police officers now have the right to see copies of complaints made against them and to sue complainants for defamation of character through the Police (Copies of Complaints) Regulations 1977. This right may have a deterrent effect not only on trivial or malicious complaints but also on bona fide complaints where there is little independent evidence. Since many complainants will learn of this officer's right only after they have registered their complaint, its introduction may have increased the number of complaints where the complainant does not wish the investigation to be proceeded with.'

(Stephens and Willis 1981: 10)

The effect of this regulation on the proportion of recorded complaints investigated has been dramatic. Thus in the London metropolitan area, nearly 68 per cent were investigated in 1970 and this fell consistently until 1977 when it reached 57 per cent (equivalent to an annual drop of 1.4 per cent). But for the two years after 1977 the proportion of recorded complaints investigated fell from 57 per cent to 38 per cent (equivalent to an annual drop of 9.5 per cent). Thus the introduction of an independent element in the complaints procedure was soon complemented by an element increasing the accused officers' rights. This has had the effect of rapidly increasing the number of complaints 'not proceeded with' (because the complainant does not want the investigation to continue) from 6 per cent in 1977 to 13 per cent in 1979. When this is added to the proportion 'withdrawn' and those 'dispensed with' (because the complainant was uncooperative) it is clear that the tendency throughout the 1970s was for the investigated proportion of all recorded complaints to drop – as indeed it did from 68 per cent to a mere 38 per cent.

Of the dwindling proportion of recorded complaints which are investigated, *more than nineteen out of twenty are unsubstantiated* because the investigator can find no grounds either for recommending disciplinary action against the accused or for submitting the case to the Director of Public Prosecutions for possible criminal charges.

Furthermore, the Police Complaints Board, the reassuring 'independent' element in the process, merely rubber stamps decisions against disciplinary action. Thus between June 1977 (when the system came into operation) and the end of 1980, the board reviewed 39,497 completed investigations. Out of these the deputy had recommended no action in 39,240 cases. The board, after carefully rereading the files disagreed in 65 cases, that is, less than 0.2 per cent of the total! This has hardly reassured a public growing increasingly cynical and disillusioned by police misconduct.

Nor is sagging public confidence in the system shored up in any way by the practices and results of the DPP. For example, allegations of assault are the most frequent complaint made against the police. But despite this, and despite the fact that the number of these complaints have risen steadily throughout the last decade (for example, the number of people complaining against the Metropolitan Police increased by 60 per cent between 1970 and 1979 although the Metropolitan Police District population declined during this period), the prosecution rate recommended by the DPP's office has actually gone down from the high level of 2 per cent in the early 1970s to the present 1½ per cent. Furthermore, less than a half of those prosecuted are convicted, which is lower than the conviction rate for ordinary members of the public charged with assault. It is this fact which the DPP uses to justify not pursuing more prosecutions against the police, although he makes no allowance for the differential quality or presentation of evidence in police-accused versus non-police-accused cases.

What effect does this system of investigating complaints and punishing offenders have on the psychology of those police tempted to assault citizens on the street or 'suspects' in police cells, or to accept financial inducements for non-enforcement of the law, or watering evidence, reducing charges, arranging bail, and any of the other criminal activities available to them by virtue of being in powerful positions? Surely if the police appreciate that the 'chances of getting away with it' are as high as 98 out of a 100, they are unlikely to be deterred. Indeed, as they gaze over the invitational edge of crime, such odds might appear to the police as a positive encouragement!

If they are tempted in this way, they might be further strengthened in their deviousness by another failure of the complaints procedure which few critics ever expose. In addition to being ineffective, the system, just like the criminal justice system, is biased against particular social groups (Box 1981a: 157–207), thus rendering these disadvantaged groups particularly vulnerable to police crime.

Box and Russell (1975) analysed complaints made during 1971 in two Midlands police forces. These may not be typical of all, particularly metropolitan forces, and therefore not a good basis for making generalizations. They do however provide a disturbing glimpse at 'who' does and does not get their complaints substantiated. The authors reported that three times as many middle-class compared with working-class complainants 'succeeded'. This ratio was doubled when the analysis was confined to allegations of police criminal behaviour. Furthermore, whereas half of the working-class complaints were about police criminal behaviour, nearly six-sevenths of middle-class complaints merely referred to non-criminal incidents. This suggests that not only are working-class citizens more likely to be 'victimized' by police crime, but they are less likely to get their allegations accepted by police officers investigating other police officers, which is, of course, the central feature and *injustice* in the system.

A recent Home Office study (Stevens and Willis 1981) of complaints within the Metropolitan Police Districts during the 1970s made an interesting comparison between ethnic minorities, particularly West Indians, and whites, which mirrors Box and Russell's inter-class comparison. Stevens and Willis found that the rate of complaint substantiation was 4.6 per cent for whites and only 1.5 per cent for those of West Indian origin. The significance of this differential can be gauged when it is realized: first, that one-quarter of West Indian complaints refer to assaults by the police, usually whilst the victims are in custody, compared with one-fifth of complaints made by whites, and second, that West Indian Britons make complaints proportionately far in excess of their contribution to the total population. In other words this ethnic minority not only feels itself to be proportionately more on the receiving end of police criminal and/or irregular behaviour, but when they do complain, their chances of having it substantiated by the police investigator are comparatively less.

This is not to argue that investigating officers simply do not bother to examine seriously complaints made by the socially powerless. The process is not that crude. Since investigation of complaints is governed by the same principle which fortifies British justice, namely that the accused is innocent until proven guilty, the situation is difficult, if not virtually impossible for complainants who cannot call witnesses to corroborate that something improper really happened. A black eye, a fractured jaw, a smashed skull, a broken leg, and a ruptured stomach are all capable of being caused in many ways other than police brutality. If a police officer denies having been abusive or incivil, or offers plausible reasons why his (or his wife's) building society account has suddenly grown – 'she's always been a very careful housekeeper' – then what the complainant heard or passed over could be merely what he or she 'thought' happened. In these and similar situations where one person's word opposes another – which is very typical in cases of complaints against the police – and where the issue has to be settled, it is normally the person who stands highest in the *dominant hierarchy of credibility* (Becker 1967) whose word is accepted.

As far as investigating officers, magistrates, judges, and most jury members are concerned, the police occupy a higher rank position on this hierarchy than the majority of complainants, who are working class and/or members of discriminated-against ethnic minorities, and who can easily be discredited. Because they are known criminals (out to get revenge on the police), have outstanding prosecutions (attempting to use complaints as a bargaining lever), were drunk (and didn't know what time of day it was) or had a long history of mental illness (and therefore couldn't distinguish our reality from their fantasy), their allegations can be easily thrown into the metaphorical waste-basket and declared unsubstantiated.

Since these social attributes frequently overlap with economic and ethnic social locations, some subpopulations are virtually 'open territory' victims for police crimes. Indeed, Box and Russell (1975) reported that none of the working-class complainants who had one or more of these discrediting attributes had their complaint substantiated. A similar finding was reported by Stevens and Willis (1979b). They stated that the rate of complaint substantiation for West Indian complainants was not only low in comparison with other social groups, but within this group it was even lower where the complainant was under arrest, had a previous criminal record, or had been reported for an offence.

Unless a complainant has witnesses whom the investigating officer regards as reliable, and unless his or her ranking on the hierarchy of credibility is higher than that of the accused, then the chances of successfully complaining are near to zero. Thus even under the most favourable conditions, where the complainant is middle class, educated, without a criminal record, sober, and has no history of mental disturbance, and the complaint refers to a fairly trivial non-criminal matter, the chances of success are not that great. But where the complainant is an easily discredited working-class or ethnic minority person, then he or she need not waste their time complaining, particularly if the allegation is that the police behaved *criminally*. The results of completed investigations demonstrate that these complainants would be better off not bothering.

Knowing that the law is not going to protect the rights of particular subpopulations is one of the most compelling reasons why police feel comparatively free to victimize them. That is why, for example, prostitutes are often 'required' to provide 'services' for free, or 'criminals' required to 'exchange' a proportion of their 'profits', or economically and/or ethnically deprived persons are sought out as objects for receiving police incivility, brutality, or 'fit-up' (frame-up) jobs, or members of politically radical groups subjected to illegal levels of police harassment, surveillance, and brutality (Douglas and Johnson 1977).

In the complaints system, there is a link between the process of considering whether to prosecute or discipline which further protects police officers from being punished for illegal behaviour. This is the 'double jeopardy' rule. Simply stated, the rule is this: if the DPP decides that the evidence is insufficient to bring a criminal charge, then no officer can be disciplined on that same evidence. In effect, the DPP's reluctance to prosecute is treated as though the officer had actually been acquitted. But of course no one has been acquitted. The DPP, guided by his convenient perception of juries' reluctance to convict police officers, operates an unusually stringent criterion for permitting prosecutions to proceed, and consequently errs on the side of excessive caution. The outcome is that many officers against whom there is sufficient evidence to justify their being disciplined escape that punishment. Sadly, this escape route is one afforded to those officers, who because of the serious charges against them are just those whose punishment would be required before the public confidence in police complaints procedure could be created. For example, it is clear that Blair Peach (to mention but one out of many) was killed by one or more police officers during (or just after) the Southall 'disturbances' in April, 1979. Commander Cass, a senior Metropolitan officer investigated this incident and 'apparently recommended prosecutions not only for homicide, but for riot, affray and conspiracy to pervert the course of justice' (Hewitt 1982: 75). But the DPP did not authorize any prosecutions and consequently the persons mentioned by Commander Cass not only escaped a criminal trial but were, by virtue of that decision, immunized against any disciplinary action which the Metropolitan Commissioner might have sanctioned.

An awareness of severe shortcomings in the complaints system has led to many suggested reforms. But tinkering with the police complaints system, as was typical during the 1970s, and as appears likely following the recent Home Affairs Committee Report (1982), will do nothing to remedy substantially the glaring defect in the present arrangements. This is not the absence of a 'truly' independent element, but the absence of justice. Far too many accused officers get away with it, and there is no guarantee that a more independent element would improve the situation; experience both in Canada and the United States, where experiments with civilian review boards have been carried out, prove that 'stubborn realities' (police non-cooperation) mire attempts to achieve results fairer to the complainants.

Whilst it is not possible to specify a level of complaint substantiation which would mollify a disgruntled public, it is clear that the present derisory level of around 3 to 5 per cent for serious allegations and three times that figure for trivial irregularities is simply not sufficient. Further, this low level of complaint substantiation discourages citizens from complaining and it is thus an inflated level of substantiation, because unreported complaints are excluded from this calculation. Under these permissive circumstances, it would take very strong, morally upright officers not to succumb, at least occasionally, when the temptation arises, as it frequently does in police-public (including criminal) encounters. This is not to relegate officers to the ranks of the wicked, but to render them as merely mortal, like the citizens they police, who would, if in their place, act with just as much rectitude and frailty.

Special investigations: throwing out the 'bad apples'

Occasionally, the smell of police misbehaviour becomes overpowering. The one or two 'bad apples' seem to turn the rest of the barrel rotten. When it is not possible to contain this smell and public conscience becomes sickened, as it did in 1969 when *The Times* provided disturbing evidence of corruption within the Metropolitan Crime Squad (Cox, Shirley, and Short 1977), then the political authorities normally respond by establishing a special investigation or inquiry. Operation Countryman, an investigation of police corruption is an example of the former, and the Scarman Inquiry into alleged police riots (amongst other issues) is an example of the latter. It is instructive to examine the Countryman saga in some detail because it illustrates perfectly the ineffectiveness of these occasional special investigations, if their function is to act as cover for gaps found in the complaints procedure.

The 'true' story of Operation Countryman may never be revealed. The semi-fictionalized account in G. Newman's play *Operation Bad Apple* may be an inspired and satisfactory guess, but its approximation to the 'truth' remains contentious. None the less, what has been discovered, through exposé journalism and the leaks of disgruntled officers, provides enough evidence for there to be glimpsed an intimate relationship between the lack of effective control and police crime.

Operation Countryman, so-called because it was conducted by members of provincial forces (an affront to the Met., who in turn denigrated Countryman as 'The Sweedy') was established in August 1978 to examine allegations of widespread corruption, particularly in the Robbery Squad. Immediate suspicions centred on payroll robberies at *The Daily Mirror* and *The Daily Express* and a security van robbery at the Williams and Glyn's Bank in the city. It was rumoured that at their best, some officers were helping culprits to evade justice (by bail-bonding, evidence-watering, charge-reduction, and wilful neglect of duty) in return for receiving part of the proceeds – known in the trade as 'taking a drink' – and at their worst, they were actively involved planning and even executing these or similar robberies. Once Countryman officers starting listening to well-known 'villains', who appeared eagerly tumbling over each other to give dates and details, these rumours began to crystallize into hard facts. Corruption, it began to appear, was historically and currently endemic rather than the abberation of a few 'bad apples' and it was widespread throughout the hierarchical command rather than confined to those below the rank of sergeant. To investigate such frightening possibilities properly, it was necessary to expand the original team to nearly one hundred officers and to accommodate them in offices outside London where their files and records could not be casually looked over by anxious Met. officers.

It was at this point that a peculiar event occurred.

The Countryman team was instructed by its political masters to confine future investigation to the three original robberies which had given rise to its existence. All other evidence was to be handed over to the Metropolitan Criminal Investigation Board (CIB).

This dismayed 'informers' because they had provided information to Countryman only on the understanding that the CIB, in whom they had no trust, would not be involved in any way. The informers were probably right to be dismayed and cynical. The Met. CIB do not seem to have pursued this evidence with the energy or enthusiasm it deserved. For instance *The Observer* (25.4.82) reported that one file handed over to them related to 'an allegation that London policemen stole part of the proceeds of a robbery at the National Westminster Bank branch in 1972. They found the bank robbers in a house with the loot, but charged them with possession of only some £500 of the £3,718 which had been stolen'. This was clearly a very serious allegation. Yet when the CIB officer allotted to investigate had an opportunity to record vital evidence from a well-placed informer (who was tape-recorded by the newspaper) he refused to do so and implied that smelly matters should be allowed to rest in peace.

Not only were existing and potential 'informers' dismayed by suddenly finding themselves up against members of the force they were attempting to implicate, but so too were Countryman officers. The CIB had not been considered the appropriate investigating body originally and there was little room for optimism that they would perform better now, since the same reasons obtained. This pessimism was indeed justified. By the end of July 1982, of nearly 200 files handed over, only one had led to a prosecution and that was against a police constable for conspiring to defraud an insurance company. This paucity of prosecutions was not because the cases were in early stages of investigation. According to Countryman officers, many were virtually completed when they were handed over nearly two years previously.

In addition to bringing in the Met. CIB to take over from Countryman the expanded (and alarming) list of officers suspected of corruption in connection with crimes other than the original three large robberies Countryman was established to investigate, it was also decided (by whom? and why?) that the Countryman team should be strengthened and assisted in its severely reduced investigation by having officers with direct and relevant experience of the Metropolitan police placed in charge of it! The very force under suspicion of widespread corruption was at last going to investigate itself vigorously and with a tenacity not seen since Robert Mark's crusade when he was Metropolitan Commissioner during the early 1970s – a crusade whose success (Cox, Shirley, and Short 1977) is highlighted by Countryman's existence. Six officers from the Northampton force immediately resigned in disgust. The team was reduced almost as quickly as it had expanded, and by mid 1982 only seven active members remained to 'tie up the odd bits of string'. But 'to complete the whitewash' might seem more accurate.

When Arthur Hambleton, the original investigation director and Chief Constable of Dorset suddenly retired, he made public his belief, based, as it must have been, on the most intimate familiarity with the strongest evidence available, that over eighty officers were under suspicion and that he expected at least twenty-five of them to be charged. According to *The Guardian* (21.7.82: 11) the list of suspects drawn up by July 1979 contained '78 officers from Scotland Yard and 18 from City of London, including the four commanders, four chief superintendents, eight superintendents, fifteen chief inspectors and six inspectors'. Yet by the end of August 1982, only nine officers had been prosecuted, and of these only two, Detective Chief Inspector Cuthbert and Detective Sergeant Goldbourn, had been convicted and gaoled for three and two years respectively. These two officers apparently demanded something like £160,000 in bribes from persons suspected of being involved in the three robberies Countryman was investigating in exchange for arranging bail and for offering weakened or no evidence. During the trial, an officer of commander rank was mentioned not only as being a possible recipient of a substantial proportion of these bribes but also of being involved in numerous other cases of bribery and corruption. This same officer was alleged to have said to Cuthbert in a tape-recorded conversation replayed to the court, 'you are going to be patsy', i.e. the person taking the blame, much the same way as multi-national corporations prematurely appoint a young executive to be responsible for going to jail. The defence barrister argued that 'unless all the members of a squad are corrupt, it suggests it would be very difficult to pursue the kind of conduct which has been alleged'. Since the allegations were believed by the jury, can we infer they also thought corruption was indeed widespread?

It is interesting to compare the success rate in prosecuting officers with that relating to 'informers'. Originally the Countryman team thought that even if informers admitted their own involvement in crimes they would be granted immunity from prosecution in return for providing vital evidence against Met. officers. Under this apparent guarantee, many London and provincial criminals came forward with more stories of police malpractice than any member of the Countryman team imagined possible. However, the DPP's office refused to honour this understanding and as a consequence more civilians who have given evidence against policemen have been arrested than the police referred to in this evidence. Was this the inevitable wheels of impartial justice turning against whoever deserved it or was it a calculated attempt to frighten informers into changing their evidence and to deter other potential informers? Certainly in the only successful Countryman trial, that of Cuthbert and Goldbourn, the major informer, Mr A. Shepard, was given immunity, but this was clearly going to be an exception once the DPP's ruling was implemented.

And so another long and very expensive investigation bit the dust. Arthur Hambleton said in an interview in *World in Action* (2.8.82) that Scotland Yard had obstructed Countryman and the DPP had failed to support it. Of course these allegations were denied, although it is true that the Met. CIB has done virtually nothing with the material passed over to it by Countryman and the DPP agreed to only four prosecutions from the first twenty-one files submitted by Countryman. The DPP argued that there was not enough evidence to justify prosecutions, but Countryman countered there would be, if immunity would be granted to informers. The DPP, with one exception, was not prepared to do this, thus making Countryman's task that much harder.

If this particular investigation and its outcome had been an exception, then little could be made of it. But it is merely one in an unending chain of investigations which have come to nothing. It is because of this history *that police officers, already tempted by the enormous opportunities and ever-present provocations, the 'rationality' of 'justifiable' short-cuts, the encouragement and support of peers, themselves deeply mired in police crimes, can feel relatively immune from criminal prosecution and therefore relatively free to engage in crimes.*

Public accountability

Attempts to make the British police accountable to local authorities – who through their rates contribute substantially to local police budgets – are also largely ineffectual (Hewitt 1982). The 1964 Police Act made it clear that chief constables were in charge of organizational and operational matters whilst the local authorities were given the supportive task of maintaining an adequate and effective police force by making certain they had the tools for the job. Attempts to establish some control have been made periodically since 1964, but without much success. However, since the Labour Party's recent success in local elections, the 1981 riots, and the police response to them, there has been an intensified effort to gain some public control, particularly in the areas of riot control, weaponry, and community policing. Struggles between local government authorities and police have been pronounced and bitter in Greater Manchester, South Yorkshire, Merseyside, West Mercia, and London (Kettle and Hodges 1982).

In London, where as yet there is no authority to whom the police are accountable except the remote Home Secretary, the struggle to achieve 'taxation with representation' has intensified with the arrival of Ken Livingstone as leader of the Greater London Council. The chairperson of the GLC's Police Committee believes that the Metropolitan police force 'is the country's most expensive and least efficient' and also has 'the lowest level of public confidence in it' (Bundred 1982: 62).

At the moment, London ratepayers contribute a massive £333 millions to the Met. police force budget and yet have no control over major policies concerning the policing of London or the disciplining of officers. The present Labour council hope to achieve some democratization of the police and hence more accountability by implementing their election pledge. This was to establish a police authority:

'consisting solely of elected members of the GLC and London boroughs to have control over the Metropolitan and City police. This authority to have power to appoint all officers of the rank of chief superintendent and above, to scrutinize the day-to-day affairs of the force and to allocate resources to the various police functions. (We believe an independent complaints procedure should be established; the proposed police committee we will set up will in the meantime investigate complaints against the police and publish reports.) The Special Branch and Illegal Immigration Intelligence Unit should be disbanded. Surveillance of political and trade unions' activity must end and all files collected for non-criminal reasons should be destroyed. All police officers will have the right to join unions and to take industrial action.'   (Bundred 1982: 72)

Whether the plans of the Labour Greater London Council will succeed is a moot point. They may have a similar fate to the proposals of Member of Parliament Jack Straw, who attempted unsuccessfully in

November 1979 to persuade the House of Commons to grant five new powers to local authorities: the right to decide general policing policies; the right to obtain more information from the chief constables; greater powers of appointment – so that non-cooperative chief constables could be more easily removed; a role in supervising local complaints against the police; and closer liaison between the police authorities and the national police inspectorate.

The failure of this attempt to introduce a new level of police accountability reflects both the present government's reluctance to interfere and hence upset an agency vital to its law and order programme, and the growing relative political autonomy of the police force, because they were strongly outspoken in their resistance to any change that introduced an element of 'political' control over the police.

It is within the context of the overall lack of effective public accountability that the ineffective control of individual police officers through the complaints procedures has to be situated. So long as the police remain relatively autonomous from public accountability they will maintain strong support for a complaints system which enables them to discredit the complainant and protect their own 'deviants'.

Police crime and the functions of the police

It should now be clear that the rate of prosecution and conviction of police 'criminals' is low. Low at least, in comparison with the judicial treatment of conventional criminals and with the standards expected in a society whose political leaders claim allegiance to establishing justice and maintaining individual rights and liberties. For it is obvious that in allowing so many police to 'get away' with brutality and corruption, conventional criminals are further insulted and many citizens' rights are rudely abrogated. In order to understand why political authorities have been reluctant and/or unable to instigate rigorous control over police misconduct it is necessary to consider the historical origins of the police in Anglo-American societies. These not only illuminate the underlying political significance of police work, but they also reveal a contradiction which makes the police a continuous problem for the authorities.

The functions of the police are numerous and not necessarily complementary. The *service* function, which we learn in childhood as 'if you want to know the time, ask a policeman', and in adulthood as the police will willingly give positive assistance after accidents, disasters, and other social/domestic misfortunes is certainly one reflecting the better, acceptable face of police work. As indeed, is another major function: that of protecting us from murderers, robbers, muggers, thieves, and other dangerous villains. But this service (to the community) function is not, and was not, the dominant function the police were established to fulfil. Numerous historical studies (Bayley 1979; Bordua and Reiss 1967; Haller 1976; Harring 1976; Harring and McMullin 1975; Lane 1967, 1979; Miller 1977) on the origins of a bureaucratic quasi-military police force contend that it was more a response by the élite to their perception of the threat posed by the 'dangerous classes' than a desire to provide an embryonic social welfare service in a blue uniform. Since the 'dangerous classes' comprised those not yet disciplined to the industrial way of life and who were consequently likely at any moment to engage in disruptive industrial action or riotous assembly, the élite had to develop an institutionalized response which would defend them and their interests. As Bordua and Reiss argue:

> 'the paramilitary form of early police bureaucracy was a response not only or even primarily to crime *per se*, but to the possibility of riotous disorder. Not crime and danger but the 'criminal' and 'dangerous classes' as part of the urban social structure led to the formation of uniformed and military organized police.'
>
> (Bordua and Reiss 1967: 82)

This *control* function, as Turk (1981: 115) calls it, has traditionally involved 'intelligence gathering, information control, neutralizing of "offenders" (specific deterrence), and intimidation of the general population (general deterrence)'. Inevitably, this function contradicts the service function because those who at times are recipients of police service work are, at other times, prime targets for control. Consequently, the community has maintained an ambivalent attitude towards the police and offered only a conditional acceptance of its monopolistic use of violence and wide discretionary powers of investigation and arrest.

This ambivalence has frustrated the state's hopes of legitimating the police. It has always chosen to emphasize the service function and graft on to this the beneficial effects of controlling conventional criminals in the hope that once this mystification was achieved, it would be possible to slip in the police's more important function – control – unnoticed. This has been achieved with only a varying degree of success, but that has not deterred the state from its quest of constructing a reliable control agency to help it demoralize, fracture, and annihilate those who through word and deed refused to accept the legitimacy of the state and its police force. These deviant 'political criminals' could then be lumped with conventional criminals and the community would remain unaware and passively idle. This quest has never been totally realized in Anglo-American societies; at times there appears to be a strong sense of community acceptance of the police as service workers, but not far beneath this cosy calm surface there has always lurked the uneasy dim awareness that the police were fundamentally more concerned with control, particularly over dissenting, or potentially dissenting sections of the population.

To prioritize analytically the control function of the police over its service function is not to accept blindly the more 'extreme' portraits of the police as mere passive instruments directly commanded and manipulated by the state for the protection, preservation, and reproduction of those whose class interests the state ultimately serves. This appears to be the position adopted by a number of radical writers. For example, O'Connor views the police as guard labour. Their purpose, he argues:

> 'is not to produce something but to avoid something. Guard labour reproduces the formal structure of capitalism and maintains and reproduces capitalist productive relations. Guard labour does not produce commodities yet without guard labour commodity production would be impossible.'   (O'Connor 1975: 304)

Similarly, the Center for Research on Criminal Justice (1977: 16) believes that 'the police serve as the front-line mechanism of repression. As such, the central function of the police is to control the working class' and to 'enforce class, racial, sexual, and cultural oppression that has been integral to capitalism development'. Just as baldly, Cook (1967: 120) assures us that 'the processes of law enforcement serve the interests of dominant groups in the society and either ignore or oppose the interests of those in lower social strata'. And Galliher (1971: 312–13) sees a similar pattern, although he adds a significant qualification. He argues that 'much police behaviour seems most easily explained when one considers that *whenever there is a conflict of interests* [my italics] between the dominant classes in a society and less powerful groups, the police protect the interests of the former and regulate the behaviour of the latter'.

Whilst this repressive control function may indeed be the inherent intention designed into the origin of police work, it does not follow that there will always be a perfect match between the blue-print and the reality. As Turk puts it (1981: 115) 'the *rationale and purpose* (my italics) of policing is to preserve against radical change those cultural and social structures which are congruent with some historically specific polity'. But that rationale and purpose need not be achieved invariably.

The lessons of history are relevant here. They provide many instances where the dominant classes may well have desired the police to protect and preserve their interests, but where the police instead chose to defend or at least not jeopardize the interests of those lower strata persons whom the élite wanted policed and controlled. Robinson (1978) documents numerous examples in the nineteenth century when local American police forces actually swore in strikers as deputies and together with them arrested strike-breakers. Police-strikers collusion often proceeded with the implicit support of local middle-class notables who resented the intrusion of industrial entrepreneurs from the East or other European countries (Gutman 1961, 1962). Indeed, so unreliable were local police that nascent capitalists frequently resorted to inviting the state governor to call out the militia, and because their invitation often fell on deaf ears, they established their own private strike-breaking, quasi-military force, the more notorious and infamous of these being the Pinkerton and Burns Detective Agencies. It was certainly this private police force which played a major part in harassing and annihilating the Industrial Workers of the World (The Wobblies) and repressing other frequent outbursts of labour unrest which were often responses to élite-inspired private-police-executed violence (Johnson 1976; Krisberg 1975: 43–6).

Not only were the public police an unreliable ally in the struggle against those who 'threatened' emerging capitalists and their interests, but they were also capable of acting *for themselves* against these interests. They formed trade unions and threatened to employ industrial action: a threat which was doubly realized in London and Boston just after World War I when both forces went on strike.

When the London police strike was beaten in late 1919, largely by Prime Minister Lloyd George pursuing a 'divide and rule' strategem – offering more money to some ranks, establishing a new grievance machinery, spying on union officials, and directly appealing to rank and file loyalty to King and Country – he made the following revealing statement to his police commissioner. He said:

> 'The police force is so essential to the stability of social order that at all hazards we must take steps to ensure that we have a body of men at the disposal of the state who can be relied upon . . . we cannot command at the present moment as long as you have thousands of men who are under contract to disobey the authorities at the behest of an outside committee.'

When the Boston police strike had been broken, also in 1919, President Wilson called it a 'crime against civilization' and said that the police should remember their 'obligations as soldiers', thus evoking images of the police defending the community against its external enemies. Governor Coolidge followed this analogy when he declared that: 'In the deliberate intention to intimidate and coerce the government of this Commonwealth a large body of policemen, urging all others to join them, deserted their posts of duty, letting in the enemy.' According to Robinson, this

> 'police strike not only exposed the lives and property of the ruling class to danger but it also clearly showed whom the police were protecting. Before the militia was called out . . . the mayor requested volunteers to defend law and order. Those who responded were for the most part . . . stock-brokers, bankers, lawyers, established businessmen, and Harvard undergraduates.'   (Robinson 1978: 144)

Thus, 'taking care of labour' (Johnson 1976) and of its own interests was just as much a feature of nineteenth and early twentieth century police forces as was the protection of privileged property rights. The only safe conclusion is not that the police were an instrument of the state but that they were an *unreliable instrument* which sometimes turned against those attempting to use it.

The police were inherently unreliable because their natural constituency was the social class from which they were drawn – in America this appears to be overwhelmingly working class and in Britain it was also this class although lower-middle class recruits were also fairly numerous (Box 1981a: 171–77). This resulted in a contradiction between the élite's intention, to be realized through the state posing as a neutral class agent, of establishing a police force loyal to the state, and the reality of having to recruit men from those very sections of the community to which they might have latent loyalties because they were born amongst them. Because this contradiction between loyalty to the state and loyalty to class rendered the police unreliable, the state had to instigate programmes to resolve it and hence make the police a more dependable weapon in future class and race conflicts.

The language and actions of Lloyd George, Coolidge, and Wilson show clearly that the police were seen as instruments of power from whom unbending loyalty and a military discipline were expected (Robinson 1978: 146). The difficulty was how to make certain this instrument did not get into the wrong hands. They had to be reformed, but in such a way that the latent purpose of this reform would be concealed from the public. Thus under the guise of 'reforming' the police and making them more 'efficient' at containing 'our crime problem', that is, establishing more careful and judicial selection procedures, instigating rigorous and politically correct training programmes, providing regular and fair opportunities for promotion, instilling the ideas and ethics of a 'profession' (thus removing them from the idea of being part of the labouring class), granting relative job security with substantial material benefits, building police-ghetto housing estates (thus isolating them from the labouring class neighbourhood), and by frowning on the idea of a police trade union and banning strikes, *the élite set about the task of building the police into a reliable instrument of class domination*. But despite all these 'reforms' the state could not hope for total enduring victory. The police continue to occupy a contradictory class position (Reiner 1978) and this has important implications for their relationship to the state.

The police always realized they had potential power over the state. It could not easily do without their service – controlling the 'dangerous classes' – and it could not easily turn to another military force, such as the army, which would be seen as blatant occupation and threatening a fragile consensus. Consequently, the state's attempt to reform the police into a reliable force against its domestic enemies could only be bought at a price demanded by the police. They wanted autonomy from gross political interference; they got this in the shape of organizational and operational control with only the hint of public accountability being anything more than a smokescreen to comfort the faint libertarian heart. They wanted to keep their own house in order if and when their men misbehaved; they got this in the form of a complaints procedure that guaranteed their control over the investigation, and through that, the judicial outcome, thus leaving police discipline essentially as an internal matter. They wanted the tools to do the job; they got them not only in the guise of modern technology, but also in the form of enormous *discretionary powers* of apprehension and arrest.

This exchange between the state and the police effectively granted the latter a licence to misbehave within tolerable limits. From the state's point of view, it implied that if you carry out your control function, we in turn will not insist that your men keep strictly within the law, providing of course you keep your deviants relatively invisible and confine the more violent and brutal outbursts to those classes and sections of the community you are controlling for us. We will turn a convenient blind eye to misconduct and defend you publicly as the 'best professional police force in the world'. There will of course be machinery for processing complaints and for holding you publicly accountable, but do not lose any sleep over these, for we will make certain they can never be effective. We do not want to be seen condoning police brutality and corruption when the public become aware of them, so if they are seen occasionally as getting out of hand we will need a few wayward junior officers as patsies in order to keep up the good appearance of having an honest police force.

Sir Robert Mark, when he was Commissioner of the Metropolitan Police, understood the nature of this bargain very well. When he took up the post, shortly after *The Times'* revelations of scandals had taken the lid off police corruption in London, he clearly had to do something. His subsequent campaign was portrayed as a clean-up job. And certainly with eight times as many officers being 'retired' as there were just prior to his appointment, there are grounds for thinking he was entirely serious and successful. But his campaign was not so much to clean up corruption as a strategic handing over of a body of scapegoats in order that the police investigation machinery would remain in police hands. As Reiner saw it:

'the essence of Mark's contribution was to protect the legitimacy, and hence autonomy, of the police force in the face of crisis. His reforms were part of a package deal in which the reward of sacrificing unprecedented numbers of bent policemen was to be the continued independence of police chiefs.'   (Reiner 1980: 393)

Through this bargain, the police institutionalized their relative autonomy. They became *conditionally* reliable. As long as the state did not interfere too much, the police in effect promised to control the 'dangerous classes'. Whenever the state has threatened to step up its level of interference, the police have effectively defended their relative autonomy. Reiner (1980) illustrates this clearly in his analysis of North America during the 1960s when a number of states attempted to introduce some form of tight civilian control over the police. This provoked a militant response; the police formed articulate, determined pressure groups which were not content merely to argue the case but actively supported legally dubious actions. In New York, for example, they insisted that the Civilian Review Board established under the governorship of John Lindsay be subject to a referendum. Not only did they get this demand granted, they also persuaded a majority of the electorate to vote against the board because it tied the hands of the police in their Holy War Against Crime.

The experience of the 1970s shows a reversal of this pattern, the state moving away from attempting to control the police directly and the police becoming less militant in their own defence. As Reiner sees it:

'The relative lack of militancy over political issues in recent years reflects rather the rightward shift in the political complexion of city governments . . . and hence the absence of non-economic issues stimulating conflict with the police . . . . Police vigilantism is less apparent because the whole society has become pervaded by the vigilante spirit.'   (Reiner 1980: 390)

The above arguments, at least with regard to police brutality, can now be presented in a slightly more theoretical way. Élites fear 'problem populations' – i.e. those surplus to the requirements of the productive process – because they pose a potential threat to social order (Spitzer 1975). Any widening of economic inequalities increases these fears because the potential might be actualized through militant subordinate organizations springing up to defend the underprivileged. Under such circumstances, increased state coercion would be expected. As Chambliss and Seidman put it (1971: 33): 'The more economically stratified a society becomes the more it becomes necessary for dominant groups to enforce through coercion the norms of conduct that guarantee their supremacy'. Increased state coercion could be achieved in numerous ways: in democratic societies by hiring more police, increasing their technological capabilities, drafting in the army. However, all these solutions are relatively more costly than one other simple possibility – the authorities could become more indifferent to police brutality in those areas where the degree of subordination is most pronounced, because it is just in those areas that riotous assembly and other forms of political resistance are more likely.

This is not to argue that the state directs the police to be more brutal. That would be too crude. As Jacobs and Britt point out:

'For inequality to lead to more lethal violence by the police it is *not* necessary to assume that élites make direct demands for harsh methods. All that is required is that élites be more willing to overlook the violent short cuts taken by "the dirty workers" in the interest of order. Of course this interpretation fits with Hughes' (1963) argument that a willingness to remain conveniently ignorant is a fundamental explanation for much official brutality.'

(Jacobs and Britt 1979: 406)

In order to test the hypothesis that police brutality will correlate positively with increases in inequality, it is necessary to control for other possible reasons why the police might use excessive force. Thus there is a need to control for the extent of violent crimes because these might provoke police violence in self-defence. It is also necessary to control for the percentage of blacks in the population because they are more likely to be killed or assaulted by the police. In addition it would be prudent to control for: the flow of immigrants into an area because strangers are more difficult to police; the proportion of the population who reside in urban areas because they are more difficult to police than rural dwellers; and of course the number of police because the more there are the more likely it is that the absolute amount of police brutality will increase.

One important study has attempted to do this. Jacobs and Britt (1979) examined police-caused homicides from 1961 to 1970 in each American state and computed the population at risk for each year so as to arrive at a standardized rate. They found considerable variations: thus Georgia has a high score of nearly forty per million persons killed by the police, but in New Hampshire, it was just under three per million. To explain these wide variations, they correlated police-caused homicide rates against economic inequality, the proportion of the population who were black, the number of police per capita, changes in the population flow, the proportion of urban dwellers, and an index of violent crimes. A number of these factors did positively correlate with police-caused homicides, but when these were controlled for, there remained a strong association between inequality and police fatal brutality. They found that the 'most important conclusion . . . (was) that the unequal states were most likely to have the largest number of police-caused homicides.'

Of course, one study in America does not prove that the police are allowed to be more violent (and corrupt) during economic crises and increased inequalities, but the results of this study are consistent with this argument. They support the view that the police are essentially a control force and when political consensus and super-subordinate social relations are threatened, police violence increases without the state intervening on behalf of those victimized.

Police violence and other crimes cannot then be understood solely in terms of the micro processes related to work experiences, occupational subcultures, and the lack of deterrence. There is also a need to situate these factors into an historically informed macro analysis because this focuses our attention on the essential role the police play in maintaining social order, and how in return, they are allowed to go beyond the limits of the law.

4 Rape and sexual assaults on females

'Missoula Rape Poem'

There is no difference between being raped
and being pushed down a flight of cement steps
except that the wounds also bleed inside.

There is no difference between being raped
and being run over by a truck
except that afterward men ask if you enjoyed it.

There is no difference between being raped
and losing a hand in a mowing machine
except that doctors don't want to get involved,
the police wear a knowing smirk,
and in small towns you become a veteran whore.

There is no difference between being raped
and going head first through a windshield
except that afterward you are afraid
not of cars
but half the human race.

Marge Piercy

Nearly one hundred years ago, Durkheim wrote that suicide is 'merely the exaggerated form of common practices' and that it 'appears quite another matter once its unbroken connection is recognised with acts, on the one hand, of courage and devotion, on the other of imprudence and clear neglect' (Durkheim 1898/1951). This relatively simple, but radical idea – that there is considerable overlap between deviance and convention, rather than the former being distinctly different and opposite to the latter – not only inspired later generations of sociologists (Matza 1969: 68–9) but it has run like a backbone through previous chapters in this book. Thus, I have argued that good business practice merges imperceptibly into sharp business practice, effective policing merges imperceptibly into defective policing, and prison discipline merges imperceptibly into prison brutality; in each case, the latter has an unbroken connection with the former. In this chapter, a similar lesson can be obtained from considering how 'normal' sexual encounters merge imperceptibly into sexual assaults of which rape is the most serious, and how the former provides just the ingredients out of which the latter can emerge.

What is rape? Legal versus a non-legal 'feminist' definition

Students of rape are immediately confronted by a definitional problem. Does the legal definition, both in principle and juridical practice, refer to a reasonably inclusive category of behaviour? Or does it exclude behaviour which is very similar to that which it includes? These are no mere academic questions. If the latter is answered affirmatively, then studies on legally adjudicated rapists *which means the vast bulk of studies* are an inadequate basis for understanding all types of rape behaviour. Furthermore, by raising the whole definitional issue, we are able to incorporate a central part of the important feminist critique of law and female sexuality (Edwards 1981; Schur 1980: 154–68).

Although there are some minor variations amongst legislatures in western countries, there is a broad agreement that rape constitutes a particular act of sexual access, namely the penis penetrating the vagina, gained without the consent of the female concerned. This legal definition and its embodiment in legal practice has been criticized by feminists and other writers on at least three counts: it contains a suppressed and unjustified major 'exclusion' clause; it reflects a male fetish with one female orifice and one instrument for its violation; its notion of consent places an unfair burden of proof on the victim, and because it is premised on the idea of a voluntary actor, it fails to include a consideration for coerced consent or submission other than under physical duress.

In the United Kingdom and in over forty states of the United States of America, and in most mid-southern European countries, there is a 'spousal exception' clause in rape laws. The exclusion of married women raped by their husbands reflects the law's view of a wife as being her husband's property rather than an autonomous self-determining person, and consequently husbands are provided with a licence to impose themselves on their wives whenever they choose, irrespective of the recipient's wishes. This 'spousal exception' has been vehemently attack-ed by feminists over the last decade or more, and the legal changes which have occurred are to some extent a reflection of this attack. However, only a small number of legislatures have sought to abolish the exclusion clause. The results have not been spectacular. The majority of legislative changes have only covered legally separated couples not living together, so that the vast bulk of marital rape remains within the law. Even the few cases that prosecutors have chosen to pursue have not enjoyed a high success rate (Drucker 1979; Geis 1978). So despite considerable press-ure and some legislative shifts, there is still a 'spousal exception' clause in the principle and practice of rape laws.

The legal principle of 'exclusion' has even wider ramifications in practice. The view of women as sexual servants, contracted willingly to serve men, gets extended beyond wives to include a whole category of 'sexually worthless' women – prostitutes, whores, drug addicts, al-coholics, sexually experienced, and divorced – who because they lack 'respectability' are considered to have no worthwhile reason for not consenting to men and therefore do not deserve legal protection (Clark and Lewis 1977; LaFree 1980; Sebba and Cahan 1975).

With few exceptions, contemporary legal definitions of rape focus only on vaginal penetration and ignore anal and oral penetration, or relegate them to acts of indecent assault (Bienen 1977). In a passionate and disturbing account of rape history and current practices which highlights the dispiriting variety of objects men manage to invent as instruments for violating a woman's physical integrity, Brownmiller argues that:

'Tradition and biologic opportunity have rendered vaginal rape a particular political crime with a particular political history, but the invasion may occur through the mouth or the rectum as well. And while the penis may remain the rapist's favourite weapon, his prime instrument of vengeance, his triumphant display of power, it is not in fact his only tool. Sticks, bottles, and even fingers are often substituted for the 'natural' thing . . . . Who is to say that the sexual humiliation suffered through forced oral or rectal penetration is a lesser violation of the personal private inner space, a lesser injury to mind, spirit, and sense of self? . . . All acts of sex forced on unwilling victims deserve to be treated in concept as equally grave offences in the eyes of the law, for the avenue of penetration is less significant than the intent to degrade.'   (Brownmiller 1975: 378)

Furthermore, by viewing the penis as the primary rape weapon, these laws reveal a male preoccupation with the risk of their respectable women getting pregnant rather than a concern for the physical and psychological injury during and after rape. This is because legislators, mainly men, see vaginal penetration by the potentially impregnating penis as the worse eventuality that can befall a woman. This merely reflects self-interest, according to Clark and Lewis, who write that:

'For a man to have his exclusive sexual property defiled by an intruder is one of the worse things that can happen to *him*, but it most assuredly is not the worse thing that can happen to a woman, even though it frequently verges on this because of its accompanying risk. What woman would not rather have a penis inserted in her vagina, even against her will, than suffer death or mutilation?'
                                      (Clark and Lewis 1977: 160)

In addition to wanting the concept of rape broadened to make it non-orifice and non-instrument specific, feminist writers also want the concept of consent re-examined, possibly with the intent of shifting from 'without the victim's consent' to 'coerced by the offender'. Because consent is legally difficult to establish, particularly if it is further complicated by the law taking into account the offender's 'honest and reasonable' belief about consent, the effect is that the law in practice is primarily concerned with sexual access achieved by the means of actual or threatened physical violence, which in turn is considered by legal practitioners to constitute proof that consent did not take place. But by making lack of consent the distinguishing feature of rape, the law misses an obvious point. It is not so much the absence of consent, although that has to exist, but the presence of coercion which makes rape fundamentally different from normal acts of sexual intercourse. In a situation where the female's choice is severely restricted by the male being able to impose sanctions for refusal, the question of her consent should become secondary to his ability to coerce. In other words, by focusing on consent under direct physical coercion, the law misses submission under threats of all types.

Thus, what in principle may already be a very narrow conceptualization of rape becomes even more restricted in practice. The result is that much behaviour which is very similar in *form*, although not *content*, is omitted and ignored by this legalistic conceptualization. There are many instances of female sexual victimization where actual or threatened physical violence is absent and where the conditions for genuine consent are also absent. A female can be threatened by economic, emotional, and social violence: that is, she may be threatened with job loss, demotion, transfer to unpleasant location, or loss of promotion chances, she may be threatened by loss of affection, supportive relationship, or the promise of marriage being withdrawn, she may be threatened by males who have the power to stigmatize her, as when for instance, a policeman can offer her non-arrest for herself (or a close relative) in return for sexual favours. For the victim's point of view, these threats can be just as real and 'costly' as can physical violence, and consequently they can be just as 'effective' in securing her acquiescence. Thus those operating with a concept of rape produced by juridical practice focus only on that type of violence which reflects man's physical superiority over females (untutored in self-defence) and ignore other types of violence which reflect man's economic, organizational, and social superiority. In doing so, they exclude an enormous amount of sexual access where the actual or threatened use of violence other than the physical variety is the means of neutralizing the victim's non-consent.

The law in practice also has a narrow view of consent. It focuses merely on the surface appearance of consent rather than considering whether or not the *conditions for genuine consent existed*. Although there is disagreement over the exact nature of these conditions, it does seem clear that there has to be relative equality, on relevant criteria, between the persons concerned. For genuine consent to sexual intimacy to be present, both persons must be: (i) *conscious* – rather than the female being unconscious, drugged or drunk, or mentally retarded; (ii) *fully informed* – rather than the female being deceived about the man's intentions, affections, or social standing; (iii) *economically independent* – rather than the female being in such an inferior position that her body can be exploited in return for male economic patronage or protection; and (iv) *positive in their desires* – rather than the female feeling obliged or socially coerced into physical acts which do not reflect her desire.

In many cases where these conditions for genuine consent do not exist, the female *appears* to be consenting because she does not overtly resist; but only in a few instances would the law regard any sexual access as criminal, namely those where the female was unconscious, drugged, or mentally retarded. Being drunk may or may not be recognized by the law as a condition preventing consent. In all other circumstances the law would regard the absence of physical damage or the absence of real physical threat as tantamount to proof that consent had been given. Yet, as Germaine Greer sees it, there is little difference between sexual access gained through the actual use of physical violence and that gained through the threatened (but uncorroborated) use of physical violence, or the actual or threatened use of economic, organizational, or social violence. All those instances of coitus gained through the use or threatened use of any type of violence and where there is an absence of relative equality between the persons involved ought to be considered as rape. To her, the definitional problems are easily resolvable. As she sees it:

> 'Those of us who have a high opinion of sex cannot accept the idea that absence of resistance sanctions all kinds of carnal knowledge; rather than rely on such a negative criterion, we must insist that only evidence of positive desire dignifies sexual intercourse and makes it joyful. From a proud and passionate woman's point of view, anything less is rape.'
> (Greer 1975: 378)

Without necessarily spreading the net of rape as wide as this and capturing every sexual act in which female positive desire is missing, it is possible to conceptualize rape in broader terms than present juridical practice permits, and yet still refer to a reasonably homogeneous and inclusive category. Thus rape could be defined as sexual access gained by any means where the female's overt *genuine* consent is absent. Of course, this would be no clearer in practice than is the current legal definition. There will always be an ascertainment problem because genuine consent – equality and the absence of coercion – is difficult to determine. None the less, the problem need not be as difficult as commonly thought nor as prejudicial to the victim as the present legal practice makes it.

A comparison of rape and theft is instructive. A person can acquire a material object because it was given by another person or stolen from them. If the previous owner brings a charge of theft, the accused's defence that 'it was a gift' rarely succeeds. In legal practice, the previous owner's accusation is tantamount to conviction, and this reflects our common-sense reasoning that there are few reasons for accusing someone of theft other than that they did it. A malicious accusation of theft is simply not part of our cultural typifications. It was for this very reason that the editor in the film *Front Page* gives his ace reporter a gold watch only to inform the police that it had been stolen. In this way he hoped to get his reporter back to Chicago and stop him getting married in Pennsylvania! When it comes to rape however, the victim's allegation that she did not consent is frequently, and, in the absence of physical bruises, usually treated with suspicion. The common-sense, and sexist assumption, is that a woman is far more likely to make a gift of her body than she is of her possessions, presumably because she too gets pleasure out of coitus. But this ignores both the pleasure derived from gift-giving and the fact that sexual pleasure for woman is nowhere near as frequent as men like to think, particularly if the intended key to its release is the mere insertion of the penis into the vagina. So if these sexist assumptions are dropped and equal treatment given to allegations of theft, whether of material or bodily possessions, then the problem of consent is not too difficult. This is not to argue that a female's accusation of rape proves the accused's guilt, any more than the previous owner's accusation of theft proves guilt. But both should be taken as establishing a prima facie case which, *in the absence of conflicting and compelling evidence to the contrary*, should settle the issue. Not to do so is to accept the view that when they accuse a man of rape, women are cunning, conniving, manipulating, revengeful, malicious, and spiteful, and that consequently the man needs protection in law not afforded to him when the charge is theft. Sometimes of course, women, just like men, are unpleasant enough to bring false accusations. But that is no reason to treat them as though it is their essential nature to behave invariably in this way.

Even if this 'feminist' definition of rape were accepted, there would still be categorization problems, just as there are in cases of theft, but none the less, the point is not to provide precision where there is now vagueness, but to de-absolutize and demystify the present legal definition: it excludes very similar behaviour, and it is only one definition of rape amongst many. Once we have escaped the reified tyranny of believing that rape is what the law says it is, we are required to consider a concept of rape which includes all those types of sexual access which have one common element, namely the lack of genuine consent, and where this is not equated with actual or threatened use of physical violence.

There is, however, an obvious danger of being too uncritical. In focusing on the similarities shared by various sexual acts we may suppress their differences. That would be a mistake, for although in order to gain a proper understanding of rape it is necessary to include more sexual acts than the law does at present, it is also important to make distinctions between those sexual acts finally included. A victim being buggered, beaten, and mutilated, before and after death, is not the same as a potential female employee resentfully, reluctantly, and mutely 'putting out' for the man who has the power to hire her. Coitus with a stranger holding a gun or knife to the victim's head is not the same as seduction-turned-into-rape between fairly intimate acquaintances where the 'weapon' is persistent verbal pressure and threatened withdrawal of affection. Being physically beaten into submitting, or doing so under threat of such a beating, is not the same as being told, in the early hours of the morning 'if you don't, you can walk home', or at the end of an evening, 'you owe me this; I've spent so much on you at the theatre and restaurant', or the plea, 'it's okay, we'll be getting married soon' (when he has no intention of doing so sooner or later). Clearly these instances all have one factor in common – sexual access where consent was not given or not genuine because it was given under conditions of relative inequality and duress; it is the absence of genuine consent that makes them all instances of rape. But since the form of rape can take different contents, it may be important to spell these out because each may require a different, or slightly different type of explanation.

The following types of rape are drawn from those established in current rape literature and do seem to have some credence:

Sadistic rape In this type of rape, both sexuality and aggression become fused into a fury of violent, mutilating acts. The rapist appears to derive eroticized pleasure not through intercourse but through an horrendous attack on the victims genitalia and body (Groth and Birnbaum 1979: 44–5).

Anger rape is a sexual assault in which sexuality, according to Groth and Birnbaum:

> 'becomes a means of expressing and discharging feelings of pent-up anger and rage. The assault is characterized by physical brutality. Far more actual force is used in the commission of the offence than would be necessary if the intent were simply to overpower the victim and achieve sexual penetration . . . such a man considers rape the ultimate offence he can commit against another person. Sex becomes his weapon, and rape constitutes the ultimate expression of his anger. In anger rape, there is little or no sexual pleasure. Indeed, in many cases, sexual difficulties rather than "satisfaction" are more prevalent. Possibly because of this, anger rapes are frequently characterized by further acts of defilement, degradation and humiliation. The victim's body is the object on which the offender projects the solution to his frustrations, shortcoming, distress, and depressing life.'
>
> (Groth and Birnbaum 1979: 13–14)

Domination rape In this type of rape, the motive of the offender is to demonstrate his power and superiority over the victim, simultaneously displaying to her 'the female's proper place' in the order of things. Because he accepts a major cultural symbolization of sex as being the equivalent of interpersonal domination, he chooses a sexual means to make his point. As Groth and Birnbaum see it, it is not the offender's desire

> 'to harm his victim but to possess her sexually. Sexuality becomes a means of compensating for underlying feelings of inadequacy and serves to express issues of mastery, strength, control, authority, identity, and capability. His goal is sexual conquest, and he uses only the amount of force necessary to accomplish this objective. His aim is to capture and control his victim. He may accomplish this through verbal threat, intimidation with a weapon and/or physical force. Physical aggression is used to overpower and subdue the victim, and its use is directed toward achieving sexual submission. The intent of the offender usually is to achieve sexual intercourse with his victim as evidence of conquest, and to accomplish this, he resorts to whatever force he finds necessary to overcome his victim's resistance and to render her helpless.'   (Groth and Birnbaum 1979: 25–6)

Seduction-turned-into-rape In this type of rape, the assault arises out of an 'acceptable' seductive situation, but where the victim decides or has previously decided that personal intimacy will stop short of coitus. The male, for a variety of reasons, but mainly a mixture of self-defined sexual urge and the need to dominate adversaries, pursues and pressurizes, cajoles and bullies, and ultimately 'persuades'. Physical force is rarely used because it is rarely needed. The victim often gets caught by her own rising sense of guilt at not letting her partner have what he wants and maybe, according to her logic of her oppressed psychology, even 'deserves', or decides that she would rather continue the relationship on his terms than risk him carrying out his threat to 'leave for good', or simply gets exhausted and unable to resist at which point she may well say to herself 'so what', although afterwards, when her energy returns, she may well regret her passivity and submissiveness. The offender does not intend to hurt the victim, but primarily seeks to pursue his own pleasure, hoping and maybe even believing that in doing so he will give pleasure to his 'reluctant and coy' partner. He firmly believes in his own masculinity and the right of men to harry and hound their prey, but within the 'gentlemanly' rules of the 'seduction game'. He also believes that a woman either needs to be pressurized, because she will feel guilty about sex, or she requires a man to make up her mind because she cannot make it up herself. Above all, he believes that men, like himself, ultimately have a right to take what they want.

Exploitation rape refers to any type of sexual access gained by the male being able to take advantage of the female's vulnerability because she is dependent upon him for economic or social support, or because, as in the case of wives being raped by their husbands, the law offers her no protection. Again, given her relatively weak position, the female often makes a rational choice that the alternatives to coitus are even more personally harmful; her consent though is not an expression of her desire, either for sexual pleasure or to please and physically comfort her male partner, nor is it genuine because the conditions under which it is given – conditions of economic or social vulnerability created by relative inequality – are not those under which consent can be said to exist.

'Exploitation' rape is endemic in our society because men's structural location puts them in positions where they can, and often do, exploit subordinate women (Farley 1980; MacKinnon 1979) and because in our culture we have a 'coercive' sexuality (Clark and Lewis 1977), in which men are encouraged to be doggedly relentless in pursuit of sex. 'Your everyday pusillanimous rapist' says Greer:

> 'simply takes advantages of any circumstances that are in his favour to override the woman's independence. The man who has it in his power to hire and fire women from an interesting and lucrative position may profit by that factor to extort sexual favours that would not spontaneously be offered to him. A man who is famous or charismatic might exploit those advantages to humiliate women in ways that they would otherwise angrily resist . . . what the men do not realize is that they are exploiting the oppressed and servile status of women.'
>
> (Greer 1975: 385)

The above five types of rape reflect differences either in the type of power employed by the offender, or his motive for committing the assault on a female's sexual genitalia. These types, summarized in *Table 4* (p. 163), do not represent a neat typology constructed out of an exhaustive combination of differences in power and motive. They are merely types in which the main feature of each is emphasized – and exaggerated – in order to distinguish it from the others. In the real world, these differences would not always be obvious or apparent, and problems of categorization would be rife. None the less, an awareness of these types does enable us to take a critical perspective on the official statistics on legally defined rape as well as providing the necessary platform from which to build an understanding of rape behaviour that relies less on the alleged difference between deviance and convention and more on the 'unbroken connection' and overlap between them.

Given the wide and unbridgeable difference between the legal and the non-legal 'feminist' definition of rape, and accepting that both are fraught with measurement problems, there is a difficulty determining the size of the problem and whether it is getting worse. If we accept temporarily the corsetted legal definition, then we find that there are about 1,200 rapes annually in England and Wales. However, this does not constitute the totality of 'illegal' rapes, for victimization surveys have shown that for every hundred females who believe they have been raped, less than twenty-five report the incident to the police. Even this under-represents the size of the problem because attempts to test the validity of victimization surveys reveal that some women who claim to have reported the incident to the police do not show up in official records. Consequently, it is more like one-fifth of incidents believed to be rape by the victim which get reported to the police. So even in terms of the legal definition of rape, the problem is far greater than official figures on recorded crime reveal. And this isn't the end of it! For as has been argued above, this legal definition is too narrow and excludes forms of sexual access gained not by the actual or threatened use of physical violence but by other forms of violence, such as verbal violence, where the female's utterances are simply ignored and her will to resist eroded by a constant verbal pressure, often into the early hours of the morning when it seems like 'getting it over with' is the only means of terminating the hassle. It also ignored economic pressure where the male is able to threaten any number of sanctions the power of employment and bureaucratic super-ordination bestows, to overcome finally the female's lack of positive desire and lack of genuine consent. It also omits those widely practised forms of fraud where the male feigns affection, love, and the prospect of marriage but vanishes once sexual conquest has been achieved. Finally, it omits, because the law generally does, all those instances within marriage where the wife is obliged, irrespective of her own desire, either for sexual pleasure or to satisfy her partner, and where refusal meets with a range of negative sanctions.

When this broader, more inclusive conceptualization of rape (and sexual assault) is adopted, it is clear that it is no longer a tiny minority of women who are raped or sexually assaulted, but a substantial proportion. This is in sharp distinction to Shorter's (1977: 481) assertion that 'the average woman's chances of actually being raped in her lifetime are still minimal', and in total agreement with Johnson, who, even using a legal definition of rape and re-analysing data from victimization surveys, concluded:

'Nationally, a *conservative* estimate is that, under current conditions, 20–30 per cent of girls now twelve years old will suffer a violent sexual attack during the remainder of their lives ... the average American woman is just as likely to suffer a sexual attack as she is to be diagnosed as having cancer, or to experience a divorce.'   (Johnson 1980: 45–6)

So, the problem of rape is far more serious than the official data implies. Understanding why some men rape and sexually assault females therefore becomes even more imperative. But in attempting to develop such an understanding, we must be wary of a trap which has snared many recent theorists; this trap suggests that females encourage men to rape them, and so the 'blame' lies with the woman and not the man.

The mystification of victim-precipitated rape

In the enormous amount of material on rape and sexual assault written recently (Burgess and Holmstrom 1974; Chappell 1976; Holmstrom and Burgess 1978; LeGrand 1973; Robin 1977; Russell 1975; Sanders 1980; Toner 1977: 115–83; Wood 1973) the emphasis, for obvious reasons, has been on the victim, particularly on how she suffers twice, first at the hands of the offender, and then at the hands of those, mainly men, who comprise the criminal justice system. Following from this emphasis there have been suggestions on how the criminal justice system could be reformed (Klein 1981; Schwartz and Clear 1980) and how women collectively, can actually lessen the likelihood of rape occurring or at least being completed, and offering genuine concern and counsel-ling to those unfortunates who have been sexually victimized. As far as the latter are concerned, the proliferation of female self-defence classes and the growth of rape crisis centres are important developments.

This feminist prioritization of the victim is obviously correct from a political perspective. However, concentration on the victim has had the negative consequence of reinforcing and encouraging a particularly pernicious view that the victim is the author of her own victimization. The belief that rape victims brought it upon themselves has thus become academically respectable with the growth of the new sub-discipline 'victimology'. But is rape a victim-precipitated offence?

A qualified but positive answer to this question was made by Amir (1967), who, after studying Philadelphia police records for 1958–60, concluded that 19 per cent of rapes were victim-precipitated. But just what did he mean by this? According to his conceptualization of rape-victim-precipitation, these were situations 'in which the victim actually, *or so it was deemed*, agreed to sexual relations but retracted before the actual act or *did not react strongly enough* when the suggestion was made by the offender' [author's italics] (1967: 266).

In a later study (Curtis 1974: 600), victim-precipitated rape was defined as: 'an episode ending in forced intercourse when a female agreed to sexual relations or clearly invited them verbally or through gestures, but then retracted before the act'.

On this definition, only 4 per cent of the victim-reported rapes in Curtis's survey could be classified as victim-precipitated. However, in noting how much lower his result was than Amir's, Curtis then proceeded to argue that Amir's high figure was 'more reliable'! He thought this for three reasons: first Amir had back-up material from police files, whereas the survey data was limited to what the victim reported; second, Amir coded his material himself whereas the survey data was coded by a team of workers, consequently Amir developed a greater in-depth understanding of his material; and third, Amir had information on the victim's 'bad reputation' which enabled him better to classify her as precipitating the events!

What can we make of the conclusion that in one-fifth of all rapes the victim's behaviour contributes towards her own victimization? Maybe we should begin by noting that these definitions of victim-precipitation do not recognize that women (and people) have a perfect right to change their minds. By implying that the assailant was unable to control himself and that the victim, by agreeing originally to sexual relations, was at fault for putting him in this state, the authors collude in supporting the assailant's refusal to recognize the victim's right to change her mind. Beyond this obvious observation, it is also clear that concealed in these definitions is a confusion between what the victim did or said and what the assailant *thought*, *perceived*, or *interpreted* her as doing and saying. Thus in a later victim-precipitation study (Nelson and Amir 1975) it was stated that female hitch-hikers amounted to 20 per cent of the total reported rape in Berkeley for the years 1968–70. This, wrote the authors, 'is a victim-precipitated offence'. But by what stretch of the imagination can getting into a car with a stranger be construed as 'clearly inviting' sexual relations, or 'deeming' to agree to them? Is accepting an offer of a lift a 'gesture' that sex is available? A sexual encounter may be what the car driver wants; it may be an option *he perceives* to exist; it may well be that he interprets all female hitch-hikers' actions and utterances as clear evidence that they are 'asking for it'. But these are his wants, perceptions, and interpretations; they are not the victim's. She was merely asking for, and prepared to accept, only a lift.

By attempting to shift the blame for rape from the offender to the victim, these theorists help deny or minimize the contribution made by the offender and behind him, the contribution of more systematic factors, such as: (i) our cultural ideas on masculinity and the structurally blocked opportunities to the realization of these cultural ideas; (ii) structural subordination of women by their relative exclusion from positions of power in economic, political, and professional spheres; (iii) our library of excuses for evading personal responsibility for the acts we commit; and finally, (iv) the low rate of prosecution and conviction as well as the comments portrayed in the media on those few dramatized cases which encourage men in the idea that they can get away with it. Furthermore, these victimology theorists collude tacitly with would-be rapists by transforming some women into acceptable rape victims by in effect saying to the offender, 'it doesn't matter, it'll be viewed as her fault'. In that sense the theory of rape victim-precipitation, through its wide dissemination in the mass media, offers men encouragement to commit sexual assaults because it provides them with a ready-made excuse. The would-be offender can gain release from any moral constraints and creeping feelings of guilt by saying to himself 'she's inviting it; she wants it. And even though she says she's changed her mind, I can't stop myself, and in any case, that's her fault for placing herself in this position in the first place'.

In addition to making those who suffer from rape and sexual assaults responsible for their own suffering, victim-precipitation theorists also encourage solutions to such deviant behaviour which further diminish female civil liberties and social freedoms, and hence compound and deepen their suffering by adding to their servility and subordination. Nelson and Amir even write that 'an assumption can be made that if there were no hitchhiking females a reduction in the total number of rapes . . . would occur' (1975: 62). Although 'after consideration' they came out against such a solution, it is easy to see how the notion of victim-precipitation can be turned into such solutions and accepted by (male) legislators and the police. Their implementation would increase control over women just at a time when they are effectively demonstrating that they want and are obtaining more control over themselves.

The whole debate confuses solutions to social problems which are policy-orientated and solutions which are based on an understanding of the problems' causes. For example, people rob banks for a variety of reasons. But as any policy-orientated banker knows, a knowledge of these reasons is not necessary to minimize the incidence of such robberies. Banks want strangers to enter their premises in order to carry out legitimate transactions, but they take precautions. They will have installed bars or unbreakable glass between the customer and the cashier, or there will be television surveillance and alarms linked directly to security or police personnel; they will also have safes and safes within safes with complicated unlocking procedures involving more than one key. In other words, banks take precautions to minimize the risk of being robbed. But these precautions are not based upon a causal understanding of why people rob banks, apart from the obvious fact that if persons are determined to rob banks, they would, if they acted rationally, choose those less well protected. If we wanted to understand why individuals rob banks, we would not emphasize the relative lack of precautions taken by a particular bank, for this would ignore all those sociological factors which constitute the motivation for such action. Of course we might think banks which did not take precautions were taking unnecessary risks, but we would not think that diminished in any way the culpability of the offender. No bank robber has ever been found not guilty, or even pleaded in mitigation, that it was the bank's fault for not protecting itself better!

Similarly, rather than argue that women should stop hitch-hiking, or putting themselves at risk in any of the various ways they are claimed to be putting themselves at risk, we could argue that women (and men) should, like banks, take precautions; they could be selective, hike in couples, not accept lifts where there is more than one male in the car, be capable of self-defence, and prepared to employ it. To be precautious in these and other ways would not diminish their freedom but facilitate it, just as banks facilitate their freedom to trade by taking precautions against robbers. However, having said that, should we also conclude that those women who did not take precautions were to blame for their subsequent victimization? Clearly, if a woman chooses not to take precautions, then she does increase the risks of being sexually assaulted, and by not being precautious she has decided to take that risk. For doing so, she might be judged unwary, unthinking, lacking in elementary 'street-sense' or even plain silly. But in no legal or sociological sense is she the cause of her victimization. For whatever a woman chooses to do or not do, just as whatever a bank chooses to do or not do, by way of taking precautions, if she is sexually assaulted or the bank robbed, it is still the person who chooses to take advantage of the woman or the bank and does the raping or the robbing who is to blame.

Although the idea of victim-precipitation has some relevance to homicide, it is erroneous to borrow the concept and apply it to any other crime which involves a victim. In victim-precipitated homicide, the victim actually started the process resulting in his or her death by being the first to introduce a weapon into the situation or by deliberately provoking the assailant. As Wolfgang defined it, 'victim-precipitated homicides' are those:

> 'in which the victim is a direct, positive precipitator in the crime. The role of the victim is characterized by his having been the first in the homicide drama to use physical force directed against (the) subsequent slayer. The victim-precipitated cases are those in which the victim was the first to show and use a deadly weapon, to strike a blow in an altercation – in short, the first to commence the interplay of resort to physical violence.'   (Wolfgang 1958: 252)

By what stretch of the imagination do rape-victims initiate the sexual assault? Do they actually start to assault sexually the persons who subsequently assault them sexually? Being rhetorical, these questions do not require answers; they point clearly to the impoverishment of taking a perfectly reasonable concept to help explain one type of crime and attempting to invoke it in the explanation of an entirely different type of crime.

Thus the idea of victim-precipated rape is both ideologically and sociologically suspect. It turns a blameless victim into the suspect, whereas, because of sex-role socialization and the 'sexist' allocation of wealth and privilege, she is relatively powerless to prevent her own victimization. And in turning the blameless victim into the culprit, it deflects our attention away from the real culprit, the man who chooses to rape and sexually assault, and beyond him, the broader macro-sociological factors which form the context in which that choice is made.

Men who rape

'The problem of rape can never be understood without an analysis of the rape offender and his motivations.'   (Clark and Lewis 1977: 133)

By dismissing victim-precipitation theory, we are left to explore at length the only and proper alternative, the offender. But how are we to discover adequate information about men who sexually assault and rape so that we can then proceed to understand the phenomena? Essentially there are three sources, and each has methodological shortcomings: (i) information derived from those persons found guilty or accused of criminal sexual assault and rape; (ii) self-report studies of rapists who have not been in official contact with the police but have been contacted by social researchers; (iii) information derived from the victims of rape and sexual assault, the majority of whom did not, for a variety of sensible reasons, report the incident to the police.

'OFFICIAL' RAPISTS

'Official' rapists are a rich source of qualitative information simply because they are a captive sample who frequently seek to co-operate in research, sometimes in the hope of getting to understand themselves, but more often in the hope that co-operation and acquiescence to 'treatment' will be rewarded by earlier release from prison. Thus recent studies (Cohen 1971; Fisher and Rivil 1971; Groth and Birnbaum 1979; Rada 1978; West, Roy, and Nichols 1978) do provide a window on the psychology and socio-cultural backgrounds of at least some rapists.

Unfortunately, they are a poor base from which to make generalizations about all rapists. This is simply because the majority of victims do not complain to the police, the police do not take seriously a substantial proportion of complaints made to them (Clark and Lewis 1977: 57–60; Sanders 1980: 86), and only a minority of police-recorded rapes are cleared up. Of this minority of men who are arrested and charged with rape over a quarter are eventually found not guilty, and of the remainder, a quarter are not sent to prison. If we take the most conservative estimate for rape, one that is based on victimization surveys, then there are about 5,000 rapes per year in England and Wales. If we call this 100 per cent, then only 25 per cent are recorded by the police as rape incidents, only 10 per cent are prosecuted, only 7 per cent are found guilty, and only 6 per cent are finally sent to prison. In other words, over nine out of ten men who rape appear not to get the punishment the crime deserves. A similar exercise on the attrition of rape cases in the criminal justice system has been made for the USA. Smithyman (1979: 101) suggests that for every 100 rape cases only 25 are reported to the police, only 13 persons are arrested, only 9 persons are prosecuted and less than 5 are convicted. Thus the prison rapists are a minute sample of all rapists.

For the purpose of obtaining information on rapists, the attrition rate would not matter if the rapes for which men were sentenced to prison were typical or representative of the universe of rapes committed in the community. Unfortunately, official rapes are a biased sample of the rape universe. The official population of rapists is likely to consist of a representative sample, indeed almost a census, of rapists who are sadistic lust murderers, and a reasonable sample of rapists who employed violence both as a means of overpowering their victim and hence emitting their 'anger'. It is also likely to include a smattering of rapists who sought to 'dominate' their victim through sexual conquest but who were unlucky enough or hadn't the wits or resources to avoid being reported, arrested, and convicted. Men who commit rape through seduction 'gone wrong' and men who use their power, wealth, position, or 'superior cunning' to gain sexual access will of course hardly ever be included in the population of official rapists.

Thus when West, Roy, and Nichols (1978) interviewed twelve – yes, twelve – rapists who were located within a special élite section of a special psychiatric facility for dangerous sex offenders they were studying men who might provide some clues to why violent forcible rape occurs, but, as the authors recognized, the results could not produce a typical biographical or socio-cultural portrait of rapists. Groth and Birnbaum's (1979) study is an improvement on this because they examined not only those in prison, but also those accused who were apprehended but for a variety of reasons were not proceeded against by the police. Overall, they managed to gather information on over five hundred rapists. Unfortunately, this report is a rich clinical study full of insights and minute details about particular rapists and types of rape, but there are no statistical breakdowns of socio-cultural factors which would enable a sociological causal model of rape or rapists to be developed. One of the rare pieces of aggregated information is that more than half (55 per cent) of the cases were rapes of 'domination', two-fifths (40 per cent) were 'anger' rapes, and 5 per cent were 'sadistic' rapes. It is quite clear from these figures that our stereotypical portrait of the 'rapist' overinflates the quantitative existence of the sadistic rapist. They are totally over-reported by the media in relation to their sheer numerical size, and although they may be more newsworthy (*sic*) they clearly are not a faithful representation of the vast majority of rapists who come to the attention of state officials. They are even less representative of the even greater number of men who rape and who remain protected under the cloak of innocence provided, on the one hand, by frightened, tired, exasperated, unsupported, cynical, and mystified victims, and on the other, by a legal system which excludes much of their behaviour from the domain of its concern.

Not only do official data provide us with a distorted picture of rapes, emphasizing the most bizarre and virtually omitting the most common, but even within those it incorporates, it further distorts reality by reflecting the selective process in criminal justice by which the powerful and resourceful suspects are better able to avoid and evade criminalization (Box 1981a; 157–212). Numerous studies have examined the judicial processing of rape cases (Bohmer 1974; Chappell 1976; Clark and Lewis 1977: 43–61; Feldman-Summers and Palmer 1980; Holmstrom 1975; Holmstrom and Burgess 1975; LaFree 1980; Jones 1973; Robin 1977; Sebba and Cahan 1975; Sanders 1980: 125–42; Toner 1977: 115–72; Wood 1973). There appears to be a unanimous conclusion that the social characteristics both of the offender and the victim are factors determining the outcome of the case even when the type of rape is controlled. Thus Sebba and Cahan (1975) report that single men rather than married men, and men with previous criminal convictions rather than none are more likely to be convicted. Official rapists are more likely to give the appearance that rapists are strangers because in the judicial process, being related or acquainted with the victim is more likely to lead to the police not proceeding with the case (Clark and Lewis 1977: 71) or not being convicted (LaFree 1980; Sanders 1980). The race of the defendant is also important. Thus black suspects are more unlikely to be able to exchange guilty pleas for a reduction in charge severity (LaFree

1980), and are likely to be sentenced more severely (Wolfgang and Riedel 1973). The conclusion is obvious to Smithyman:

'Some serious limitations must be placed on the generalization of findings from prison populations to the general population of rapists. Prison populations are biased in favour of offenders who do not have the kind of social status or the financial resources to influence judges and prosecutors to use alternatives to penal confinement. In addition to containing a disproportionate number of persons from the lower socio-economic class, imprisoned rapists are likely to have extensive criminal records in terms of frequency of arrest. It should also be pointed out that imprisoned rapists may also contain a larger proportion of those who have committed violent and brutal rapes.'

(Smithyman 1979: 101–02)

Further support for this argument comes from Clark and Lewis's study of rape in Toronto. They note that most studies on official rapists report a lower-class over-representation, yet, they argue, we should be cautious before drawing any conclusions about the socio-cultural characteristics of rapists. They believe that:

'If the rapist is better placed in the social hierarchy than the alleged victim, it may not seem credible that he would have to, or want to, rape her. If the reverse is true, especially if the victim is a "respectable" witness, it will appear much more believable that the offender would have to resort to physical violence to achieve his purpose. Generally, suspects from lower socio-economic groups are more likely to be perceived by a jury and officers of the Court as the sort of men likely to have committed rape, and therefore, they are more likely to be convicted and labelled "rapists".'   (Clark and Lewis 1977: 99–100)

Finally, Rada makes a similar point after reviewing a mass of relevant literature. He argues that:

'the ramifications of social status and race are so great and so diverse that the influence of these variables impedes our efforts to study rapists and rape. In particular, it is likely that differences in social status and race are associated with differences in the probability of arrest, prosecution, conviction, and sentencing of alleged rapists. Thus, rape incidents and rape offenders that become available for study are biased samples from the total populations of rape incidents and rape offenders.'   (Rada 1978: 77)

So the only reasonable conclusion is that neither the types of rape for which men are imprisoned, nor the socio-cultural background of imprisoned rapists, affords us a reasonable basis for making generalizations about either the distribution of various types of rape or the types of men who commit them.

SELF-REPORTING RAPISTS

Although there have been hundreds of self-report studies conducted over the last twenty years (Box 1981a; Braithwaite 1979a) not one has included an item on rape or sexual assault. This might be explained by the fact that the vast majority of these studies were conducted on adolescent school children and that since such a population would be unlikely to contain individuals who had engaged in such criminal behaviour its inclusion would not produce worthwhile data. But even those studies on adults (Stark and McEvoy 1970; Tittle and Villemez 1977; Wallerstein and Wyle 1947) failed to include rape or sexual assaults as items to be reported. Since these studies usually include other criminal acts of such a serious nature that the respondent, if caught by the police, would have been liable for a long prison sentence, it is curious why these researchers left rape off the list. The outcome is that we are forced to rely on only one study which has attempted to gain some information on rapists by directly interviewing the men concerned. Smithyman (1979) advertised for men who had committed rape (defined as non-consenting penetration of vagina, anus, or mouth) to volunteer themselves for a confidential interview. Fifty self-reported rapists living in the metropolitan area of Los Angeles in 1976 were subsequently interviewed. The results were quite startling; these self-reported rapists, none of whom had been arrested, were quite unlike rapists in prison. The majority of them had college or university degrees, and 84 per cent had completed high school; the education of official rapists is much lower than this. According to the New York Mayor's Committee Report (undated), of 3,162 sex offenders (of whom 13 per cent were rapists) 36 per cent did not complete elementary school, 44 per cent completed elementary school only, 10 per cent entered but did not complete secondary school, 9 per cent completed secondary school, and only 2 per cent had some collegiate or professional education. Similar reports on the relative educational impoverishment of serious sex offenders have been made by Apfelberg (1964), Gebhard *et al.* (1965), and Guttmacher (1951). Only 12 per cent of the self-reported rapists were unemployed. This is much lower than the 22 per cent unemployed reported in the New York Mayor's Committee, or the 37 per cent unemployment rate amongst whites and 26 per cent amongst blacks reported by Amir in his study of Philadelphia of 833 rapists reported to the police in 1958 and

1960. Nearly half (42 per cent) of Smithyman's self-reporting rapists were employed as white-collar workers whereas amongst official rapists the comparative per cent is much lower – 10 per cent amongst whites and 5 per cent amongst blacks (Amir 1971), 15 per cent in Gillen's (1935) study of eighty rapists in Wisconsin State Prison. Finally, only 10 per cent of the self-reporting rapist population were black, which is about the total per cent of blacks in the American population. However, amongst official rapists the proportion of them who are black is much higher: 36 per cent (Frosch and Bromberg 1939) 82 per cent (Amir 1971).

Of course Smithyman's study is unique and small and it too had a biased sample. 'It included only males who read the advertisement for the research project in a selected paper and who were willing to risk sharing the details of their participation in criminal behaviour with an unknown researcher' (1979: 112). It may well be that it attracted more educated, resourceful, and hence secure (from legal harassment) rapists. None the less, it does key in with our conclusions from the section considering the social construction of rapists in the criminal justice system. It too reveals that reliance on convicted and imprisoned rapists will give a distorted view of the phenomena. Thus whereas certain types of rapists, namely those who have lower educational achievements, lower occupational attainments, and oppressed ethnic status will figure prominently amongst the official population of rapists, it can be inferred from Smithyman's study that rapists appear to be much more evenly spread throughout the male population and not confined to one particular, and in this case, deprived stratum. This is not to infer however that there are no discernible differences in the *types of rape* committed by men in different stratum. Thus, as will be explained in detail later, it may well be that the 'subculture of violence' might give us a firm theoretical grip on the rapes committed by official rapists, but we need to look beyond it to the 'culture of masculinity' if we want to understand the common theoretical bond between *all* types of rape.

VICTIMIZATION REPORTS

In recent years, there have developed two important methods by which we might improve our knowledge on the incidence of crime: these are victimization surveys and victims reporting directly to some organization not formally part of the state's control apparatus.

In victimization surveys, a representative and stratified sample of the public are asked to report if they have been the victim of any crime in the recent recallable past, and where possible, to provide information on the assailant and a number of other related issues. The results of numerous surveys lend overwhelming weight to the view that rape is a highly underreported offence; according to Winslow (1969: 2), 'forcible rapes were more than three and a half times the reported rate'. This finding has been echoed in later survey reports (Hindelang 1976).

Although it is clearly difficult for a rape victim to observe an offender's social class background or employment status, she is able to provide information on one highly visible criterion of stratification: namely ethnicity. The results suggest that negroes are over-represented in the population of victim-reported rapes. Although they only constitute 11 per cent of the United States' male population they constitute 39 per cent of the population reported by victims of forcible rape. In the light of this finding, it seems clear to Hindelang (1978) that negroes are more likely than caucasians to be involved in these types of rape cases. This however does not necessarily contradict the previous argument on the over-representation of negroes amongst the population of official rapists. It may well be that the rate of rape committed by negro males is higher than amongst the caucasians – if we confine ourselves to forcible criminal rape – but even so, it is nowhere near as high as is suggested in studies of official rapists.

However, there are at least three flaws in this technique for us to place too much reliance on it generating valid data on the social characteristics of rape-assailants. First, the victim can only report the most obvious social characteristic – skin colour; she cannot guess accurately social class, income, area of residence, marital status, and so on. Thus although negroes may be over-represented in the population of victim-reported rapists, they are also over-represented in the population of low-income, low-educated, unemployed males, and consequently we cannot control for these other possibly more important social charcteristics. In other words 'rapists' might be more working class than middle class, poorly educated, and unemployed, but these social characteristics are masked by virtue of the victim being unable to identify them in the often fleeting and terrifying moments of a rape encounter.

Second, the victim can only report the assailant's social characteristics if she sees him. In a small minority of cases, she doesn't; the attack is swift and she may be rendered unconscious.

Third, this technique relies entirely on the victim recognizing their own victimization. In many instances, the perception of victimization is simply not made. As Clinard points out:

'While theft of some small object of little value or a small sum of money is remembered by some as a theft, it is forgotten by others. Under what conditions is a vague tampering with a door or a window, or footsteps outside a dwelling at night defined as an "attempted burglary"? Often an attempted assault or an actual assault of a minor nature is considered to be too trivial to be reported, or perhaps even remembered.' (Clinard 1978: 223–24)

This inability to recognize or recall her own victimization is highly likely in those cases of seduction-turned-rape, for in these the female is very likely to blame herself because she must in some sense have consented, either by the looks she gave, the clothes she wore, the physical encouragement she gave, and, given the very fact that sex occurred, by the very failure to 'guard her treasured possession' properly. Greer (1975) has called the female capacity to interiorize her own victimization, and hence not even interpret the event as a rape, as a symptom of the pathology of oppression. She writes:

'I have not entirely emancipated myself from the female legacy of low self-image, self-hatred, and identification with the oppressors, which is part of the pathology of oppression. The girls who have been mistreated, subjected to seduction-turned-into-rape, often take the fault upon themselves. They think they must have made a mistake somewhere, that their bodies have provoked disgust, that they were too easy in their conversation. The internalization of injury is what makes seduction-turned-into-rape such an insidiously harmful offence against women. What men have done is to exploit and so intensify the pathology of oppression.' (Greer 1975: 388)

Furthermore, victimization surveys exclude completely 'exploitation-rape' because in most of these instances, although the victim would have experienced various threats (refusal to hire, willingness to fire, refusal to promote or increase salary) she will not have been coerced physically. Consequently she will, in the majority of cases, view the event not as rape but as her deciding to 'put out' in order to secure some slight economic advantage or security. It will not therefore appear as a rape statistic on victimization surveys. But the overlap between this type of 'rape' and other types is simply too great for us to exclude it. It is excluded by most criminologists on the ground that when physically coerced females have no choice (except to provoke their own death), whereas when they are economically coerced they have a choice (change jobs, become unemployed, etc.) But this is too simplistic. It accepts the sexist assumption that female resistance to rape is useless, and would result only in their death. Available evidence suggests otherwise; women who resist tend not to get raped as frequently as do those who fail to resist (Sanders 1980: 73–9). It also minimizes the social and economic damage and disruption which women, particularly single mothers, experience when made un-employed, demoted, or in some way economically diminished by a refusal to 'come across'. In other words, women about to be raped – as the law recognizes it – have more choice than submission or death, and women about to experience 'exploitation-rape' – which the law hardly recognizes except possibly as sexual discrimination – have less choice than is commonly imagined, because economic deprivation is a serious and expensive cost even when set beside unwelcome and undesired coitus. In neither situation does the condition of consent – relative equality – exist, thus separating them both off from a decent and humane sexual encounter.

Another type of 'exploitation-rape' not tapped by victimization surveys is rape within marriage. Since this is still not included in most countries legal statutes (although this is changing, for example in Sweden, South-West Australia, and some states in America – Bienen 1977) it means that wives whose husbands 'force' or 'oblige' them – by the implicit threat that if she resists she will lose his economic and physical protection – will not necessarily see it as rape and will therefore not regard it as something required to be reported in a victimization survey.

Finally, victimization surveys miss out entirely many 'anger' and 'domination' rapes which are exported. Brownmiller (1977: 86–113) gives a disturbing account of rapes by American soldiers on Vietnam's female peasants. Of course she is not able to state accurately how many rapes were committed, but the considerable evidence she does adduce, mainly from ex-GI's, leads her to conclude that it was a very prevalent form of sexual amusement and revenge. She also presents evidence from other wars to support the view that during such occasions, rape incidents increase alarmingly. The relevance of this to the present argument is that by asking American women about their rape experiences, victimization surveys remained incomplete in their coverage because they failed to tap rape committed by American men abroad. During a period of war – as was the case when many victimization surveys were conducted – 'ex-ported' rapes would be numerous. Furthermore, Brownmiller's evidence supports the view that war-time rapes were committed by men of whom others would not think it possible, for they were on most criteria reasonable and respectable persons.

Since there are good reasons for believing that 'seduction-rapes' and 'exploitation-rapes' constitute the majority of rapes, victimization surveys are clearly a very unreliable source for information on the type of men who commit these rapes. Of course this criticism does not apply to men who commit 'anger' and 'domination' rapes (except for the 'exported' variety). Considerable information on these has been thrown up by victimization surveys, and, on the assumption that socio-cultural factors are causally relevant, this provides us with considerable clues as to 'why' they sexually assault females.

Another important source of information has been provided by victims reporting direct to various organizations which form part of the Women's Movement. Amongst other exercises, these organizations have attempted to gauge how widespread sexual harassment and assaults are in the work place. Thus theWomen's Section of the Human Affairs Program at Cornell University sought to discover the extent of 'any repeated and unwanted sexual comments, looks, suggestions or physical contact that you find objectionable or offensive and causes you discomfort on your job'. Of the 155 respondents, who, it has to be pointed out, were not a random sample of the American population, 56 per cent reported physical harassment. The Ad Hoc Group on Equal Rights for Women managed to get 875 members of the United Nations secretariat to complete a questionnaire on sexual harassment at work. Nearly three-quarters of them reported that they had experienced some form of sexual misconduct. Interestingly, nearly a third of these were in connection with promotion, which of course was primarily a male prerogative to dispense. Finally, over 9,000 readers of the *Redbook* magazine in America replied to a questionnaire on sexual harassment and over 92 per cent reported it was a problem.

Of course, sexual harassment includes a wide range of behaviour, from verbal innuendoes and lewd suggestions – 'petty rapes' – through to attempted or completed forcible rape. But what this and other evidence (Farley 1980; MacKinnon 1979) demonstrates is the widespread existence of sexual aggression and access without the consent or willing enthusiasm of the female concerned. They also demonstrate that at work, many women are in a position where they can be exploited and taken advantage of by their superiors, who are, of course, primarily men.

Explaining rape

Having now categorized the major types of rape and documented their widespread existence through the community, we are in a position to attempt an explanation not only of rape in general, but where possible of particular types of rape. To achieve this latter objective, we need not search for entirely novel explanations for each type, but merely explore the possibility that they spring from the various ways in which the major causal factors of rape can combine to cause particular types of rape.

SEXIST CULTURE

One of the major dimensions important for understanding rape is the nature of sexist culture. The ideal stereotypes for men and women in our culture prepare *those who accept them* to place themselves unwarily into a 'rape trap'.

The 'culture of masculinity' and the 'subculture of violence'

> 'James Bond alternately whips out his revolver and his cock, and though there is no known connection between the skills of gun-fighting and love-making, pacifism seems suspiciously effeminate.'
>
> (Susan Griffin, *The Politics of Rape*)

To be a 'real' man in our culture is to realize that 'a man's gotta do what a man's gotta do'. He has to be strong, powerful, and independent; he should be prepared to be tough in overcoming adversity, to be forceful and never flinch or show cowardness, to be dominant by fair means or foul, to be constantly striving for achievement and success, even at the expense of others if necessary, to be competitive and determined to win although prepared to take defeat 'like a man' and above all, never, never to be seen acting or talking like a girl. In a man's world, to be a 'sissy', or 'mother's boy' is the stigmatized fate that awaits those who lack the manly qualities of ambitious striving, shrewdness in outsmarting others, and moral flexibility to secure a desired end. These qualities are acted out in the world of sport (e.g. football, rugby, and poker), in the occupational world (e.g. take-over bids, mergers, career striving, and corporate crime – see Chapter 2), and particularly in war, whether with the nation's 'enemies' or with men's 'enemy', women. In sexual matters, the 'real' man must dominate his partner by charm, connivance, or cunning, and if these fail, by coercion. When it comes to the 'fair opposite sex', masculine success, just as in the Vietnam War, is measured by the 'body-count'; women are reduced to the object of a prey, with man as the active predators. The number of 'birds pulled' often becomes the benchmark of a man's masculinity, the measure upon which his status with peers is based (Clark 1965: 71; Rainwater 1970: 285–309). As one of Liebow's respondents put it (1967: 144): 'where "pussy" is concerned, a man should "take what he can get"'. And writing directly on the 'masculine mystique and rape', Hills argues that (1980: 70): 'Especially for males *who have internalized the importance of appearing virile*, and who are unsure of their masculinity, scoring with a sexually attractive woman – the more frequently the better – may become a kind of ritualistic test of their manhood'.

The 'body-count' ritual is certainly a base cause of rape as far as some feminist writers are concerned. Men are socialized into regarding sex as not only their goal, but also *their right*. And that means, write Medea and Thompson:

> 'sex under whatever conditions the particular man can stand. Whether in a whorehouse or the back seat of a Toyota, the object is to score. However, your score counts more if you don't pay for it in cold hard cash. The most respected player in the game is the one who best outwits the most females by coaxing, lying, maneouvring; the one who, with the least actual cost to himself, gets the most females to give him the most sex.'   (Medea and Thompson 1974: 32)

Masculine sex-role socialization is a cultural precondition of rape because, first, it reduces women in men's minds to the status of sex-objects, and second, it instructs men to be the initiator of sexual encounters and to be prepared for strong, even if deceitful, resistance. Because of this, men come to view women 'as the hoarders and miserly dispensers of a much desired commodity and men must constantly wheedle, bargain, and pay a price for what they want' (Clark and Lewis 1977: 128). Out of this (misogynistic) view, it is but an easy step to link sex with aggression and assertiveness, and hence see rape and seduction as the same sexual act of conquest over a reluctant and coy adversary. No matter how 'impolite', 'ungentlemanly', or 'primitive', the socialized male feels it proper to pursue his 'natural inclinations' and take what he wants, rather than beg or admit defeat. Thus, in pursuing 'normal' sexual relationships, men often find themselves in a situation where a reluctant female has to be overcome, not only because that's what 'real men' do, but because that's what 'real' women really want. In other words, 'normal' and 'coercive' sexual encounters become so fused in the masculine mystique that it becomes possible to see rape as not only normal, but even desired by the victim. Such is the double-think of the oppressor's psychology.

Men who accept this view are reinforced in it by the way in which rape is portrayed in popular films such as *Blume in Love*, *Clockwork Orange*, *Frenzy*, *Dressed to Kill*, *High Plains Drifter*, *Kiss*, *Going Home*, *Save the Tiger*, and *Straw Dogs*. According to Curtis (1975: 77), there were during the period 1971 to 1973 no fewer than twenty major films in which rape was graphically presented. The rapes generally involved white males who were frequently portrayed in flattering and sympathetic terms. A similar cultural message on the 'permissibility of rape' is also contained in numerous 'soft-porn' video films, which have now become a staple viewing diet in many homes. In these, the victim is typically characterized as resisting the man's strong arms, urgent passions, and verbal seduction until finally a button is touched which releases the whole of her physical emotions and her 'real' but until then concealed desire – for him! In so-called 'hard-porn', the female is invariably the object of men's brutal, sadistic, lust-rape fantasy and she is frequently whipped, beaten, and violently assaulted.

Whether or not the recent upsurge in the availability of pornography has had a direct influence on increasing the incidence of sex offences in general and rape in particular is a topic of heated debate. Two governmental reports (the US President's Commission on Obscenity and Pornography, 1970, and the UK government's Commission on Obscenity and Film Censorship, 1980) both concluded that the alleged relationship between pornography and sex offences was not supported by the available evidence. This unanimity amongst official bodies is not reflected in the academic community. Thus Court (1976) claimed after examining data from Copenhagen, Sweden, USA, London, England and Wales, New Zealand, Australia, and Singapore that a 'predisposed individual with problems of sexual relationships would be provoked into a sexual reaction, which might sometimes be illegal, if he came into contact with pornographic material'. However, Cochrane (1978) after re-examining some of this data concluded that there was no evidence supporting such a conclusion. The problem as he saw it was not one of increasing pornography, but one of a totally sexist environment. If rape and sexual assaults were increasing it was because of a totally sexist environment in which some men were reacting violently either out of fear of their sexual privileges being undermined by the Women's Movement, or because, during times of economic recession, they were experiencing economic problems or unemployment, reduced standard of living, and taking this out on women. In other words, pornography, though arguably intrinsically objectional, was not the cause of rape, and by focusing on it the broader macro-structural factors prefiguring rape were being left unanalysed.

Although Cochrane's point may be more ideologically pure, the most recent reanalysis of evidence available to the Commissions (Diamond 1980) and recent experimental evidence (Donnerstein and Hallan 1980; Malamuth 1980) all support the view that *some* men, mainly those already predisposed towards violence, are likely to victimize women subsequent to their exposure to pornography. None the less, what needs to be stressed, is not the pornography but the predisposition, for if this exists, rape and sexual assault might be triggered off by any number of factors other than exposure to pornography.

Men already predisposed to assaulting women, both physically and sexually, are not only those who are totally entranced by the 'masculine mystique' but within this group will be many men socialized into the 'subculture of violence' (Wolfgang and Ferracuti 1967). Where the 'masculine mystique' meets the 'subculture of violence', there exist the necessary but not sufficient conditions for many 'seductive' rapes and probably a disproportionately large number of 'anger' and 'domination' rapes. The 'subculture of violence' is not discontinuous with the dominant conventional culture, but it gives it a distinctive interpretative twist. According to the authors of this concept, the subculture of violence is mainly located at the bottom of the stratification system, amongst the lower skilled and unemployed in which there is an over-representation of ethnically oppressed males. These young men do not reject the 'masculine mystique' but find themselves in situations where its realization through culturally prescribed modes are blocked or at best severely restricted; in these circumstances, explosive physical force may be viewed not merely as the only available means of dominating others, but as *the* test of masculinity when it comes to reluctant women. It may also be the symbolic means whereby the male expresses his frustration and resentment at being on the losing end of the distribution-reward system. As such, it may be a crucial factor enabling us to understand why some men adopt a particular type of means, i.e. physical violence as opposed to verbal harassment, economic, or social exploitation.

Female socialization and the preparedness for rape

In our culture, the idealization of feminity involves the notions of passivity, dependence, submissiveness, and mindlessness; women are taught to need men, to be emotionally and economically dependent upon them, and to look to them for protection in a harsh brutal world of male predators. These notions are both taught within the family and schools, and reinforced through the mass media, particularly in the numerous magazines devoted to female (but not feminist) concerns. These elements in her socialization prepare a woman to be a rape victim (Weis and Weis 1975). She is told that men are there to protect her and she needs their protection; of course she is warned that some men are rapists, but they are a mindless, mentally ill, small minority. Unfortunately when she turns to men for protection many more than she was prepared to expect turn out to be men willing to rape in order to have sex or to symbolize their notion of masculinity. She is taught that to be normal she has to be heterosexual; this means she has to be actively engaged in getting and capturing her man. To do this, she has to look, dress, smell, and speak in a feminine and sexual manner: hair coiffed, straightened,

waved, permed, tinted, bleached, sprayed, eyebrows plucked and pen-
cilled, eyes lined, lashes curled, mascaraed and shadowed, ears pierced,
nose powdered and bobbed, teeth capped and braced, mouth lipsticked,
chin lifted, neck and shoulders pancaked and suntanned, underarms
deodorized and shaved, breasts bound and siliconed, nipples rouged,
wrists perfumed and braceleted, midriff bared, abdomen girdled, finger
nails painted, cuticled, filed, and manicured, fingers ringed, buttocks
girdled, vagina deodorized and perfumed, pubic hair trimmed and
shaped, thighs gartered and stockinged, legs shaved, and toenails
painted. The whole body has to be soaked in oils, creams, and moisturiz-
ers. No wonder women don't make works of art, says Dworkin (1974:
117), they are works of art! In doing all this preparatory work, the typical
female is not only saving the embalmer a job, but in making herself
desirable to men, she is not consciously pursuing her desire. The risk is
that in making herself desirable, she may be desired too arduously; in
appearing sexy she may be mistaken for someone willing to have sex.
Thus a woman has to be prepared to be seduced, but to hold out as long
as possible for the best possible outcomes (promotion, love, marriage). If,
however, things don't go according to plan, that is, if in attempting to
meet, talk, and entice men, she is thought to be talking 'too freely', or
appearing 'too sexy', and 'available', then she is instructed by our cultural
standards not to resist. Struggling, fighting, and fleeing are all hopeless,
for men are so superior physically that women who resist will only get
injured more than they need, and besides, it is important to keep her
looks in good condition if she wants to compete for men successfully in
the future. Finally, in this social preparation for becoming a rape victim
she is told to 'be forgiving'; after all, the man can't really help himself, his
sexual urges are so powerful that it is not really his fault if they overcome
him. In any case, it is the female's job to help him control them by not
exciting him and encouraging him too much. And so, by this final, ironic,
and sadistic twist, the alleged masculine sexual burden become the
victim's strict responsibility. If matters get out of hand, it is entirely her
own fault. No wonder many 'seduction-turned-into-rape' victims have
an enormous sense of guilt (Schwendinger and Schwendinger 1980:
4–17) and blame themselves, and hence misperceive it as not being rape
but something they brought upon themselves and thus deserved. It's like
a Jew on the way to the gas chamber declaring 'it's all my own fault'; such
is the pathology of oppression, that the sufferers see themselves as the
oppressors see them.

Of course, it would be wrong to emphasize and perhaps exaggerate the
degree to which women and men internalize these cultural stereotypes.
There is always a grave danger when discussing the cultural determi-

nants of behaviour of slipping easily into a frozen, lifeless, oversocialized view of people. Clearly, in the real world, there are different degrees of socialization into sex-role stereotypes; if there were not, there would never be people to join the Women's Movement or Men Against Sexism. On the other hand, it is just the existence of these movements which testifies to the widespread acceptance of cultural (in this instance, sexist) norms. So although the tendency to present a puppet theatre view of society has to be resisted, the fact remains that a substantial proportion of individuals do regard cultural prescriptions regarding masculinity and femininity as being relevant and applicable in numerous situations. It is in just those situations where individuals willing to take seriously the options afforded by cultural sexual stereotypes meet, that rape (or sexual assault) becomes a possibility, and from that it sometimes slips into a reality. As Clark and Lewis see it:

> 'The socialization of both men and women takes coercive sexuality as the normal standard of sexual behaviour. Men are expected to apply a certain amount of pressure to have women submit ("agree") to sexual intercourse, and women are expected to resist such pressure, whatever their own desires might happen to be. Men are expected to be sexually dominant and to initiate sexual activity; women are expected to be somewhat passive and to agree to sex reluctantly. *Understandably, those men who most strongly identify masculinity with sexual dominance and aggression are not likely to see any difference between what they call seduction and women call rape* [my italics].'   (Clark and Lewis 1977: 141)

Beneath the convention of femininity is a subterranean lesson; rape is not the opposite to normal sex, but a grim, grinning caricature of it.

THE SOCIAL DISTRIBUTION OF WEALTH, POWER, AND STATUS

Economic inequality, both between men and women, and between men, is a contributory factor to rape. Without other factors, such as sex-role socialization, a library of cultural excuses, and the relative lack of deterrence, economic inequality would not necessarily lead to rape or sexual assault; but in combination with them, it becomes dangerously potent.

If we compare the social locations of adult women with men, we find that statistically they differ considerably, and always to women's disadvantage. Thus, the rate of 'economic activity', i.e. paid labour, is twice the size for men than it is for women. Indeed, less than half of women potentially available for employment are in the active labour force. The majority, being part of the reserve army of labour, are mainly house-bound captive mothers and/or unemployed. Women are also over-represented in the 'secondary labour market' (Barron and Norris 1976). This means that the typical female job is low paid and often part-time, it is insecure both in absolute terms and in relation to jobs in the primary labour market, and it offers few, if any, career prospects. Even in those professions and semi-professions in which women are a large compo-nent – teaching, medicine – the effect of institutionalized sexism makes its indelible mark. For example, within the medical profession, the small minority of female consultants cluster in the 'feminine' specialities of 'child and adolescent psychiatry', and 'mental handicap'; there are hardly any in the 'big boy' specialities of neurosurgery and general surgery (Oakley 1981: 154). As ever, women are located in caring and nurturing roles, even within the medical profession's 'higher' status groups. Furthermore, women hardly ever enter professions in the first place. Thus in 1977, the profession with the highest proportion of women was dentistry – but only 15 per cent were women. Amongst other professions the female 'share of the cake' was minuscule: barristers (6 per cent), architects (5 per cent), university professors (2 per cent), chartered surveyors (1 per cent).

The civil service is a microcosm of institutionalized sexism at work, despite the equal opportunities legislation. The civil service becomes a male fortress the further one ascends the career structure. All permanent secretaries are male, as are nineteen out of twenty deputy and under secretaries. It is only at the other end of the hierarchy that women form the majority: they constitute 66 per cent of clerical officers and 80 per cent of clerical assistants.

Even in trade unions, where one hopes to witness socialist *practice*, women fail to achieve high status. Thus although they form 38 per cent of the membership, they are only 18 per cent of the Trade Union Council delegates, 11 per cent of executive members, and a mere .05 per cent of full-time officials.

The upshot of these sexual divisions in the labour market is that as a group, women are economically worse off than men. Furthermore, their power at work and the status it confers is low compared to men with similar class backgrounds, education, and qualifications. Most of the minority of women who have paid work (as opposed to unpaid domestic labour) tend to be concentrated in those service jobs – nurses, maids, canteen assistants, typists, secretaries, shop assistants, cleaners, office machine operators, hairdressers, telephone operators, waitresses, bar-tenders – where men are typically in an immediate supervisory and physically proximate position. The combination of these factors means that women at work are vulnerable to the whim and fancy of male employers or organizational male superiors, who are in a position to reward or punish their female subordinates economically. The majority of women, being economically inactive, are dependent upon husband and lovers, and beyond them other related men or acquaintances. For their continuing economic support and protection, many of these males may occasionally demand a sexual price beyond the level the female is willing to go without feeling it to be coerced from her rather than given freely.

Economic inequality also helps us understand why men commit one type of rape rather than another. Men with wealth, organizational power, and social status (as well as 'good appearance' and 'cultural charm') are in a different and advantageous position to gain access sexually to females, than are those relatively powerless men, holding poorly paid jobs (if any), lacking respectability, and possessing those physical attributes which, given our cultural 'standards', confine them to a stigmatized identity. When men from this latter group rape, they rely primarily on physical violence because this is the resource they command. Being relatively unable to 'wine and dine' females or place them in a position of social debt, and being less able to induce in women a sense of physical and emotional over-comeness, these 'socially' powerless men are left with a sense of resentment and bitterness, which is fanned and inflamed by cultural sex-role stereotypes of 'successful' men being sexually potent. In these circumstances, should they decide to be 'successful' men, they have to rely on actual or threatened use of physical violence to gain sexual access to women.

It may also be the case that the sheer fact of economic inequality is experienced by some disadvantaged men as unfair, and out of anger and frustration, they assault women, a vulnerable and easy target, rather than attempt collectively to alter the economic system of wealth creation and distribution. Klein argues:

'Male physical power over women, or the illusion of power, is none the less a minimal compensation for the lack of power over the rest of one's life. Some men resort to rape and other personal violence against the only target accessible, the only ones with even less autonomy. Thus sexual warfare often becomes a stand-in for class and racial conflict by transforming these resentments into misogyny.'

(Klein 1981: 72)

Finally, economic inequality between men helps us to understand why the official population of rapists, that is those legally adjudicated and imprisoned, are characterized by an over-representation of men from oppressed ethnic minorities and the lower or economically marginalized social class. These are just the men who are much more likely to commit those types of rapes – mainly 'anger' and less so 'domination' – which the law recognizes as rape and is prepared sometimes, depending on the social characteristics of the victim and the suspect, to prosecute. Commenting on the fact that mainly poor and black men go to prison for rape, whilst others, mainly powerful men get away with it, Greer says that (1975: 379): 'neither the judges nor the prosecuting attorneys are hampered in their dealings by the awareness that they, too, are rapists, only they have more sophisticated methods of compulsion'.

MAKING RAPE SUBJECTIVELY AVAILABLE

Our sexist culture is replete with a library of accounts (Scott and Lyman 1968) and techniques of neutralization (Sykes and Matza 1957; Matza 1964) which enable the potential rapist to proceed without feeling inhibited by guilt. He evades guilt by redescribing his or the intended victim's motives and intentions in such a way that his behaviour appears 'conventional'. This cultural legerdemain can be accomplished in numerous ways.

Since rape, like all crime, implies responsibility, the potential rapist only has to convince himself that he is not responsible and then rape can occur without guilt. This *denial of intention* can be achieved by viewing himself as temporarily insane, although this carries the risk of being found insane and sectioned under the Mental Health Act 1959 (UK) or one of the numerous North American Dangerous Offenders Acts. Consequently it is better for the rapist to take refuge in the cultural construct of men – in this they are portrayed as having overpowering, biologically determined sexual urges. As Carol Smart sees it:

'One of the most pervasive myths which feed our distorted understanding of rape is the belief in the urgent sexual potency of men. Men are believed to have a virtually uncontrollable sexual desire, which once awakened must find satisfaction regardless of the consequences.'
(Smart 1976: 95)

Empirical support for the widespread acceptance amongst rapists of this comforting myth has been reported by Taylor (1976). In a study of ninety-four sex offenders either appearing in court or located in an institution, he was able to document eighty-six accounts which 'neutralized' their motives. Three-quarters of these accounts (sixty-five out of eighty-six) consisted of attempts to deny intention either by reference to 'breakdown in mental functioning', or 'inner impulse', or 'defective social skills'. In each case, the offender viewed their offence as being involuntary.

Failing these possibilities, potential rapists can utilize the available 'social meaning of alcohol' consumption. According to MacAndrew and Edgerton (1970), our culture is one in which the ingestion of alcohol is *believed* to cause breakdown in moral inhibitions, so that drunken persons are more willing to behave licentiously and violently. Consequently people who have been drinking alcohol can take advantage of this belief and ease themselves into a state of diminished control not over their behavioural co-ordination, (because alcohol consumption definitely impairs this) but over their moral comportment (because alcohol consumption does not impair this unless the consumer mediates the available cultural meaning of alcohol consumption to be applicable to him in his present situation). That sex offenders frequently take advantage of the option offered by the social meaning of alcohol consumption is clear from a study of people in prison for such offences. McCaghy (1968) interviewed 158 sex offenders. Of these, 32 per cent denied being responsible for their behaviour by claiming that at the time, they were under the influence of drink. Typical of these accounts were: 'When I drink, I get that I don't give a damn attitude'; 'I have no intention of hurting them . . . but . . . every time I committed a crime I was drunk'; 'I'd never have done it if I were sober'; 'I was drunk. I didn't realize their age and I was half blind. I've always been a drinker'. In other words, these sex offenders denied that they had any intention at the time of the offence to commit a crime; they merely admitted to another minor deviation all too normal in our society, namely being in the grip of that magical chemical, alcohol.

Finally, a man about to rape can avoid feeling guilty by convincing himself that 'she really wants it'. Since it is widely believed that beneath the socialized coyness of the reluctant female there is a burning desire to be possessed by the strong, dominant, and forceful male – as every rape scene in films portrays it – some men find it relatively simple to transform a female's 'no's into 'yes's; through the distorting lens of the myth that women really want it, every act of refusal becomes an unambiguous sign of encouragement, every discouragement an invitation to persist but more strenuously. In the daily drama of seduction-turned-into-rape, the offender renders himself guiltless by acting out the male fantasy that females want to be raped, and consequently, despite every sign to the contrary, he sees nothing but tacit consent. According to this script, men see sex as merely the instrument for enabling the female to overcome her inhibitions and express herself totally and gratefully. As Herschberger argues:

> 'When the man turns to the sensational image of rape he learns of an act which, if effected with any unwilling women, can force her into a sexual relationship with him. She can be forced into a psychological intimacy with him. The unwilling women magically becomes willing, her sensory nerves respond gratefully, stubborn reflexes react obediently, and the beautiful stranger willy-nilly enters into a state of sexual intimacy with her aggressor.'   (Herschberger 1970: 24)

In our common-sense notions of crime, the existence of a real victim figures prominently to such an extent, that it is possible to convince ourselves that where there is no victim, there is no crime. Consequently all a potential rapist has to do, if he wants to minimize guilt and facilitate the commission of his intentions, is to transform the victim into a non-victim. This can be accomplished, to his satisfaction, in a number of ways.

First, he can relegate the victim to the ignominious position of being a non-person, such as a prostitute, whore, or 'promiscuous bitch' for whom 'one more fuck wouldn't mean anything anyway'. Since in his mind, she will not be upset or genuinely hurt by it, he may as well impose sex on her and be indifferent to whether or not she actually consents.

Second, he can convince himself that since he does not intend to hurt her, and indeed, he would not persist if he met with physical resistance, and since she is not offering any, it follows, according to his logic, that she is not being criminally victimized. That the female may be paralyzed with fear, that she may be shocked into dumb submission, or that she simply doesn't fancy her chances of struggling successfully can all be neatly evaded by the man's belief that if she is not fighting about it, she must be willing, although not admitting it verbally. In denying her a victim status, the offender is simply blinding himself to the considerable disabling effects his expressed intention to commit rape has on her.

Third, he can transform the rapist-victim relationship into something more conventional. Thus some rapists report that they honestly thought the female wanted money for sex, others that she really enjoyed it and was eagerly desiring him, and others that they were lovers merely doing what lovers ought to do. Some claim it was purely part of the normal dating scenario; thus Gibson, Linden, and Johnson (1980: 62) report rape victims who claimed that the rapist asked them if they enjoyed it, requested to be allowed to drive them home, to have their telephone number, and enquired about the possibility of another date.

Finally, males intent on committing rape can attempt to shield themselves from their intentions, by condemning the person who would, when raped, condemn them. He may view the victim as in some way responsible for her fate. 'The principle that governs this,' according to Jackson:

'is that, while rape is wrong, some women *deserve* to be raped. The victim is seen as a "cock-teaser", the cruel woman who leads men on only to reject them. She has acted provocatively and can hardly expect any other response, she "had it coming". The provocation may be slight or non-existent from the point of view of the victim. It is enough, insofar as accounting for the rapist's motives is concerned, that he is capable of construing her actions in this way. It is possible for a man to see his prey as a legitimate victim even where no sexual invitation is perceived, where, for instance a woman is too aloof and refuses to respond to sexual overtures.'   (Jackson 1978: 83)

Alternatively, he can condemn her for her *contributory negligence*. If she must walk dark streets at night, if she must be in a public drinking house without male protection, if she insists on hitch-hiking, then she only deserves what she gets, and 'I may as well give it to her'. Having thus elevated himself to the dubious rank of vigilante, the potential rapist then feels morally licensed to do society's 'dirty work'. Similarly, he can condemn the female for being 'out of place' – for being too free with her manners, speech, or beliefs, for not accepting in other words the subordinate, submissive place females have been allotted in our society. Indeed, any woman who steps out of line and challenges the established sexist order of things becomes a potential rape victim because she threatens to 'demasculinize' some men, and consequently has to be put in her place. This has led many feminists to interpret rape as a social control process as well as a sexual assault. Thus Weiss and Borges argue:

'The woman is consistently taught that she is both defenceless and responsible for the prevention of her victimization. She is encouraged to stay at home after dark. To avoid molestation, she is instructed not to spell out her first name on door bells and in telephone directories, but to use an initial and to hide behind her father's or husband's last name. In so doing, she forfeits a symbol of her femininity and personhood. Rape operates as a social control mechanism to keep women in their "place" or put them there. The fear of rape, common to most women, socially controls them as it limits their ability to move about freely. As such, it establishes and maintains the woman in a position of subordination.'   (Weiss and Borges 1973: 94)

And Griffin believes that:

'rape is a form of mass terrorism, for the victims of rape are chosen indiscriminately but the propagandists for male supremacy broadcast that it is women who cause rape by being unchaste or in the wrong place at the wrong time – in essence, by behaving as though they were free.'
                                                          (Griffin 1973: 30)

And Brownmiller echoing the same point:

'Women have been raped by men . . . for many of the same reasons that blacks were lynched by gangs of whites; as group punishment for being uppity, for getting out of line, for failing to recognize "one's place", for assuming sexual freedoms, or for behaviour no more provocative than walking down the wrong road at night in the wrong part of town and presenting a convenient, isolated target.'
                                                   (Brownmiller 1975: 254–55)

THE LAW'S 'UNWITTING' CONTRIBUTION

These techniques of neutralization are not private constructions thought up by potential rapists. They are part of *our* cultural repertoire for evading personal responsibility. Potential rapists merely stretch and extenuate these techniques to fit their current situation. But even in constructing these permitting excuses for rape or sexual assault, men are assisted considerably by the criminal justice system and the media's dramatic representation of rape cases. In relying and accentuating the judge's summing up, or his utterances justifying the sentence, the media faithfully record the 'sage's views', and more often than not, these reinforce one or more of the above techniques of neutralization.

Thus in a study of British newspaper reports, Smart and Smart (1978: 98–102) show the following judge's statements to have been widely publicized: 'he drank two gallons of beer', 'the pregnancy of (his) wife may have been one of the reasons for his committing the offence', 'the accused (a window cleaner) . . . was sex-starved', 'it was not unusual for young men to take advantage of a girl, or for young men to behave totally out of character after having something to drink', 'you (the accused) . . . were overcome by your own sexual urges to do something you deeply regret'. This list could be endless, but maybe just one more will suffice: 'Here is a young man of previous good character whose career as an excellent soldier would be completely destroyed if this sentence of three years were to stand . . . . Clearly he is a man who on the night in question allowed his *enthusiasm for sex* to overcome his normal good behaviour'. The judge was describing a man who, among many grossly indecent assaults, had forced his multi-ringed fist into the victim's vagina and twisted it until she fainted with pain and was ripped internally.

By reading these and numerous similar accounts, which in many tabloids are often set next to photographs of half-naked ladies, just to give the story a spicy and racy aura, many men, and particularly those already viewing women as sexual objects, will learn that the law itself permits forceful sexual encounters which it will not recognize as rape simply because the accused was 'sex-starved', 'drunk', 'provoked', or simply too 'enthusiastic'. Some men are thus prepared to use these notions of irresponsibility, provocation, and irresistible urges to excuse themselves in advance. So excused, they then proceed to force themselves upon an unwilling women.

The enforcement of rape laws makes another encouraging contribution to potential rapists by informing them, unwittingly and indirectly, that they will be relatively immune from arrest, prosecution, conviction, and imprisonment if they rape *certain* types of women. By offering 'vengeance' to only some rape victims, the law reflects and reinforces the sexist view that women are not sexually autonomous. The victims recognized by the law in practice are those women who have communicated through their behaviour and commitments (to men and children) that they recognize their place in the established order of things. In this order resides a dehumanized conception of female sexuality – it is not hers, she does not possess it, it is only held in 'trusteeship' until the right man comes along to claim what has been rightfully his all along (Clark and Lewis 1977: 125–27). Women who have the liberated cheek to claim sexual autonomy, who choose to explore their sexuality with whomever they please and under whatever conditions interest them, are not the kind of women likely to be protected by the law. In effect it says to them, if you are not prepared to behave yourself – according to male criteria – then don't come complaining to us that you have been sexually attacked. It's your own fault! What do you expect if you insist on behaving as you do?

Potential rapists do not have to attend courts to gain an insight into the judicial distinction between women. The media operates as a highly selective and sensitizing information channel through which the courts' distinction between the 'legitimate' and the 'illegitimate' rape victim is communicated (Weis and Borges 1973). Male recipients of this information immediately recognize it, for it resembles the sexist dualities learnt in adolescence between 'good' girls, the type you try to marry, and 'scrubbers', who are only 'good for one thing'. The distinction the law and the ordinary man make between members of the 'fair' sex are bound to overlap because they are cut from the same cultural cloth. But the former, being authoritative, coming from the mouths of learned judges, reinforces and makes it even more 'real' for men already enamoured with the 'masculine mystique'.

There is yet another way in which the operation of the legal system helps to foster rape. In the vast majority of incidents, the legal system is not evoked by the victim because she believes, often with good reason, that it will not be effective and that it would put her through an ordeal possibly as bad as the rape itself. Furthermore, even when rape incidents are reported to criminal justice officials, it is only a small proportion of cases in which the law attempts to obtain 'revenge' for the victim and 'protection' for those like her. Because these facts are not "official secrets", but widely disseminated, potential rapists realize that this is a type of crime for which there is a very low rate of being convicted and imprisoned. Indeed, there was a New York Times headline in 1972 which said: WHEN ROBBING WHY NOT COMMIT RAPE. As the article explained, it was not advocating rape, but pointing out that the enforcement of rape laws was so poor that the chances of being caught, prosecuted and punished appropriately were minimal, just as they were for robbery. So, the newspaper asked, where is the deterrent?

This question could properly be asked of the British legal system. Only a minority of rapes are reported to the police. Thus even though two-thirds of all *recorded rapes* in 1981 were cleared up, this represents a small percentage of all rapes committed. Furthermore, even when a case is cleared up it does not necessarily mean the culprit is justly punished. Even where a man is apprehended, he still has good chances of not being prosecuted because the victim often decides she cannot face another ordeal, or the police decide the allegation is 'unfounded', a decision which may reflect their sexism or their accurate prediction of the court's sexism; even if arrested, he still has a good chance of plea-bargaining – pleading guilty to a lesser sexual crime, such as 'indecent assault', which carries a lighter average sentence; even if prosecuted for rape, he still has a good chance of not being found guilty – in England and Wales for the year 1981, 112, or 28 per cent of the 406 prosecuted men aged seventeen or over were acquitted. Only when there is an 'unlucky' convicted rapist – unlucky, that is, considering the chances against conviction – does the law take a serious view of the offence. Thus in 1981 in England and Wales, 293 men were found guilty and of these, 269 or 92 per cent were imprisoned, 11 were given suspended prison sentences, 9 were placed on a probation order, and 1 was fined £2,000 because, according to Judge Richards, the victim was guilty of *contributory negligence* by virtue of the fact that she accepted a car-lift from a stranger late at night.

Judge Richards' sentence, plus a few other maverick performances by colleagues, such as a double rapist of a seven-year-old girl not being imprisoned for more than six months, sparked off a debate over the possibility of a mandatory prison sentence for all rapists. The government came out against such a 'reform'. The grounds for this decision appeared to be that it would encourage the suspect and the police to engage in more plea-bargaining than now exists, it would discourage jurists from convicting, and it would prevent judges taking into account any mitigating or extenuating circumstances. The outcome of the 'reform', implied the government, would be that more rapists would get away with it. Against this is the view that there are no excuses for rape, and police discretion should be more circumscribed. In any case, too many rapists get away with it now, and introducing a mandatory sentence would introduce a new factor into any calculations being made by potential rapists.

As matters stand at the moment, only a small minority of all rapists are imprisoned, and even then they are not imprisoned for long. Thus in 1981, 20 per cent of imprisoned rapists were sentenced to less than two years in custody, and a further 27 per cent for between two and three years. In other words, nearly a half of imprisoned rapists, and much more than a half of all convicted rapists, are not gaoled for more than three years. With good behaviour, parole, and remission the majority of imprisoned rapists are back in the community less than two years after leaving it. Not only might this seem a modest average sentence for a crime which in principle carries a life sentence, but it is so *varied*: from fines, to probation orders, to suspended sentences, to lengths of imprisonment from less than six months to ten years or more. A potential rapist contemplating such a variety of outcomes surely could not predict accurately what the likely cost to him would be in terms of conviction and imprisonment for a long time. Given the frame of mind he would be in when contemplating rape, it is likely that if he considers the crime rationally – and many rapes are planned – he would take the range of sentences passed by the court and turn this variety to his advantage. Not being able to predict what he would get, he may well imagine that it would not be *that* serious. So encouraged, he may well go ahead and leap this final 'rational' hurdle.

In the preparation-for-rape, the law plays a not inconsiderable part: it operates with a restricted definition of rape; it achieves a low clearance rate; its procedural system puts off many victims and makes conviction less likely; it entertains a dual conception of legitimate and illegitimate victims; and finally, its arbitrary sentencing practice guarantees the dramatization of the most bizarre cases, thus encouraging the 'normal' calculating rapist.

It has to be repeated that the majority of rapists, according to either the legal or feminist definition, are not touched directly by the actual operation of the law. Once these men have raped, and then realize that the experience can be handled, that the fear of apprehension was relatively groundless, and that the act itself can be easily neutralized beforehand and effectively excused afterwards, then they are prepared to commit it again, should a similar situation present itself. Given our sexual mores, a re-occurrence is more than likely.

Concluding comments

Figure 2 attempts to represent the above arguments. Hopefully, it makes clear that understanding each of the five major types of rape requires a slightly different emphasis to be placed on the four factors – 'masculine mystique', 'structural inequalities', 'cultural library of excuses', and the 'law's unwitting contribution'. Thus, in order to understand the small number of sadistic rapes, it is essential to emphasize the offender's attachment to being 'manly' and his location within the distributive system of social rewards. His use of techniques of neutralization do not appear to be extensive or important, although in some instances an appeal to such 'severe forms or mental illness' as 'paranoiac schizophrenia' will undoubtedly be encountered – as they were in the Peter Sutcliffe (Yorkshire Ripper) case. At the other end of the continuum is 'exploitation' rape: this can be understood by emphasizing a man's willingness to take refuge in the numerous cultural excuses that enable him to evade responsibility; there is also a need to emphasize his location within the system of inequality, and to a lesser extent, his mesmerization by the 'masculine mystique'. This last point however, should not obscure the major thrust of this chapter's argument, which hopefully *Figure 2* brings out: *each type of rape is primarily committed by men from that population who are relatively more attached and identified with notions of 'manliness' and feel the need to demonstrate this essentializing view of themselves whenever they experience some identity doubts or anxieties.* The engine of rape is not to be found between a man's loins, but in his mind, and this in turn reflects cultural definitions of gender.

The view that rape is fundamentally a cultural expression, a means by which 'stressed, anxiety-ridden, misogynist' men can assert their 'cherished notions of masculinity' is opposed to the view put forward by Brownmiller (1975). Her assertions come close to viewing rape as an expression of anatomical and biological possibilities. Thus she argues:

'Men's structural capacity to rape and woman's corresponding structural vulnerability are as basic to the physiology of both our sexes

Figure 2 A typography of five types of rape and factors associated with their causation.

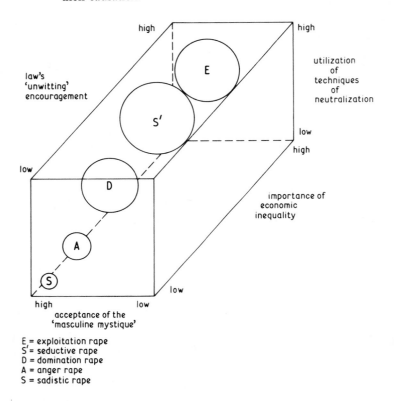

E = exploitation rape
S'= seductive rape
D = domination rape
A = anger rape
S = sadistic rape

Table 4 Types of rape and their recognition by law

type of rape	primary type of power employed to coerce victim	offender's primary motives	proportion of victims recognized by law
sadistic	physical (actual)	aggression/sex	all*
anger	physical (actual)	aggression/revenge	most
domination	physical (threatened/ actual)	sex/conquest	many
seduction	emotional/social some physical	sex/manliness	few
exploitation	economic/ organizational/ social	sex	none

* Many are transformed into murder charges

as the primal act of sex itself. Had it not been for this accident of biology, an accommodation requiring the locking together of two separate bodies, penis into vagina, there would be neither copulation nor rape as we know it . . . we cannot work around the fact that in terms of human anatomy the possibility of forcible intercourse incontrovertibly exists. This single factor may have been sufficient to have caused the creation of a male ideology of rape. When men discovered that they could rape, they proceeded to do it – man's discovery that his genitalia could serve as a weapon to generate fear must rank as one of the most important discoveries of prehistoric times along with the use of fire and the first crude stone axe.'   (Brownmiller 1975: 13–14)

From this assumption of biological primacy, she goes on to argue that rape exists universally and serves an invariable function. Thus:

'From prehistoric times to the present . . . rape has played a critical function. It is nothing more or less than a conscious process of intimidation by which *all* men keep *all* women in a state of fear . . . (furthermore) men who commit rape have served in effect as front-line masculine shock troops, terrorist guerrillas in the longest sustained battle the world has ever known.'

(Brownmiller 1975: 14, 209)

Not only do these statements biologize what is essentially a social phenomena, but by employing the metaphors 'longest sustained battle' and 'from prehistoric times', Brownmiller implies that men are rapists because it is in their nature. The argument in this chapter has been that in industrialized societies it is not men's nature to rape, but that it is an historical conjuncture of 'sexist male culture', coupled with gross inter- and intra-gender inequalities in wealth, power, and privileges, and firmed up by techniques of neutralization and a legal system in which institutionalized sexism is embedded that forms the roots of rape. Curiously, Brownmiller rejects the sexist image of females ingrained in our culture, but seems not to reject the masculine image as cultural phenomena. As the Schwendingers rightly argue:

'Brownmiller's erroneous interpretation of history is particularly evident when she analyses the causes of rape. That analysis depends heavily for its credibility on the sex stereotyping of men. Paradoxically, such stereotyping originates in sexist ideologies, where both sexes are caricatured. Men are depicted as natural predators; and all women, by nature and at heart, are either dangerous creatures or willing subjects. In Brownmiller's . . . work, however, this heritage is obscured because she only rejects the sexist typing of women. She, therefore, wrests the typification of men from its original ideological context, which refers to dominant as well as submissive relations. She then uses the typifications to rationalize a radical, bourgeois, feminist view of social reality. Rape, in that view, cannot be attributed to any cause other than natural law; man is oppressive by nature and rape maintains male supremacy and privilege.'

(Schwendinger and Schwendinger 1976: 82)

This willingness to biologize rape and grant it a universal social function led Brownmiller to conclude that all men's interests are served by keeping women in their place through rape-fear intimidation. It is difficult to see how the interests of many men (e.g. sons, husbands, brothers, fathers, and lovers) are furthered or supported by having related women (e.g. mothers, wives, sisters, daughters, and lovers) raped or intimidated by other men. Of course in our society, many men benefit by 'their' women behaving well. If fear of rape plays a part in these women's motivations for behaving well, then these men are rapists' allies. But not all men want or desire women to be 'in their place' or behaving well according to sexist criteria. Some men experience sorrow and grief, and have an emphatic sense of pain and agony for rape victims, and this human response need not only be confined to those with whom they have a social relationship. To deny that men are capable of transcending the 'masculine mystique' and to be blind to the fact that some men have actually accomplished this transcendence is to be guilty of inverted sexism. Unfortunately, for the liberation of people, it is an offence radical feminists, including Brownmiller, seek to commit and defend.

5 Powerlessness and crime – the case of female crime

Thirty years ago, Pollak claimed that female crime was masked by its relative invisibility and that because 'crimes of women remain underreported to a greater extent than do the crimes of men', (1950: 44) the 'numerical sex differentials . . . furnished by the official crime statistics' (1950: 56) are mythical. He came to this peculiar conclusion – that women commit as many crimes as men – by way of arguing that illegal abortion, prostitution, and shoplifting were reported very infrequently to the police. Because these offences were either female-specific or female-related, the contribution females appeared to make to crime was significantly deflated. Of course, he was aware that some male crimes were also invisible. For instance, white-collar crimes were, by virtue of the superior cunning of those perpetrating them, rarely brought to the attention of officials. But Pollak considered that these and other examples were always offset by comparable female crimes, such as, in this instance, domestic servants stealing from their employers. And naturally, there were always those demonic figures haunting his and all guilty men's consciousness – wives who practise the dark, undetectable art of murdering husbands and lodgers by poisoning their steak and kidney puddings. Finally, he argued that even where some crimes were committed equally by either sex but not reported or prosecuted, this diminished the relative female contribution to crime; if there were more prosecution, then the proportionate increase in female crimes, starting from a smaller absolute base figure, would be much greater than in male crimes and the result would be a narrowing in the sex-differential.

Because most criminologists had neglected the study of women criminals (Smart 1976), Pollak's portrait of the 'masked female offender' gained a certain credibility – indeed, it was almost the only authoritative view available. However, both Pollak's evidential base and his arguments have been re-examined recently, and it is clear that in comparison with men, females commit very few crimes, particularly 'serious' conventional crimes (Scutt 1978). Consequently it is Pollak's image of the 'masked female offender' which is fast being turned into a myth. This is not simply because 'permissive' legislation has resulted in prostitution *per se* being decriminalized and abortion becoming legally available in private clinics and National Health hospitals, although obviously both these juridical changes mean that thousands of women, whose behaviour would have been described in the past as criminal, are now no longer at risk of being so labelled. But rather, it is because criminologists have attempted during the last twenty years to overcome Pollak's claim (true at the time) that 'undiscovered crime is beyond the reach of any quantitative assessment'. Their results – from self-report studies and victimization surveys – show that the 'numerical sex-differentials . . . furnished by the official crime statistics' are, if anything, a very good guide to the actual sex-differential, at least as far as 'conventional' crimes are concerned.

First, what sex-differential is furnished by official crime statistics? If the data provided in the *Criminal Statistics for England and Wales, 1979* are standardized by controlling for the relative size of the male and female population aged between 15 and 64 years (see *Table 4*), then the following observations seem warranted. The only offence where the female rate of conviction approximates that of men is shoplifting – no surprises there. A long way behind comes fraud and forgery – out of every five persons convicted, only one is female. For all the other serious indictable offences, the ratio is even lower. Only one impression is possible: the official statistics, controlled for population size, show that the female rate of conviction for serious 'conventional' criminal activity is much lower than that for men – approximately only eighteen females are convicted for every hundred males convicted.

This conclusion would hardly have surprised Pollak. He simply believed sex-differentials in conviction rates were invalid because they 'masked' the true, much higher rate of female crime. However, measurement techniques developed over the last twenty-five years cast doubt on

Table 5   The ratio of conviction between females and males for selected
indictable crimes, England and Wales, 1979

indictable crime	female/male ratio controlled for population aged 14–65 years
shoplifting	.802
fraud and forgery	.221
handling stolen goods	.157
murder/manslaughter/attempted, etc.	.125
thefts (exc. shoplifting/handling)	.112
woundings and serious assaults	.086
criminal damage	.070
robbery	.057
burglary	.039
sex offences (rape/assaults etc.)	.011
all indictable crimes	.178

Pollak's view. Reporting one's own crime or criminal victimization to
social scientists are both techniques claimed to measure criminal activity
independently of those state bureaucracies whose routine practices and
procedures generate official criminal statistics. Recent interpretations of
self-report and victimization studies on such 'conventional' crimes as
murder, assault, arson, robbery, theft, and burglary support the view that
sex-differentials in conviction rates *reflect*, albeit distortedly, real differences in male and female criminal behaviour.

This is an ironic conclusion, since these independent techniques were
initially introduced because official data were considered to be so
hopelessly invalid that no inferences concerning either the distribution
of crime or its aetiology could be drawn from them. Certainly, many
earlier studies using these techniques appeared to contradict the *patterns*
of contribution to crime made by women and men. However, the current
view is that the contradiction between official and self-report data is
more apparent than real. These data tap similar and *different* domains of
behaviour. But where they do overlap, which is mainly in the measurement of serious conventional criminal behaviour, as opposed to trivial
and status offences – the main areas measured by self-report studies –
then their sex-differential rates in criminal behaviour are not dissimilar
(Elliott and Ageton 1980; Hindelang, Hirschi, and Weis 1979).

Self-report studies first became fashionable amongst criminological
researchers after Nye, Short, and Olson's (1958) work in the late 1950s.
Since then, there have been hundreds of such studies, and although most

have been conducted in North America, there have been others in Australia, Britain, New Zealand, Scandinavia, and Switzerland (Braithwaite 1979a: 45–50). This measurement technique is not without its critics (Box 1981a: 65–75), but it is safe to argue that the majority of respondents are *honest* when they complete questionnaires or reply to interview questions concerning their own criminal behaviour (Clark and Tifft 1966; Gibbons, Morrison, and West 1970; Gold 1966; Hackler and Lautt 1969; Hardt and Peterson-Hardt 1977).

The present question is: do the results of self-report studies support the conclusion of official data that women commit very few serious conventional crimes in comparison with men? The most methodologically sound answer to this has been given by Smith and Visher (1980). They took 'every instance in the literature which reported a relationship between gender and various deviance/crime indicators including self-reports of actual deviance and official recordings of arrest, police contact, conviction, or incarceration' (p. 692). From an analysis of forty-four studies, they were able 'to reduce the available evidence to 1,118 separate measures of association that serve as independent indicators of the magnitude and direction of the sex-deviance relationship' (p. 693). Although there were interesting differences between the gender-crime relationship when self-reported data are compared with official data, none the less, the overwhelming similarity is that the contribution females make to serious conventional crime is about the same in both data sets. It appears that with non-serious offences, the official data under-reports the involvement of women, particularly young females, who are more like their male age peers than the official statistics reveal.

A similar conclusion on the female contribution to serious crime was arrived at by Hindelang, who examined the results of victimization surveys in North America from 1972 to 1976. He states that:

'When we move back from arrest data . . . to reports of victims about crimes that may or may not have been reported to the police, we get a picture of female involvement in common-law crime . . . (robbery, aggravated assault, simple assault, burglary, motor vehicle theft, larceny, and rape) . . . that is strikingly similar to that portrayed in arrest data. In general it appears that even at the earliest stage in the offending process for which data is available the conclusions we can draw about sex and involvement in crime from victimization survey data are essentially the same as those derived from arrest data for the same types of crimes.'   (Hindelang 1979: 152)

On the best available 'scientific' evidence, it would appear safe to conclude that females commit far fewer serious 'conventional' crimes than do men. However, this conclusion probably *exaggerates* the female contribution! For example, women play virtually no part at all in corporate crime (Chapter 2), governmental and social control agency crimes (Chapter 3), or organized crime (Block 1977, 1980; Ianni 1974; Steffensmeier 1983). Furthermore, since these crimes are more injurious and harmful in their physical, social, and economic effects than 'conventional' crimes, their incorporation into this analysis would further deflate the real contribution females make to *all* serious crimes.

However, before accepting this conclusion, it might be prudent to deal with a major objection which is made of official, self-report, and victimization data sources. Because labelling behaviour criminal is essentially a social process (Schur 1979, 1980), it is frequently argued that the outcome may be determined less by the person's actual or presumed behaviour than by their personal attributes, real or imagined. This interplay between the symbolic meanings attributed to personal characteristics and the presumed relevance of abstract meanings typically associated with particular behaviour is evident whenever an individual classifies her own actions or has them classified by others, including members of the public, victims, police, or judges. It may be that the typical beliefs we share concerning gender affects how a person's behaviour is labelled – by us or them – just as much as any apparent consensus on that behaviour's inherent meaning. Consequently, intersex difference in criminal behaviour may be more imagined or socially constructed than reflecting a 'real' difference in actual criminal behaviour. They may result from labelling process in which 'meaningless' behaviour has a meaning attributed to it after the audience, including the self as audience to its own behaviour, has taken account of the person's social characteristics and biography. It may be 'who' you are rather than 'what' you actually did that determines whether your behaviour is seen by others, and you, as criminal.

Thus, there are some writers who argue that gender affects the outcome in judicial cases and that this enables women rather than men to escape criminalization. Other writers however, take the opposite view; they believe that women being processed by the criminal justice system are likely, as they are everywhere else, to be discriminated *against* and thus receive more punitive treatment in comparison with men even when their criminal behaviour is similar.

The former sentimental and romantic view is typified by Pollak (1950) and Reckless and Kay (1967). In their view police and judges are 'chivalrous' and 'protective' towards women. They are reluctant to harm or punish them either because they believe women are not 'really' criminal or because it would be 'unmasculine' to impose pain and hardship on women. In the latter cynical and sceptical view, this judicial paternalism is seen as a thin veil glossing over sexist patterns of suppression. Thus a number of female/feminist criminologists (Anderson 1976; Armstrong 1977; Chesney-Lind 1973, 1974, 1977, 1978; Conway and Bogdan 1977; Datesman and Scarpitti 1977; Rogers 1973; Shacklady-Smith 1978) have all sought, with varying degrees of success, to expose one particularly insidious sexist practice carried out under the guise of 'chivalry', and which inflates the apparent 'criminality' of women, namely the judicial view that young females are in need of 'protection'. The outcome according to these authors is that young females are far more likely to be institutionalized, and hence appear more criminal, than are boys whose delinquent/criminal behaviour is similar but who, because they do not need protection, are left in the community. Indeed, what is particularly disturbing about this 'protection' is that it is often afforded to females who have *not* committed any serious delinquent act at all, but are simply 'ungovernable' or 'unmanageable', *as far as* their parents or teachers are concerned (Teilmann and Landry 1981). Thus, rather than concern themselves with dispensing justice, juvenile courts are often transformed into stern parental surrogates who lock up their naughty daughters for behaving in ways which gain scarcely concealed approval when committed by sons. As Datesman and Scarpitti see it:

> 'The juvenile court has utilized its discretionary power in the service of traditional sex-roles. While particular female juveniles referred to the court for criminal offences may benefit in the short run, the long-term effect is the same – to reinforce and perpetuate outmoded sex-roles. In the final analysis, the juvenile court appears to be less concerned with the protection of female offenders than the protection of the sexual status quo.'   (Datesman and Scarpitti 1977: 73)

These two views are not necessarily contradictory for they appear to focus on *different* types of crime. The first argues that when women commit *serious* crimes, they will be less severely sanctioned than men: Steffensmeier (1980a) proposes a number of reasons why this might occur – judges do not want to separate a mother from her children because they view social reproduction as an important female job; judges, police, and the public have difficulty conceptualizing serious female crime and prefer to believe that 'she didn't really do it' or 'wasn't really capable of it', or, as Millman (1975) puts it, 'she only did it for love', poor demented little thing; women are not generally believed to be really criminal and hence an occasional, even serious criminal act is more likely to be viewed as an irrational or emotional response to a passing situation, and therefore not *predictive* of further criminal behaviour; finally, if severe penal sanctions are a direct response to the perceived *dangerousness* of the offender, then it is believed that they need not be applied so often to women because on the whole they are not really dangerous. In other words, when the concept of 'chivalry' is dissected, it reveals a series of beliefs which when acted upon tend to deflate the contribution women make to serious crime, because members of the public report female suspects less, the police arrest or prosecute them less, and even then often after making a reduction in the seriousness of the charge, and judges and juries return relatively more not-guilty verdicts, or if this is not possible, tend not to impose the severest penal sanction.

On the other hand, according to the cynical view, many women do not commit serious crimes, but instead commit merely 'status' or minor sexual offences, or no offences at all. None the less, they are more severely treated by the criminal justice system which, by locking up more women for 'their own protection' than is required by the normal demands of justice, inflates the apparent criminality of women.

Because the issues being considered in this chapter are centred on serious female crime, it is only the first of the above arguments which is relevant: the question is, 'do women suspected of committing serious "conventional" crimes get away with it more than men, and thereby produce a sex-differential in criminal behaviour statistics which is more illusion than reality?' This can only be answered by considering the best available evidence. Unfortunately, all of this comes from North American studies and the results may not be generalizable to Britain, although reasons for holding such a belief are hard to imagine.

Victimization surveys provide an extremely interesting window on the public's willingness to report female suspects to the police. Thus Hindelang reports that 'of the victimizations surveyed in the overall 1972–76 period, almost one-half of those involving male offenders and only one-third of those involving female offenders were reported to the police' (1979: 150). However, apparent preferential treatment disappeared when the seriousness of the offence was introduced into the analysis. After taking into account the extent and nature of bodily injury, weapon use, intimidation, forcible sexual intercourse, and financial loss suffered by the victims, Hindelang was able to make two important observations: first, females contributed far less than men to serious crime, but ironically, the most serious crimes committed by female offenders were *slightly more* likely to be reported to the police than male-offender crimes, and only for the less serious crimes was there a small trend in the opposite direction; second, if 'chivalry' existed it appeared to be a female virtue, for females reported female-offenders less than did male victims!

Three studies on the reporting of shoplifters either by customers to store detectives (Steffensmeier and Terry 1973) or by store detectives to the police (Cohen and Stark 1974; Lundman 1979a), and a study of traffic citations (Lundman 1979b) controlling for type of offence, prior record, holding valid licence, and being sober, were all unable to locate any evidence supporting the view that women were favourably treated. The offence rather than gender seemed to be the major determinant of social response.

A study on police referrals to juvenile court for a formal hearing (Thomas and Sieveres 1975) and another on police willingness to prosecute on a reduced charge (Bernstein, Kelly, and Doyle 1977) both show that sex had only a slight and even then not direct effect on female offenders being protected. And for later stages in court proceedings, the bulk of the evidence (Baab and Furgeson 1967; Bedau 1964; Bernstein, Kelly, and Doyle 1977; Green 1961; Judson *et al.* 1969; Lotz and Hewitt 1977; Martin 1934; Myers 1979, 1980; Nagel 1969; Nagel and Weitzman 1971; Simon 1975; Teilmann and Landry 1981) supports the contention that sex plays a negligible role in determining judicial response. But most of this work, and certainly all of that published more than five years ago, has to be discounted because it contained no controls for other factors known to affect sentencing outcomes, such as the seriousness of present charge(s) and the length and quality of prior charges/convictions.

Against this body of research-based opinion has to be balanced two contradictory studies. The first (Swigert and Farrell 1976) is an analysis of nearly 450 persons suspected of murder in a large urban jurisdiction in the north-eastern United States. The authors argue that decisions to grant bail, engage in plea bargaining, allow a trial by jury, convict, and imprison, were all directed by the imagery of the 'normal primitive', one of whose characteristics is 'maleness'. Consequently women, who on the whole did not approximate the 'normal primitive' were treated more leniently throughout the judicial process. Thus:

'even when male and females are charged with the same offence, males are more likely to be convicted on more serious charges. In this way, the imagery of the violent male is reinforced by statistics concerning violent criminality, statistics that reflect the failure of officials to perceive and label females involved in violent crimes.'

(Swigert and Farrell 1976: 443)

In another study, Nagel (1981) analysed the data on nearly 3,000 defendants prosecuted for a wide variety of offences, but excluding prostitution or rape, in the state Criminal or Supreme Court in a major American city in New York State. After controlling for a large number of legal and extra-legal variables, and examining their effects on different stages in the criminal justice process, she concluded that her data failed to reveal any:

'evidence that females were more harshly treated. Females were no more or less likely than males to have their cases dismissed, and were somewhat more likely than males to avoid probation or prison sentence after an adjudication of guilt . . . females charged with a crime were significantly less likely than males similarly charged to spend any time behind bars. Thus . . . the "paternalistic" thesis which suggests that females were more leniently treated is more consistent with our findings.'

(Nagel 1981: 111)

However, she also found that this conclusion did not apply across the spectrum of offences, for where a female's offence exhibited 'inappropriate sex-role behaviour' the penal outcome tended to be harsher, thus supporting the view that courts act to protect 'traditional' women by punishing those who are 'unconventional'.

Given the variability both in the methodological adequacy and the contradictory results of the above research, it would be wise to avoid dogmatic assertions. None the less, the weight of relevant evidence on women committing serious offences does not give clear support to the view that they receive differential, and more favourable, treatment from members of the public, police, or judges. Consequently, it would not be unreasonable to conclude that the relative contribution females make to serious crime is fairly accurately reflected in official statistics, although it is slightly exaggerated by differential labelling. Police-public attitudes may favour women marginally, but more important, women appearing in court do not possess so frequently those disadvantageous social characteristics – particularly unemployment not compensated for by such integrative social roles as being a mother or housewife – which adversely affect the judicial disposition towards male offenders (Kruttschnitt 1980).

A similar conclusion can be reached after considering whether self-report data is distorted because of sex-related rates of concealment and exaggeration. There is some evidence that females do feel more guilty and ashamed of their misdemeanours and that consequently they tend to under-report them, particularly in comparison with boastful boys, who proudly exaggerate their daring, exciting, illegal acts (Erickson and Smith 1974; Morris 1964). However, subsequent studies (Box 1981a:

66–72; Braithwaite 1979a: 54–8) have not been able to replicate this finding, at least not to the extent of supporting the argument that self-report data seriously underreport the female contribution to serious 'conventional' crimes. Consequently such data cannot be used to shore up the validity of official statistics. In other words, it is possible that a small portion of the sex-differential in self-reported delinquency is accounted for by the way in which girls view themselves. But this would not begin to explain away the large gap between female and male rates of self-reported delinquency; this gap must reflect something of the actual difference in their behaviour.

Having established that the contribution females make to serious 'conventional' crime, as measured by official statistics, victimization surveys, and self-report studies, is very small, the intriguing question is 'why?'.

Why do women commit so few serious crimes?

There is disagreement within sociological criminology as to how this question might be answered. There are those, mainly feminists (Cloward and Piven 1979; Harris 1977; Klein 1973; Leonard 1982; Rodmell 1981; Smart 1976, 1977), who argue that a *special* theory of female criminality is required. The reason for this is very simple. As Leonard puts it:

> 'Theoretical criminology was constructed by men, about men. It is simply not up to the analytical task of explaining female patterns of crime. Although some theories work better than others, they all illustrate what social scientists are slowly recognizing within criminology and outside the field: that our theories are not the general explanations of human behaviour they claim to be, but rather particular understandings of male behaviour.'   (Leonard 1982: 1–2)

'Feminist' criminologists appear to argue that the key to understanding female crimes lies in sex-role socialization and social scripts and beyond these, the forms of male domination to which female law-breaking is either a response of accommodation or resistance (Cloward and Piven 1979).

Alternatively, there are others, amongst whom some feminists can be found, who assert that 'any who champion the contention that female . . . attributes have been mischieveously expunged' (from the analysis of female crime) 'must demonstrate that analytic losses have been inflicted' (Rock 1977: 393). This latter position can be put more positively: if the existing general theories of deviance, which have been applied predominantly to males, were now applied to females and found to be just as predictive, then there would be no need for a special theory to account for female criminality.

It is possible to take these two positions and assess their relative merits in the light of available, and relevant, evidence.

DOES SEX-ROLE SOCIALIZATION EXPLAIN THE SMALL CONTRIBUTION FEMALES MAKE TO CRIME?

Many writers (Haskell and Yablonsky 1974; Hoffman-Bustamente 1973; McCord 1958; Oakley 1972; Payak 1963; Sandhu and Irving 1974) have argued that sex-role socialization is linked to criminality in such a way that it accounts for the much lower rate of female compared to male crime. Thus Oakley asserts that:

'criminality and masculinity are linked because the sort of acts associated with each have much in common. The demonstration of physical strength, a certain kind of aggressiveness, visible and external proof of achievement, whether legal or illegal – these are facets of the ideal male personality and also much of criminal behaviour. Both male and criminal are valued by their peers for these qualities. Thus, the dividing line between what is masculine and what is criminal may at times be a thin one.'   (Oakley 1972: 72)

Appealing simplicity coupled with frequent repetition has resulted in this view becoming the orthodoxy. Yet there are at least two serious difficulties which should make more reflective readers at least sceptical.

First, many writers, including Oakley, *assume* that the independent variables – the sex-role stereotypes of 'aggressiveness' and 'competition' for males, and 'passivity' and 'dependence' for females – are so well known that no documentation is needed. Of course, gender differences exist, but it cannot be taken for granted that female offenders originate from those – presumably a minority – who are not successfully socialized into their traditional sex-role scripts. Rather this alleged relationship – between poor sex-role socialization and female delinquency – has to be documented by *measuring* both variables and then discovering their inter-relationship. Unfortunately, some commentators have substituted speculation and rhetoric for the necessary hard-graft of empirical research. The result is ideas, often good ones, which remain just that because they lack supportive evidence to persuade the doubtful.

Second, adherents to this position often assume that the subjective meaning of criminal activity to the offender can be inferred merely by knowing their sex. Thus Cohen (1955) portrayed girls as committing crimes because they are preoccupied with boys, and boys were viewed as committing crimes because they are preoccupied with aggressive and competitive pursuit of occupational and worldly success. This is indefensible because it takes refuge in 'artificial polorisations . . . which . . . totally obscure and distort what is known about variability' (Shover and Norland 1978: 117).

In view of these two difficulties, the only research reports eligible for serious consideration are those which have attempted to document gender differences and relate these to measured delinquency/crime. There are not many of these!

Shover *et al.* studied over 1,000 public-school students in grades eight through twelve in a large south-eastern American city during the year 1976–77. They conceptualized gender roles as 'behavioural expectations which people hold for themselves, expectations about such matters as appropriate conduct or plans for the future' (1979: 166). The results were consistent with the view that 'for both boys and girls, the more traditionally feminine their expectations, the less extensive their involvement in property offences' (1979: 173). Some of the sex-differential in crime could therefore be accounted for by the fact that more girls than boys were traditionally feminine. However, the results were not strong and very little delinquency was accounted for by gender role differences. Furthermore, Thornton and James re-analysed the same data and concluded that 'for females, the masculine role, whether in terms of self or other's expectations, does not relate to the frequency of delinquency' (1979: 243).

Another study, this time of less than 200 students attending a mid-western university in the late 1970s required respondents to state how far they perceived themselves as possessing the 'stereotypically masculine traits of aggression, independence, objectivity, dominance, competitiveness, and self-confidence'. The authors conclude that 'in general the findings showed an effect of masculine traits on delinquency behaviour' (measured by self-report techniques) 'and that . . . independent of sex, male traits increase a person's propensity to engage in various forms of delinquency . . . but . . . while male traits seemingly increase the likelihood that members of both sexes will engage in delinquency, their effects are greater for males than females' (Cullen, Golden, and Cullen 1979: 306–07). Clearly, their operationalization of 'masculinity' differs considerably from that of Shover *et al.*, and it appears to be infused with 'sexist' images, i.e. masculinity = 'objectivity!', 'self-confidence!' However, since the authors admit that their attempt to test the masculinity hypothesis is a 'modest and partial one', it might be better to have a modest and partial faith in its conclusions!

Three other studies are relevant to the current issue, but because they confined themselves to females and not male-female comparisons, they are only indicative of gender-delinquency relationships. Giordano and Cernkovich found that amongst 186 institutionalized females and 740 school attenders, there was a positive correlation between those who thought that traditional female behaviour patterns were not appropriate to them and the level of their delinquency, and this corroborates the view that 'more delinquent girls are more autonomous in their behaviour generally than their less delinquent counterparts' (1979: 479). However, James and Thornton concluded, after analysing responses of 287 girls attending schools in a small city in a north-western state during the 1977–78 academic year, that 'a girl's positive attitudes towards feminism have little influence on her involvement in delinquency. If there is any effect at all, it is negative' (1980: 236). Finally, Widom (1979) studied 73 women awaiting trial in Massachusetts, and in comparison with a control group of 20 non-offenders, was unable to locate any difference in 'masculinity' – the offending population was not more 'masculine' – and there was only slight support for the view that young female offenders subscribe to feminist beliefs.

What evidence there is – and it is not consistently sound – is that there is no unambiguous support for the view that female offenders come from that small minority of women who do not identify with traditional female values. Poor and inadequate sex-role socialization does not appear to be a plausible account of why a small minority of females commit delinquency/crime. Consequently, it may be that a better understanding of the low rate of female criminality can be gleaned from examining how they fare on those variables which have proven to be predictive of male delinquency/crime. But before doing so, a cautionary note has to be sounded. Most of the following theories and the bulk of supporting evidence refer primarily to adolescent females. This concentration is not entirely unreasonable for females aged 14 to 20 years commit just over a third of all serious (i.e. indictable) offences in England and Wales, which means that their contribution is far in excess of the proportion of all women they represent. None the less, the outcome of this concentration is that there is little illumination of why adult females commit so few serious crimes in comparison to the total committed by men. But where there is some relevant evidence, it will be added for illustrative purposes.

WHAT ABOUT CONTROL THEORY AND DIFFERENTIAL ASSOCIATION?

In the original formulation of control theory, Hirschi (1969) argued that adults, as carriers of conventional culture, attempt to overcome the problem of preventing their young committing deviance by seducing them with affection, trapping them with physical and social possessions, and mystifying them into accepting cultural myths as personal beliefs. Young people are induced into conformity by growing *attached* to adults, particularly parents, by becoming *committed* to future conventional lines of activity, such as academic achievement and occupational advancement, and by coming to *believe* in the moral superiority of conventional legal standards. To the extent that adolescents are *socially bonded* in these three ways, they remain insulated from the temptations of deviance and effectively controlled to resist them should this insulation be penetrated.

However, after testing this theory on boys, Hirschi concluded that it 'underestimated the importance of delinquent friends' (1969: 230). Consequently, the recent expansion and modification of the original formulation has concentrated on the incorporation of peer groups, or more technically 'differential association' (Box 1981a: 121–56). These reformulations have been subjected to rigorous testing (Aultman and Wellford 1979; Cernkovich 1978; Conger 1976; Hepburn 1976; Hindelang 1973; Johnson 1979; Krohn and Massey 1980; Linden and Fillmore 1981; Minor 1977, 1978; Poole and Regoli 1979; Thomas and Hyman 1978), and the outcome is that control/differential association theory is now widely recognized as providing a major contribution to our understanding of why adolescents get involved in delinquency *in the first place*. Briefly, the central argument is that the more adolescents are attached to and supervised by their parents, teachers, and conventional friends, the less likely they are to become involved with or influenced by delinquent peers and their associated delinquent values. Furthermore, they are less likely to accept the risks inherent in much deviant behaviour, not necessarily because they fear being caught by state officials, although that apprehension is unlikely to be absent, but because they fear upsetting those of whom they are fond or afraid. Finally, they are more able to resist the temptations inherent in much delinquency behaviour because, being 'properly' socialized by conventional adults rather than 'delinquent' peers, they do not perceive delinquency as being 'fun' or 'exciting', nor do they accept those symbolic meanings commonly attached to it, such as a 'masculine verifier', as being appropriate or attractive to them.

The relevance of these ideas to explaining the relatively small contribution females make to serious crime has been examined by numerous researchers (Hagan, Simpson, and Gillis 1979; Jensen and Eve 1976; Johnson 1979; Krohn and Massey 1980; Shover *et al.* 1979; Smith 1979). All report results in broad agreement with control theory's major lines of argument, and show that the social locations of females typically contains more of those factors which act as constraints on delinquent behaviour.

For example, Hagan, Simpson, and Gillis (1979) questioned 611 students in four Toronto high schools on attachment to father/mother and willingness to take risks and the perception of delinquency as fun. They argued that Wrong's (1961) indictment of sociology for having an oversocialized conception of man was valid if limited to *men* but it did not extend to *women* because:

'if our findings are generalizable, then there may be reason to assume that women *are* oversocialized; more specifically, overcontrolled. The point . . . is to place this finding within the context of a larger stratification system – a system which makes women the instruments and objects of informal social controls, and men the instruments and objects of formal social controls. Thus . . . in the world of crime and delinquency, as in the world of work, women are denied full access to the public sphere through a socialization sequence that moves from mother to daughter in a cycle that is self-renewing.'

(Hagan, Simpson, and Gillis 1979: 34)

Thus it appears that young females are more closely supervised than their brothers, and that the burden of this supervision falls more on the mother's shoulders. First, as the object of parental, mainly maternal control, and later as the instrument of that control, women find themselves more encapsulated within the nuclear family and consequently, less free to explore and cope with the tensions and temptations of the world beyond the family boundaries.

In another original and sophisticated testing of control/differential association theory, Johnson considered that it helped to account for some of the sex-differential in delinquency. First he concluded that although (1979: 124): 'there are numerous minor difficulties in the respective magnitudes (and in some cases the significance) of the male and female coefficients, many undoubtedly attributable to sampling and measurement error . . . most of the general patterns remain similar'. Second, the lower rate of delinquency amongst females was at least in part a reflection of their social location – they were more controlled and supervized by their parents, and hence they were more willing to accept conventional values and be less influenced by or involved with delinquent peers. The last point is probably worth stressing because recent extentions of control theory have brought it 'closer to differential association in that it emphasizes the need to take into account the type of association as well as the quality of the association' (Krohn and Massey 1980: 530). Relating this point to female delinquency, it appears that amongst the small minority who deviate, delinquent friends and their values play a major part, but that in comparison with boys far fewer female friends are themselves already into delinquency. Indeed, what evidence there is supports the view that female friendships, being more home- than street-centred, play a distinctively protective role. Consequently, female peer groups 'reinforce dependence, compliance and passivity among their members' (Hagan, Simpson, and Gillis 1979: 35), thus keeping down the frequency of female peer delinquency, whilst, from all the available evidence, male peer groups are important causal factors of delinquency, particularly amongst boys less socially bonded.

DO FEMALES HAVE FEWER OPPORTUNITIES TO COMMIT DELINQUENCY?

Of course, an individual's social bonding and friendship network creates constraints which diminish the opportunity to commit delinquency. But there are other types of structure which have interested 'opportunity theorists'. Thus Cloward and Ohlin (1961) moved beyond Merton's theory of anomie by highlighting the relevance to delinquency causation of *both* legal and illegal opportunity structures. In their argument, they assumed that most adolescents aspire to get jobs. Those who were unsuccessful would experience frustration which, because they *externalized* blame on to society, would in turn operate as a strong motivation to adopt illegitimate means of acquiring money, possessions, and status.

It is not difficult to see how this explanation might help unravel part of the reasons why girls make a relatively lower contribution to delinquency than boys, or why women contribute so little to organized crime.

In the first place, only a minority of girls come to regard work as more important than marriage and child-rearing. If and when they discover blocked occupational opportunities, they might well respond in a fashion different to that adopted by boys with thwarted ambition. These girls are more likely to *internalize* the blame for this situation, unlike many boys who, according to Cloward and Ohlin, are socialized to be outward looking and more inclined therefore to *externalize* the blame on to others including 'the system'. Relatively more girls blame themselves for 'failure', not because they are to blame in any objective sense, but they have been socialized to *endure* the female's lot in life. This capacity however must have limits; some women find themselves unable to endure any longer the hardships, oppression, and domination that is often passed off as conditions 'natural' for women to experience. Trained to blame themselves and pushed beyond endurance, pro- portionately more females turn to self-destructive and individualistic responses, such as alcoholism, drug-addiction, mental illness, and suicidal behaviour. In other words, in a patriarchal society like ours, women's disorganized and spontaneous 'protests' are more likely to be channelled away from innovative criminal behaviour and into retreatist and self-defeatist adaptations (Cloward and Piven 1979).

Second, the majority of girls do not see themselves essentially as workers or careerists. Proportionately fewer girls than boys aspire to jobs because they have been socialized into viewing work as secondary to marriage and child-rearing. Consequently, fewer of them would be frustrated by the lack of opportunities for work or further education to secure higher status employment. In addition, the rate of unemployment among young males tends to be higher than amongst females because relatively more males enter manufacturing industries, whilst females tend more to enter secondary and tertiary industries and are relatively protected from the worst effects of recession and unemployment. Thus one implication of Cloward and Ohlin's argument (1961) (which was directed at explaining *male* gang delinquency) is that girls commit fewer delinquency acts than boys partly because they experience a lower rate of thwarted ambition.

This would be theoretically neat but for the argument that work itself provides illegal opportunities: employee theft is impossible unless one is first employed! But more important, by fracturing the family's tight surveillance over its female members, work provides just that release from informal social control which would otherwise dampen down women's involvement in delinquency.

However, there are at least two reasons for thinking that employment *per se* may not be as criminogenic for women as it is for men. First, men are vastly over-represented in high status occupational positions, particularly in national and transnational manufacturing, commercial and financial corporations, as well as in the dominant professions and governmental social control agencies. It is just in these prestigeous occupations that work-related crimes are most prevalent. Thus the employment of women may enable them, like their male counterparts, to steal from their employers. They may also be freer to commit other crimes away from the stern, transfixing, familial gaze. However, because of their confinement to the traditional female lower-status work-positions, they will be relatively less able to engage in either serious forms of white-collar crimes or corporate, professional, and governmental crimes which are much more socially, physically, and economically harmful than conventional crimes.

Second, Cloward and Piven (1979) argue that the frequency and pattern of an individual's crime depends very much on whether they find themselves separated from or aggregated with other similarly disposed individuals; that is, whether people commit crimes in response to domination, stress, or opportunities by themselves, or with the collusion, tacit or otherwise, of others who share a similar position, depends on how far structural factors enable them to interact. Thus women at work are less segregated than their female counterparts at home and this may facilitate collectivist or at least co-operative opportunities to bend rules or break laws. But even so, the aggregation of male workers and their collectivist responses has a longer history and a greater impact, so that again, on the assumption that work aggregation was criminogenic, it would be plausible to predict that more males than females would use that opportunity resource to commit criminal acts.

The other type of opportunity structure Cloward and Ohlin discussed was the 'illegitimate' variety. They argued that even though a person might experience a plausible motive to deviate, he or she might be unable to do so simply because there was no opportunity. In other words, if a person already prepared to break the law was unable to form contacts with others who were already into a semi-criminal career, then that person might not be able to engage in violence against others (conflict subculture), or property offences (criminal subculture), or consume illegal drugs (retreatist subculture). When the argument concerning the availability of illegal opportunity structures is applied to women, it is clear how it might help explain their lower serious crime rate. In our culture, illegal opportunity structures, just like their legal counterparts, are sexist. Indeed, they are, if it is possible, more sexist, simply because sex discrimination legislation may have some slight effect on the legitimate work world – although it might be more symbolic than real (Coote and Campbell 1981). In the world of organized, careerist crime, sex-segregation and discrimination are traditionally established operating norms. Sexism in the cultural world of organized crime is not merely a question of women being untrained to take part in various 'capers', although on the whole women are not trained to be as agile and physically aggressive as men. Nor is it merely a matter of not being trained to employ weaponry or technology associated with much modern crime, although this factor too plays its part. But more important are the attitudes and beliefs of those already established in criminal activities, for these men are likely to view women through traditional sex-role stereotype lenses – women are likely to be seen as emotional, unreliable, illogical, and untrustworthy, as altogether not the type of person you want along on an armed robbery. Organized crime is not 'an equal opportunity employer'; there are glorified Godfathers, but whatever happened to Godmothers? They are relegated to subordinate participatory positions in which they function either as an exploited sexual object of exchange value or they are required to act as sexual covers to entice victims or as partial pay-offs to business accomplices. For the most part they are kept out of sight and out of power by the processes of 'homosocial reproduction', 'sex-typing', and male responses to the demands and contingencies emerging in the 'environment of crime'. Indeed, Steffensmeier contends:

> 'men who in large part populate and control the world of crime, prefer to work with and associate with and to do business with other men. In fact, because of high risks and a hostile environment, the tendency to keep out "outsiders" may be greater in the underworld. Male criminals reproduce themselves, particularly, in leadership and skilled criminal positions.'   (Steffensmeier 1983: 4)

Furthermore, male criminals tend to view crimes they commit as too hard or dangerous for a woman, or consider that such behaviour would degrade or coarsen her, or believe that she lacks the necessary skill, or – and this may be the most important – would not be willing to submit their masculine pride to 'the show being run by a woman'. Finally, the environment of crime is both uncertain and threatening. Not only are there the police and informers, but there are other criminals who have not heard that there is honesty amongst thieves. In such a world, strength, toughness, and ability to handle oneself are at a premium, and male criminals prefer to rely on other men to cope with the dangers. Thus women are rarely recruited into organized crime, and on the occasions they are, it is merely to play subordinate, sexually-infused roles, mirroring their subordinate position in the legitimate world.

The above brief consideration of both the legitimate and illegitimate opportunity structures indicates that there are plausible grounds for predicting what we already know: the rate of female crime will be much lower than that of males.

DOES SOCIETAL REACTION REDUCE THE LIKELIHOOD OF FEMALE CRIME PERSISTING?

Proposals to explain the *origins* of delinquent behaviour may not necessarily be adequate to account either for its *persistence* or *development* into more serious crimes. Once a person has *experienced* delinquency there are problems to be tackled. Not only must s/he attribute a *meaning* to that experience and then cope with that meaning, but s/he has to practise the shameful art of deception – in order to avoid being caught – and if caught, s/he then has to cope with the meaning of apprehension and possible *stigmatization*.

According to labelling theorists, it is the *reaction* to one's deviant behaviour, or more properly the attribution of 'deviantness' to one's behaviour (Schur 1979: 197–271), that is a necessary, although not a sufficient factor preceding the drift towards *being* deviant. Once a person's actions are labelled deviant – either by others or by him/herself – this becomes another possible criminogenic circumstance in that person's life, much like, say, delinquent friends, absent parents, or alienation from school are 'causes' of delinquency; but it only achieves this causative function if the person mediates the experience of being labelled in such a way that the fear of being caught is reduced – i.e. 'if I can get away with it once, then why not again' – or the sense of injustice becomes so inflamed that deviance becomes the chosen instrument of revenge – 'I'll show them they can't do this to me and get away with it' – or, if legitimate opportunity structures close down as illegitimate opportunity structures open up – 'what else can I do, but do it again'. If the experience of being labelled deviant and the consequences of that are mediated in these or similar ways, then further delinquent activity is predictable.

This argument does not propose a deterministic process. It does not suggest that once labelled an individual will inevitably become more deviant; it merely indicates that more deviance *may* occur, but does not *have* to (Matza 1969: 143–97). There is though, a strong underlying implication that many individuals who have been labelled deviant will, because of altered opportunity structures and a heightened sense of injustice, slide into more, and possibly even serious deviant behaviour.

The crucial *external* factors in this process of becoming deviant seem to be *imprisonment* and *stigmatization* (Box 1981a: 208–43). Furthermore, there is a strong empirical, although not theoretical link between these two factors: stigmatization is usually greater after a person has been convicted and sent to prison than when the person is merely convicted and receives a less severe penal sanction, such as suspended prison sentence, fine, probation, community service order, or conditional discharge.

The application of these labelling/interactionist arguments – very briefly and crudely rendered here – has been largely confined to male offenders, so that its utility for explaining why the sex-differential exists and persists has not been explored in any depth. Yet it has obvious relevance. If the labelling argument is plausible (its truth-value is difficult to determine given the insistence by its adherents that it remains vague and sensitizing) then a possible reason why women's contribution to crime remains relatively small may be that they are imprisoned far less than comparable male offenders, and that the minority who are imprisoned fail to experience or internalize the criminal code, unlike their male counterparts who do appear to be attached to this code whilst in Her Majesty's prison.

Although fewer women go to prison – the average daily female prisoner population in England and Wales is about 1,500 compared with 45,000 for men – there is no substantive evidence that when the nature of the offence and prior criminal record is controlled, women are incarcerated less than men. There is however evidence that female prisoners become less 'criminalized' than do male prisoners. This is partly because the female prisoner population has relatively fewer 'hardened' career criminals than the male prisoner population and hence there are fewer criminal role-models to emulate. But it is also because a large proportion of incarcerated females attempt to reconstitute their socio-sexual life in order to cope with the pains of imprisonment (Bowker 1981; Foster 1975; Giallombardo 1966; Ward and Kassebaum 1966) and this facilitates a relatively easy reintegration into normal society after release.

However, since the vast majority of female offenders are not imprisoned, the vital issue is whether, none the less, they experience stigmatization in the community which might propel them further into deviance or whether their deviance is allowed to remain so unobtrusive that it is not further compounded. Indeed, if female crime/delinquency is not commonly viewed as an *essentializing* act, one that enables us to know *who* the person is *really*, then most female offenders will be treated as though it was merely a 'mistake' or an 'accident' or 'just something that happened'. These culturally provided excuses enable the offender to mediate the experience and meaning of being apprehended in such a way that she maintains a normal conventional self-image.

On this vital issue, there is both experimental and 'naturalistic' data which are consistent with the claim that compared with male offenders, female offenders are less stigmatized. Consequently, if labelling analysis is plausible, this enables us to understand why men rather than women are more likely to get further involved in criminal activities and careers.

For example, Steffensmeier and Kramer (1980) conducted a survey in America on 189 students and 271 persons living in the community to assess how far they would stigmatize female felons. On the whole, the results could be interpreted as supporting the view that because most people fear female offenders less than male offenders – maybe women are perceived as being less dangerous and less aggressive – they declare that they would be more prepared to allow female felons to work in the same job, or join the same social club, or be a neighbour. Assuming that 'saying is doing' – always a dubious assumption with human beings – then it would be predicted that female felons returning to or allowed to remain in the community would not be so stigmatized that a slide into more deviance became the only viable option for them. Evidence consistent with this prediction has been reported by Horwitz and Wasserman (1979) who showed that when individuals were matched for prior crimes and previous judicial sentence, men were still rearrested much more than women for committing further crimes. Thus, amongst those released from prison, 85 per cent of the men were subsequently arrested, but not one woman!; of those on probation, 92 per cent of men compared with 55 per cent of women were subsequently arrested; and for those who had been given a lighter sentence originally, 55 per cent of the men compared with only 28 per cent of the women were subsequently arrested.

Of course, these differences could be the result of the police's 'chivalrous' treatment; maybe the police simply do not arrest or harass as many female ex-convicts as they do men. But the review of relevant literature earlier in this chapter does not give much support to this point of view. It is probably more plausible to argue that female offenders are less stigmatized and consequently do not experience simultaneous closing of legitimate opportunities and an opening of illegitimate opportunities. Furthermore, they are less likely than male offenders to be gripped by a sense of injustice because, being less stigmatized, they do not experience 'punishment' in excess of that imposed by the court, whereas men often do experience this form of injustice.

Given their lower experience of stigmatization, the relative unchanging nature of their opportunity structures, and the comparative absence of a sense of injustice, women are less likely to recidivate and hence the level of their involvement in criminal activity will remain low.

Of course, judicial labelling may not be the only social reaction which affects further delinquency. The attribution of positive or negative evaluations to others is a permanent feature of social life, and again, if labelling theory is correct, those individuals who receive mostly positive evaluations are more likely to remain relatively conventional whilst those who experience more negative evaluations may well spiral deeper into deviance. If, say, there were gender differences in the degree to which girls received fewer negative evaluations than boys, particularly from significant adults, such as parents and teachers, then this too might be an additional factor in accounting for the lower rate of female delinquency.

A study by Simons, Miller, and Aigner (1980) was designed in part to test this line of reasoning. From the data provided by nearly 4,000 children attending public schools in Iowa during the autumn of 1976, they concluded that boys are more negatively labelled, both by parents and teachers, and it was just this group of boys who scored high on self-reported delinquency. Because far fewer girls had to cope with being stigmatized by teachers and parents, their rate of self-reported delinquency was comparatively lower than the boys' rate.

CONCLUSION: SO WHAT DOES IT ALL ADD UP TO?

All the theories discussed briefly above – sex-role socialization, social bonding, differential association, differential legitimate and illegitimate opportunity structures, and labelling – have all traditionally been proposed as explanations of male delinquency, although this limitation applies less to labelling theory. However, it now appears that with varying degrees of success these explanations, particularly if combined, equally account for young female criminal deviance and some of them, particularly illegitimate opportunity structures, offer more than a clue to explaining the low incidence of adult female serious crime. The single exception apparently is sex-role socialization, for there is not much empirical support for the view that female offenders are more 'masculine' than their conventional sisters. If however the argument were that successful sex-role socialization prepared 'traditional' females to engage in 'traditional' female crimes, then that suffers from an embarrassing 'abundance of riches' for it simply predicts far more female crime than ever exists.

It seems reasonable, in the light of the best available scientific evidence, which admittedly is far from satisfactory, that the sex-differential in rates of delinquency/crime can be accounted for by the fact that in comparison with their male age peers, adolescent girls are relatively less *powerful* and this crucial social difference persists into adulthood. Their potential autonomy is hedged in by parental close supervision; they have fewer legitimate opportunities through which they might obtain some escape from this manifestation of patriarchal control; rarely are they able to gain entry to those positions of organizational power where large-scale socially and economically injurious crimes are pursued with virtual immunity; they are excluded from entry into the higher echelons of sophisticated organized lucrative crime, although from the use of their bodies – as prostitutes – might be extracted the surplus value which helps to finance other criminal enterprises; even when they do gain legitimate employment, it is normally as nurses, teachers, clerical assistants, shop-servants, social workers, secretaries, and similar lower white-blouse occupations where supervision by male superordinates either replaces or reinforces parental control; they are diminished by parents, teachers, police, and other state officials who refuse to recognize their equality with men, who believe in their relative 'goodness' – that they will behave like nice girls – and who will not take them seriously even when they do occasionally deviate.

Because of their relative social *powerlessness* women rarely find themselves in positions where they are free to execute major crimes; their resources and opportunities simply do not facilitate it, and the level of surveillance and social control inhibit it. Consequently, the incidence of female crime is low, and when it does occur, it is trivial in terms of the persons killed, injured, or deprived. Furthermore, even this minor show of resisting domination is often not attributed to their own authorship. Instead it is viewed, mainly by a male dominated judiciary and medical profession, as a symptom of some underlying disorder, normally sexual in nature, which requires help, understanding, and possibly medical intervention. All of this is of course a further turn on the screw which keeps women hedged in and dependent rather than free and autonomous.

Of course, these various theories of criminal deviance do not explain why females differ from males in their exposure to or possession of just those factors which are more criminogenic. But to answer that requires moving beyond middle-range theories to search for sociological theories of sex-roles and related power-distribution in industrialized societies. That is a vital theoretical exercise, but one which is both clearly beyond the specific issues raised in this chapter, and better left to those more astute at that type of theorizing.

There is however, one related issue. If the above factors help to explain sex-differentials in criminal behaviour, then if the social position of women changes in such a way that they come to share the same privileges and resources as men, if they come, in a word, more *powerful* then it follows that there should be a convergence between the sexes on the frequency and pattern of crimes they commit. It is to just this intriguing issue that we now turn.

Does emancipation mean females will commit more serious crimes?

A supporter of feminism might regard women's social existence in our culture as bad enough without their collective attempts to achieve liberty and equality being viewed pejoratively as criminogenic. Yet historically, it is just this irony that has haunted and terrified the imagination of criminologists from Lombroso onwards. Thus Cecil Bishop wrote:

'In the fight for emancipation women have won most of their objectives and they have good reason to be jubilant at their success. Yet could they have foreseen the future twenty years ago, they would probably have relinquished the struggle, afraid of the consequences of their coming triumphs ... it is true to say that the women of this country were never in a more unhappy state than they are today ... many more women have become criminally minded during the past years than ever before.'   (Bishop 1931: 3–4)

And twenty years later Pollak reminds us:

'ever since the 1870s (they) have predicted that the progressing social equalization between the sexes and particularly the entrance of women into ever-wider fields of economic pursuits would lead to an increase in the volume of female crime and thereby to a decrease, if not a disappearance, of the sex-differential apparent in criminal statistics.'   (Pollak 1950: 58)

It might have been possible to dismiss this ironic slur as yet another attempt by male criminologists to shore-up patriarchal control by warning women and politicians of the dreadful consequences which follow any concession to feminist demands for more social integration and economic equality. Yet this particular ploy is no longer so obviously available, because in recent years female criminologists too claim to have seen the 'darker side' of the Women's Movement (Adler 1975; Simon 1975). However, the possibility of women, unwittingly and unintentionally, colluding in the oppression of their sisters should not be ruled out; it may be that those female writers who adduce evidence to support a connection between emancipation and female crime in fact gloss over a more fundamental truth, namely that increased arrest or conviction rates reflect the increased willingness of members of the public and the criminal justice system to criminalize 'deviant women' as a disciplinary action whose effect, hopefully, is to get them to realize their right place in the 'natural' order of things – 'get back to the nuclear family'.

Although there is a babble of voices over the emancipation-leads-to-crime issue, a major claim, around which protagonist and antagonist collide, appears to be that as women come to free themselves from familial constraints, such as child-rearing and patriarchal controls, such as economic and psychological dependence upon husbands or male lovers, and as they simultaneously explore extra-familial territory by taking advantage of educational and occupational opportunities, and by reflecting on feminist issues and personal change, so sex-differences in the level and pattern of criminal activity move towards convergence. One particularly clear rendition of this argument comes from Simon. She claims that:

'as women become more liberated from hearth and home and become more involved in full-time jobs, they are more likely to engage in the types of crime for which their occupations provide them with the greatest opportunities. (Furthermore) . . . as a function both of ex-panded consciousness, as well as occupational opportunities, women's participation role and involvement in crime are expected to *change* and *increase*.'   (Simon 1975: 1)

More specifically, she believes that female crimes of violence will not increase relative to men, because:

'such acts typically arise out of the frustrations, the subservience, and the dependency that have characterized the traditional female role . . . . When women can no longer contain their frustrations and their anger, they express themselves by doing away with the cause of their condition, most often a man, sometimes a child. As women's employment and educational opportunities expand, their feelings of being victimized and exploited will decrease, and their motivation to kill will become muted.'   (Simon 1975: 2)

Conversely, Simon believes that property offences, and particularly those which are occupationally related, will increase relative to men because as women enter the 'man's world' so they experience the accompanying tensions, which motivate crime, and the inherent temptations, which facilitate it. This view is echoed by Henson who suggests that:

'women cannot, or anyhow should not, claim that there is nothing constitutionally different about them which is relevant to their as-similation into the labour market – insisting that they can perform with equal competence and vigour whatever tasks men perform, yet that they will be (somehow constitutionally) impervious to the frustrations, pressures, and temptations which corrupt men.'
(Henson 1980: 77)

However, this portrayal of changing female crime does not enjoy a consensus amongst other writers. Indeed they spread across a con-tinuum from sceptical critics to those who make a variety of claims for liberation and criminality. At one end are those who deny any positive relationships between female emancipation and crime (Crites 1976; Datesman and Scarpitti 1980; DeCrow 1974; Feinman 1979; Klein and Kress 1976; Morris and Gelsthorpe 1981; Smart 1976, 1979; Weis

1976). Spread out at the other end are a motley assortment of authors who assert that contemporary women are committing more *masculine* crimes (Adler 1975; Gibbons 1977), more *violent* crimes (Adler 1975; Austin 1981; Bruck 1975; Deming 1977; Nettler 1974; Roberts 1971; Rosenblatt and Greenland 1974; Woodward and Malamud 1975; Vedder and Sommerville 1970), more *serious* crimes (Datesman and Stephenson 1975; Loving and Olson 1976; Sandhu 1977), more *male-dominated* crimes (Adler 1975; Inciardi and Siegel 1977), more *white-collar or occupational* crimes (Henson 1980; Simon 1976; Widom 1978), and becoming involved in *drug addiction* (Greenberg and Adler 1974).

This debate is bewildering because rhetoric and anecdote often substitute for rigorous analysis of relevant data. Most commentators rely on crude manipulation of official arrest or conviction data. In doing so, they make one or more of the following errors:

(i) failure to control for the changing population base of females available to commit crimes – even those aware of this requirement tend to control for the whole female population rather than that segment likely to account for the vast bulk of it, namely those aged 15–64;

(ii) failure to control for the changing rate of male crime, for if this is also increasing, then although female crime may be increasing *absolutely* it may not be increasing *relatively* to male crime – if both increase at the same rate, then the sex-differential does not converge;

(iii) failure to disaggregate the dependent variable into different types of crime, particularly into those which are more theoretically relevant – all too often authors rely on gross data, such as the American Uniform Crime Index, which consists of homicide, rape, robbery, aggravated assault, burglary, larceny over $50, and car-theft, or the British category of indictable offences, which involves violence against the person, sexual offences, robbery, burglary, theft, fraud, forgery, criminal damage. This methodological move is inappropriate because the theoretical assertions in the literature refer to fairly specific crimes *within* these broad categories;

(iv) failure to specify theoretically and measure rigorously either the dependent or the independent variable;

(v) failure to apply relevant statistical tests to the data so that significant changes and relationships between the independent and dependent variables can be identified.

Thus, the arguments of those who are tempted to prove a causal connection between emancipation and female crime by merely documenting the historical overlap between these two social events seem

to be fatally flawed. Something more than simple concurrence is required before the alleged causation becomes convincing.

An extensive literature search reveals only three studies which come
close to meeting the above criteria. In a number of papers analysing
arrest trends in America for standardized age-sex-population data for
periods between the 1930s and late 1970s, the authors (Steffensmeier
1978, 1980b, 1981; Steffensmeier and Cobb 1981; Steffensmeier and
Jordon 1978; Steffensmeier, Rosenthal, and Shehan 1980; Steffensmeier and Steffensmeier 1980; Steffensmeier, Steffensmeier, and
Rosenthal 1979) concluded that female crimes of violence against the
person have increased absolutely but not relatively to the male rate,
whereas female property offences have increased faster than the male
rate. However, this last significant finding is accounted for almost
entirely by non-occupationally related crimes, such as shoplifting,
cheque, and welfare fraud. Furthermore, they were unable to find
any evidence to confirm the existence of liberated female criminals
either during the World War II period, when the female labour force
participation rate increased enormously, or for the decade following
1968, when feminist activities and organizations expanded.

This same research team separately analysed arrest trends for adults
and adolescents, and were unable to locate any empirical support for
the other varieties of argument linking female emancipation to crime.
They did not detect any female gain over men for *masculine* crimes,
male-dominated crimes, or *serious* crimes (once shoplifting had
been removed from this category). Consequently they felt able to conclude:

> 'The new female criminal is more a social invention than an empirical
> reality and that the proposed relationship between the women's
> movement and crime is, indeed, tenuous and even vacuous. Women
> are still typically non-violent, petty property offenders (Steffensmeier
> 1978: 580) . . . . Female arrest patterns have changed very little over
> the past decade and . . . whatever changes have occurred appear to be
> due to changing law enforcement practices, market consumption
> trends, and the worsening economic position of many females in the
> US rather than changing sex-roles or the improved occupational,
> educational, and economic position of women.'
>
> (Steffensmeier 1980b: 1087)

With any luck, this would have terminated this particular debate. But
the cozy silence of agreement is rare in sociology. Thus a recent
Canadian time-series study (Fox and Hartnagel 1979) for the period
1931–68 implicitly criticized the methods and contradicts the results of

Steffensmeier's research. Rather than taking a particular year as a watershed in the Women's Movement, Fox and Hartnagel attempted to measure directly such indicators of female emancipation as *the rate of labour force participation, educational involvement, fertility*, and *'being single'*. They argued that both the ideas and the influence of the Women's Movement have a longer, even if desultory history than the recent upsurge in feminist activity and organization. Consequently, by taking actual indicators of female emancipation and correlating these against female criminal convictions, they hoped to test more exhaustively the hypothesis that 'liberation leads to crime'. The results of this analysis were that as the indicators of female emancipation increased so did the rate of female convictions, particularly for female theft.

A recent study of US data by Austin (1982) also conflicts with Steffensmeier and his colleagues. Austin examined the effects of women's emancipation and the women's liberation movement on burglary and robbery for the years 1959–78, and on car-theft, larceny, and fraud/embezzlement for the years 1960–75. As indicators of women's emancipation, he took the *divorce rate* and the *female labour force participation rate*. For the Women's Movement, he took 1966 as the watershed year because NOW (National Organisation of Women) was established then. His study was therefore a combination of methods adopted by both Steffensmeier's research team and Fox and Hartnagel. After considering changes in the percentage female contribution to the above five major crime categories, he concluded that all the evidence demonstrated:

> 'an association between female emancipation and female criminality, an increase in emancipation accompanying an increase in criminality. Further, accelerated increases in criminality that begin in 1968, 1969, and 1970 occur at the same time as, or follow closely, accelerated increases in female emancipation in 1967 and 1968. Therefore, the temporal sequence criterion for demonstrating a causal relationship is also satisfied . . . and . . . contrary to the dominant position in the literature, the evidence does not show a stronger or more likely effect of female emancipation on larceny-theft than on more serious offences.'
> (Austin 1982: 423)

Austin does not claim that his study proves conclusively any causal connection between emancipation/liberation and female crime, but 'the data does satisfy the causal criteria of association and the temporal order for this proposition' (Austin 1982: 427).

The best three North American empirical analyses then, appear to have contradictory results. All three are not sound methodologically (Box and Hale 1983b). But it is not this shortcoming which has been the central focus of substantial critics. Instead they have concentrated on the growing economic marginalization of females and the effect this has on their criminal activity, particularly on their propensity to engage in property crimes. Thus Crites argues:

'employment benefits derived from the feminist push for equal employment opportunities accrue predominantly to white, middle-class females. The women's rights movement has largely swept over the subpopulation group of poor, minority females, into which the female offender falls. These women, rather than being recipients of expanded rights and opportunities gained by the women's movement, are, instead, witnessing declining survival options.'

(Crites 1976: 36–7)

and Klein and Kress argue similarly that:

'In the current economic crisis, with the likelihood that women . . . will be the first fired, one may expect that women may begin to commit more 'street offences' as they are thrown out of work . . . we can expect greater pressure on the wives and lovers of working class men who are laid off from their jobs and perhaps an increase in crime-related activities such as welfare fraud and prostitution.'

(Klein and Kress 1976: 41–2)

The applicability to England and Wales of the liberation v. marginalization theses remains virtually unexamined. Simon and Sharma (1979) and Simon (1975) argue that it does apply, but their manipulation of gross conviction data covering scarcely more than a decade is simply inadequate, and they fail to meet any of the above five critical criteria. Smart (1979) argues, on the basis of a longer period of analysis (1953–75) that liberation has not caused an increase in crime. But she is convincingly criticized by Austin (1981) for misinterpreting her results, which he claims, are consistent with the view that women contribute more now to violent crimes. However, the Smart-Austin disagreement is based on analysis too weak to sustain either position (Box and Hale 1983a).

It is therefore of some interest to examine how far, if at all, female emancipation in England and Wales can be causally linked with changes in the pattern and rate of female crime, or whether these changes are best explained in terms of increasing economic marginalization or some other, as yet, unexplicated factor.

Female crime patterns in England and Wales: liberation or marginalization?

The British press does not seem to have any intellectual doubts over the relevance of liberation to female criminality. 'Equal Crime for Women' blared *The Daily Mail* (23.2.77), whilst *The Evening Standard* (27.10.77) declared that 'Girl Muggers as Bad as Men', and *The Sun* (1.9.75) saw the connection, when it revealed a 'Crime Wave of the "lib" Girls'. Five years later *The Daily Mail* (1.2.80) was in no doubt that 'Women's lib "pushes up crime"'. Recently the Yorkshirewomen Conservatives re-commended that girls aged 10 to 17 who commit criminal offences should receive the same punishment as boys, including military-style short-sharp prison sentences because 'during the last 20 years the level of serious crime committed by girls has risen out of all proportion to their male counterparts. It is a fallacious argument to think of all girls as sweet, tender, gentle things. Girls are as bad as boys' (*The Guardian* 25.5.82). Finally, the pronouncements of high-ranking police officers, prison governors, and judges have further legitimated the image of the new violent liberated female offender (Morris and Gelsthorpe 1981). For example, Joe Whitney, a male governor in a female prison was reported by *The Sunday Times* (30.3.80) as saying that 'Women offenders are changing. Previously they tended to be non-aggressive; jailed for fraud, shoplifting, and theft. In recent years we've experienced a new, aggressive, liberated criminality in women'.

The claim that female crime has increased dramatically in England and Wales over recent years looks plausible enough. The rate of conviction for indictable offences since 1951 has indeed gone up, particularly the crimes of violence against the person. Data in *Table 5* show that whilst the conviction rate for all indictable offences has increased fourfold during the last thirty years, it has increased twelve and a half times for violent offences, and this rise has been particularly steep during the last decade when female liberation was more influential than the preceding two decades.

However, this table is misleading. If liberation is causing more female crime than the relevant data is a comparison of inter-sex differentials in conviction rates (assuming these reflect something of the reality in inter-sex difference in criminal activity). When this is constructed (see *Table 6*) we find that females contributed hardly any more to crimes of violence than they did in 1951. On the other hand, they do seem to have made a significant increase in the contribution they make to property offences.

Thus an examination of changes in the level of *absolute* and *female-relative-to-male* conviction rates reveals a contradictory finding. The

Table 6   Females found guilty of indictable crimes, England and
Wales, 1951–79. Rate per 100,000 population aged 15–64

year	all indictable offences	violence against personal[1]	property offences[2]	standardized 1951 = 100		
				all	violence	property
1951	1.04	.002	.96	100	100	100
1956	0.92	.002	.84	88	100	88
1961	1.54	.003	1.44	148	150	150
1966	2.01	.006	1.90	193	300	198
1971	2.94	.010	2.72	283	500	283
1976	4.21	.020	3.70	405	1,000	385
1979	4.00	.025	3.51	385	1,250	366

[1] Includes murder, manslaughter, conspiracy to murder, causing death through dangerous driving, grievous woundings, malicious assaults, etc. i.e. official categories 1–15 in *Criminal Statistics England and Wales*
[2] Includes robbery, burglary, theft, handling, fraud, and forgery, i.e. official categories 28–31, 34, 39–49, 54, 51–3, 60–1, in *Criminal Statistics England and Wales*

former supports the orthodox consensus view that liberated violent female offenders are increasing whilst the latter supports the view that women are making a greater contribution only to property offences. But neither of these data enables us to consider properly the influence of women's liberation on criminal activity. To do this, we need to measure

Table 7   The relative female to male contribution* to persons found guilty of committing indictable offences, per 100,000 population aged 15–64, 1951–79, England and Wales

year	all indictable crimes	crimes of violence against the person	crimes against property
1951	.13	.08	.13
1956	.13	.05	.14
1961	.14	.04	.16
1966	.15	.06	.17
1971	.15	.06	.18
1976	.19	.09	.22
1979	.18	.09	.22

* Calculated as

$$\frac{\text{number of females convicted}}{\text{number of females aged 14–65}} \quad \frac{\text{number of males convicted}}{\text{number of males aged 14–65}}$$

liberation and see if this correlates with changes in the *female-relative-to-male* conviction rate for *various* offences.

Box and Hale (1983a) constructed four annual indicators for female liberation for the period 1951–79. These were (i) the number of live children per 1,000 women aged 14–45; (ii) the number of unmarried women per 100,000 aged 15–65 (i.e. those who are single/divorced/widowed); (iii) the rate of higher education experience per 100,000 women aged 15–65; and (iv) the rate per 100,000 women aged 15–65 of participation in the labour force. They took fertility and 'being single' to be indicators of women's emancipation from the patriarchal family, and pointed out that both the proportion of women not married and the birth rate have steadily declined during the last thirty years. The result, they argued, is that fewer women have become captive housewives and/or mothers. Their other two measures are indicators of women's involvement in extra-familial activity which provide both the socio-psychological space to explore independence as well as experience temptations and tensions at work which often give rise to male criminal adaptations.

In addition, Box and Hale were aware that numerous critics of the thesis that liberation-leads-to-more-female-crime argued instead that economic marginalization was more important. These critics believe that although some upper middle-class women have made inroads into formerly male professions, the vast bulk of women have become increasingly economically marginalized – that is, more likely to be unemployed or unemployable, or if employed, then more likely to be in insecure, lower paid, unskilled, part-time jobs, where career prospects are minimal. This marginalization, particularly in a consumer-orientated status-conscious community, continuously conditioned by aggressive mass media advertising, is possibly a more important cause of increases in female crime rates than advances in female emancipation. Furthermore, anxieties concerning their ability to fulfil adequately the social roles of mother, wife, and consumer have been heightened during the 1970s because the welfare state, on which proportionately more women than men depend, has tightened its definition of who deserves financial assistance and at the same time has become increasingly unable to index these payments in line with inflation.

In order to examine this thesis Box and Hale took the rate of female unemployment (i.e. the number of women per 100,000 registered as unemployed) as the indicator of economic marginalization.

Finally, they pointed out that any attempt to locate an empirical relationship between liberation or marginalization and female crime would have to be tempered by a recognition that official statistics of criminal activity might be sensitive to changing social practices and routine bureaucratic procedures. Following Steffensmeier (1980a) they argued that some of the absolute and relative changes in female crime might be accounted for by changes in the social processes of constructing official data. For example: (i) attitudinal changes, brought about either by the changing sex-roles or the greater attention media give to female crime, may result in more willingness to shift from being sympathetic and protective to being harsh and punitive; (ii) the political move towards *equality* between the sexes, partly as a consequence of pressure mounted by the Women's Movement, may have been extended to the official processing of offenders so that their sex becomes a less relevant factor than it was previously; (iii) the trend towards professionalism and bureaucratization of the police may result in the more consistent applications of universalistic criteria; (iv) changes in how crimes are categorized may increase the female conviction rate – for instance, Rans (1978) argues that until quite recently the police did not record a female crime if the female was merely an accomplice to a male offender, but this particular act of 'chivalry' has now changed, thus producing the illusion of reduced sex-differentials in criminal behaviour; and finally, (v) there may have been changes in crimes to which the police and public pay particular attention, and some of these may be sex-related crimes – if they pay *less* attention to public drunkenness then the sex-differential decreases, and if they pay more attention to shoplifting – 'We Prosecute All Shoplifters' – then the sex-differential decreases.

Consequently, they had to make some statistical control for the view that women are treated less 'chivalrously' now than previously, since this change would directly increase the female conviction rate and produce a slight reduction in the crime-sex differential. The problem of course was the absence of relevant time-series data. However, they argued that annual changes in the police force's sex-composition could be used to fill this gap, not because female police will necessarily perform their duty more strictly according to universalistic and professional criteria, but because the fourfold increase from 1951 to 1979 in the proportion of the force who are female is itself an indicator of the extent to which the force has increasingly recognized demands for sex equality, and that this recognition might have extended to the routine processing of female suspects.

The results of their attempt to test the liberation versus marginalization effects on female crime rates theses was that liberation *per se* had no direct effect either on crimes of violence or property offences. Most of the increase in female convictions for *violence* seemed to be explained by changes in social labelling practices; i.e. the public being more willing to report female offenders, increased willingness of the police to prosecute and a greater preparedness of magistrates and juries to convict. In this sense, female liberation may have an indirect phenomenological effect. The behaviour of the public, police, and magistrates is influenced by their image of female crime, and if this image has changed recently, largely because of its portrayal in the media and the publicized link between female liberation and violent aggressive crime, then what is believed as real becomes real in its consequences. If women are believed to be more violent, then those suspected of being violent will be seen as conforming to a new stereotype, and deservedly convicted. The relative increase in female conviction rates for violent offences is then a self-fulfilling prophecy, rather than a reflection of any real change in female propensity for violent crime.

The major factor accounting for most of the increase in *property offences* seems to be economic marginalization. In other words, as women become economically worse off, largely through unemployment and inadequate compensatory levels of welfare benefits, so they are less able and willing to resist the temptations to engage in property offences as a way of helping solve their financial difficulties. Under these circumstances it is increasing female economic marginalization, brought on by the current economic crisis and a government headed by a woman determined to restore the family with a full-time, non-working mother, that has caused any slight reduction in the inter-sex differential property offence rates.

Female liberation does not appear to have been the demonic phenomenon described by criminologists and accepted by the media, police, and criminal justice officials. This may of course reflect that whatever liberation has occurred is marginal indeed (Coussins 1977, Oakley 1980). If women did really become equal to men in terms of social and economic power would they behave just like men? Without for one moment claiming to know the answer to this question, it does appear from the best available evidence that women's deteriorating economic circumstances and not emancipation have been 'responsible' for their increased contribution to property offences. Furthermore, and this needs to be emphasized repeatedly, even if the Women's Movement and/or female liberation were discovered ultimately to be a cause of women's slight gains over men in the rate of property offending, it would still remain true that the vast bulk of these offences would be trivial in terms of the value of goods stolen or handled. In comparison with the value of goods stolen by men, including of course men acting in the name of multi-national corporations, female property offences are, and probably would remain insignificant. For the only circumstances under which women would be in equal positions to men would in all probability be those where the motive and ability to commit crimes with immunity would be relatively absent. Since this would be such a totally different economic and political system to the present one, we cannot claim to predict the type and quantity of crime it might produce for either males or females.

Finally, although it would appear that female culturally and structurally constructed powerlessness produces comparatively less serious criminal behaviour, it should not be concluded that powerlessness is therefore a social disability to be cherished. Whilst it may dampen the rate of female criminal behaviour, it appears to enhance other forms of deviance, such as prostitution, alcoholism, drug addiction, mental disorder, and suicidal behaviour (Al-Issa 1980; Brown and Harris 1978; Chesler 1972; Smith 1974). It also renders women a favourite and easy target for the massive victimizing behaviours of men with economic, social, and physical power (Chapman and Gates 1978; Dobash and Dobash 1981).

Of course, powerlessness ought to be inherently insupportable in a society espousing democratic ideals. But when idealism tarnishes, maybe an increased awareness of the brutalizing, degrading, and self-annihilating effects of powerlessness will brighten up beliefs and provoke action. If slight increases in trivial property crimes were to be the cost of women's liberation being achieved, and from the evidence it is not certain that even this cost would materialize, it would be well worth it in comparison with the price paid now by powerless women at present.

6 Crime, power, and justice

If people know anything about Lord Acton, it is likely to be that he believed that 'all power corrupts, and absolute power corrupts absolutely'. The previous substantive chapters attempted to put ugly pockmarked flesh around these solid bones of democratic common sense. In them it was shown that: (i) the growing concentration of economic power in national and transnational corporations is sometimes utilized to victimize large numbers of employers, consumers, and the general public; (ii) the enhanced legal powers of apprehension and investigation coupled with improved technological capacity of the police is sometimes used by officers to victimize criminally citizens and business, and; (iii) men who are powerful economically, politically, and physically occasionally impose themselves sexually on relatively powerless and vulnerable women. As opposed to all this unpleasantness, it was argued that women, a relatively powerless group, commit hardly any serious crimes in comparison with the endless spread-eagled trail of lifeless, injured, and robbed victims left in the path of predatory powerful men.

Had this book been longer – God (and my publisher) in Her infinite wisdom forbid – it would also have documented further the positive relationship between power and crime by exposing the enormous amount of criminal victimization carried out by members of the Home

Office and the Prison Service against those supposedly in 'their protective custody' (Coggan and Walker 1982; Cohen and Taylor 1976; PROP 1979; Geary 1980; Thomas and Pooley 1980). It would have examined the inherent links, not only in North America, but also in the United Kingdom between politicians, police, business financiers, and 'racketeers' in that form of organized crime – supplying illegal goods at monopolistic prices – commonly called the 'Mafia', described by Cressey (1969) as *The Theft of a Nation*, and documented in fine detail by Chambliss (1978). The crimes of businessmen and professionals (Johnson and Douglas 1978; Leigh 1982; Levi 1981) that victimize shareholders, clients, and citizens would also have been presented. Lord Acton may not have had these forms of corruption (and crime) in mind, but such was the force of his wisdom that it illuminates dark corners everywhere.

The possible clue to our understanding most serious crimes can be located in power, not weakness, privilege, not disadvantage, wealth, not poverty. This is not an idea that has found much elbow room within traditional criminology. Indeed, even within radical criminology, it is an issue over which there is a curious, although not quite total silence (Liazos 1972; Pearce 1976; Thio 1978). However, it should be clear by now that analysing the positive relationship between power and crime, a task pursued in previous chapters, should be a priority on any criminology agenda.

If power is so potentially dangerous (and criminogenic), what to do about it? Democracy was invented to tackle this problem (Benn and Peters 1959). In a truly democratic society, the problem of power is not solved, but it is contained. There is no way that people determined to behave badly, and having mastered the shameless art of deception, can be prevented from occupying positions of power. There is probably no way in which positions of power can be designed so as to avoid contradictions that impose tremendous pressure on their incumbents to deviate from the path of decent behaviour. None the less, it is possible to take two important precautions. First, by spreading power thinly, just as a good farmer would spread manure over a field, instead of concentrating it in one place, the stink of rotten absolute power can be avoided. Second, by establishing institutionalized checks and balances, all power-users become accountable to those or their democratically elected representatives directly affected. The adoption of these two precautions significantly reduces the chances of people in powerful positions inflicting too much avoidable and technically illegal damage on citizens lives, limbs, and property. The trouble in our society is that power has been increasingly 'exported' and the remainder concentrated. Institutionalized methods of making the powerful accountable have withered like grapes on autumnal vines.

Democratic power bestowed in trust to parliament has been 'transferred' to the European Economic Community, the International Monetary Fund, American-dominated transnational corporations, and the Pentagon. These bodies increasingly make decisions affecting the quality of life in Britain. British critizens are powerless under the present political climate to make these distant decisions makers accountable, but a collective democratic struggle to assert our rights could succeed (Benn 1981). An already shrunken legislature seems to be increasingly incapable of checking the executive, and part of the legislature – the House of Lords – is neither elected by nor accountable to the public. The governing political party seems increasingly unable to check the cabinet. The cabinet seems no longer to have tight reins over the prime minister, a position which has moved from being 'first amongst equals' to being simply 'first' full stop. The executive has lost its grip over its social control agencies such as the prison service, which appears increasingly to be run by the Prison Officers Association, and the police, which seems to be driven mainly by the Chief Police Officers Association and the Police Federation.

The public seems to have little awareness of democratic principles and the rights and duties these impose on citizens. The state seems determined not to relieve this ignorance but actually compounds it further by introducing or firming-up 'authoritarian' control devices. For instance, the Official Secrets Act is used to prevent the public gaining information on issues 'sensitive' to the government, such as 'defence', 'national security', and 'domestic security'. Thus on the prison system, there is little information concerning prison discipline, drugging of prisoners, parole procedures, brutality against prisoners, and prisoners' general contacts with the outside world. Consequently British prisons operate behind a shield of undemocratic secrecy (Cohen and Taylor 1976; Wright 1982). Fitzgerald and Sim argue that:

'successive Home Secretaries have used the lack of public knowledge and scrutiny of prisons to support their particular needs. On the one hand they have argued for substantial popular interest and support for the aims of an enlightened penal policy and for the methods we use to carry it out. On the other hand, they have systematically denied the public access to information on and debates about penal affairs. Uninformed and 'reactionary' public opinion is then claimed to be the barrier to the introduction of enlightened policies.'

(Fitzgerald and Sim 1979: 6)

Another authoritarian device is the existence and interpretation of the Contempt of Court Act, 1981. Originally intended by those draughting it to liberalize the law of contempt in line with recent European Court's rulings, this particular act has now been so interpreted that *The Sunday Times* would still be prevented from publishing articles on such national scandals as the thalidomide affair – which led to the European Court's initial involvement – and so effectively it minimizes the degree of public information and thereby provides an undemocratic cover for culpable powerful institutions and persons to shield behind (Hewitt 1982: 91).

The outcome is that large sections of the public lack the inclination, ability, or power to make accountable those wielding political power, and through them, those wielding economic power. Ironically, for a nation that went to war against fascism, the democratic will to solve the problem of power has been lost; we have people in political and economic power who are not accountable to those whose lives they control. A result, as previous chapters have shown, is that this power is occasionally used to victimize criminally those who are primarily powerless.

Government penal policy and judicial sentencing practice

What is the government and its criminal justice system doing about crime? Well, they are not idling. According to its *Observations on the Fifteenth Report of the Expenditure Committee* (1980), the government appeared to hold out hope. In this report, it promised 'to publish a review of the present parole system during the first ten years of its operation'; it said it was 'considering whether there is any way in which . . . section 47 of the Criminal Law Act 1977, which enables a court . . . partially to suspend a sentence of imprisonment . . . could be implemented'; it declared the government were in no doubt that 'there would be difficulty in assessing any offender's means with sufficient accuracy . . .' but, this would be 'proceeded by a comprehensive review of financial penalties . . .' and 'as soon as it is possible to undertake such a review, the government will ensure that the possibility of changing to a day fine system is fully explored'; there was a pledge 'to continue to examine ways in which the numbers (or persons in prison for fine or maintenance order default) might be further reduced'; there was a promise to keep 'the four existing day training centres under review, but because of high running costs . . . there were no plans to approve the setting up of any more experimental centres'; there was a belief that 'more day centres should be provided and both the statutory services and voluntary organizations . . . given further encouragement to undertake the task. It has to be recognized, however, that this will require additional resources which will necessarily limit the rate of progress'; and it will bear in mind 'the possibility of extending weekend detention schemes . . . especially for young offenders'.

The present Conservative government promised, when it was elected in 1979, to look into this, explore that, consider something else, and wonder about the possibility of *almost* anything and everything. But while it was gazing up to the blue sky for inspiration, it took some positive steps on the ground. The following *action* the then Home Secretary Mr Whitelaw informed the House of Commons in early 1980, has been taken:

'First, we must ensure that the prison estate is adequate for the job that it has to do. We have every sympathy with the May Committee's recommendation that the building programme, together with a considerable maintenance commitment, is substantial. Work already in progress will produce about 3,400 new or refurbished places by 1985, including a major new dispersal prison, which should come into use next year. Firm plans are being made to start two new major projects in both 1981–82 and 1982–83, which will provide 1,500 further places by the later 1980s. I hope to continue the programme on that basis in 1983–84, and preliminary planning is now proceeding.'

In other words, six new prisons will have been started by the mid-1980s and this programme coupled with work already in progress will result in nearly 6,000 new places for prisoners being made available. That equals an increase in prison capacity of about 16 per cent.

More prisons is not the only weapon in the state's strengthened armoury. Whilst unemployment has risen sharply to around 3.5 millions in early 1983 (or nearly 14 per cent of the available labour force), the government has been busy making significant and not unrelated exceptions – the police and prison service have been allowed to swell their ranks. As the following table (see *Table 7*) shows, the police in England and Wales rose by 23 per cent during the decade 1971-81, whilst the respective figures for Scotland and Northern Ireland were 15 and 78 per cent respectively. During the same decade, the prison officer class were allowed to increase from just over 13,000 to nearly 20,000, or approximately 48 per cent. Neither of these manpower increases reflect purely demographic changes in the general 'client' population. In fact, during this period, the numbers of population per police officer fell from 529 to 434, and the prisoner per prison officer fell from 3.4 to 2.82. For reasons which are clarified below, there are more police per citizen and more prisoner officers per prisoner now than there were a decade ago.

Furthermore, whilst there was no money to maintain decent standards of health, education, transport, and social welfare, the government

Table 8   Increases in police and prison officer personnel, 1971–81

	1971	*1981*	*per cent change*
police			
England & Wales	97.3	119.5	23
Scotland	10.8	12.4	15
Northern Ireland	4.1	7.3	78
total	112.2	140.0	25
prisons			
prison officer class	13.1	19.4	48
others	5.4	7.4	37
total	18.5	26.8	45

Source: Central Statistical Office (1983: 177).

managed during the first two years of its office to 'magick' up sufficient 'filthy lucre' to increase the capital expenditure *in real terms* on the administration of justice by 10 per cent, and on the police by a massive 67 per cent (Central Statistical Office 1982: 226). These increases were 'to reflect the government's priority for law and order services' and to 'allow an improvement in regime and in standards of security and control' (Cmnd. 7841: 84, 87).

Whilst the government were pumping money into shoring up its defences against 'the rising crime wave', the judiciary were doing their bit to stem this 'black tide'. They were sending more and more people to prison. Thus between 1971 and 1981 the number of persons received into prison under sentence rose from 60,429 to 88,110, an increase of 46 per cent (see *Table 8*). This increase cannot be explained away merely by the rise in convictions for serious crimes; these rose from 340,000 in 1971 to 437,000 in 1981 (excluding motor offences), a rise of only 29 per cent. Rather it appears that courts are increasing the rate of imprisonment per 100 convicted persons for particular offences and concentrating this harsher penal practice on the young. Thus between 1977 and 1981 the rate of imprisonment for burglary rose by 21 per cent, for theft and handling by 16 per cent, and for robbery by 7 per cent (Home Office 1982: 166–67). The rate of incarceration in detention centres and borstals for young convicted males aged between 14 and 17 years rose during the period 1971–81 from 6 per cent to 13 per cent. During the same decade the rate of sentencing to immediate imprisonment more than doubled for convicted males aged 17–21 years, rising from 3 to 7 per cent. As these data refer to *rates* and not absolute numbers, they mean that *proportionately* more young offenders *now* are being 'put away' than ten years ago.

The courts have also been sending offenders to prison for longer periods. The average length of prison sentence rose during the period from 1961 (=100) to 1973 (=151), it dipped slightly at the end of the decade but rose again in the early 1980s. The outcome of this judicial practice is that England and Wales have a higher prison population per 100,000 general population than many other European countries, including France, Netherlands, Belgium, and Switzerland (Fitzmaurice and Pease 1982).

Finally, but not least pernicious, the judiciary have been remanding more persons to prison who were not later received as convicted and sentenced to prison. This remanding in custody, for a sharp lesson, of those males who arguably did not commit crimes deserving imprisonment, increased from 29,560 in 1977 to 37,311 in 1981. Furthermore, the average time spent in custody increased from between 14 to 20 days before 1970 to about 38 days in 1981.

Clearly, prisons are being used to punish more and more offenders and particularly the young. They are also serving as a warning to those not deserving imprisonment this time round. Given the usefulness of prisons both for incapacitating offenders and deterring some potential offenders, there can be no doubt that the number of prisoners will rise to fill the capacity made available by the government's prison building programme.

Unemployment, crime, and imprisonment: an illustrated understanding of government penal policy and judicial sentencing practice

Government penal policy and judicial sentencing practices do not emerge out of a vacuum; rather they both reflect changing patterns of social relationships, particularly between the powerful and their subordinates. During the last decade, Britain has been experiencing a deepening economic crisis and this has affected the way governments and the judiciary have 'criminalized' subordinate groups. This crisis has produced those groups called 'unproductive elements' by Mathiesen (1974: 77), 'surplus population' by Quinney (1977: 134) and 'problem populations' by Spitzer (1975: 642). Despite these different images, each of these authors is referring to the same phenomenon – that group of people 'unrequired' by the productive process and who therefore become a 'nuisance' eligible for state intervention. If they are 'social junk', as Spitzer graphically puts it, such as the elderly, sick, or mentally

Table 9 Receptions into prison, 1971–81, age, immediate sentence/fine defaulter, England and Wales

	1971			1981			percent increase		
	under 21	21 & over	total	under 21	21 & over	total	under 21	21+	total
males									
under sentence	18,396	29,641	48,037	27,782	36,368	65,150	51	23	34
fine defaulters	991	9,395	10,386	4,108	15,958	20,046	315	69	93
total	19,387	39,036	58,423	31,890	52,306	84,196	64	34	44
females									
under sentence	391	1,130	1,521	720	2,087	2,807	84	85	85
fine defaulters	70	415	485	282	825	1,107	302	99	128
total	461	1,545	2,006	1,002	2,912	3,914	117	88	95
all									
under sentence	18,787	30,771	49,558	28,502	40,542	66,957	52	32	35
fine defaulters	1,061	9,810	10,871	4,390	16,783	21,153	314	71	95

disturbed, they have to be *managed*; if they are 'social dynamite', such as the under- and unemployed, or unemployable, they have to be *controlled.* The former groups represent a fiscal problem which has been intensified with the growing inability of modern capitalism to generate sufficient surplus to pay for its welfare state (O'Connor 1973). In response to this fiscal crisis, governments have attempted to pursue a policy of *decarcera-tion*, that is, removing people from mental hospitals and similar institutions, closing them down and diverting potential inmates by encouraging 'community treatment', which happens to be comparatively cheaper (Scull 1977). The latter groups present a more intractable problem because they are actually or potentially more troublesome. Spitzer argues that this problem population – the able bodied, mainly young unemployed and unemployable – throws into question the ability of the capitalist mode of production to generate enough work and wealth, and this helps contribute to a situation conducive to the creation of a legitimacy crisis. Furthermore, it is just this problem population who, because they can distance themselves from the consent to be governed, are likely to be *perceived* by those in positions of power and authority as potential disruptives, thus constituting a threat, real or imagined, to social discipline, law, and order. Consequently, this problem population has to be suppressed or eliminated in order to preserve ideological and social hegemony. The criminal justice system, with its elastic ability to expand into areas not previously subject to its jurisdiction, its preparedness to parachute forces into this expanded territory and increase the rates of apprehension and prosecution, its apparent willingness to be partially blind to the police's disregard for law when their violations are against the 'enemies of the state', and – the issue to be magnified shortly – its capacity to extend the use and length of prison sentences, is *one* of the first line defences available to the powerful.

The government is aware that its economic policies, like those of its Labour predecessor, are reducing the living standards of large sections of the community. For example, household disposal 'real' income (that is after the effects of inflation, tax, and social benefits have been taken into account) fell by 2 per cent during the year 1980–81. But this fall was not evenly spread throughout the British population. It was concentrated almost entirely amongst manual workers, who therefore experienced a much sharper fall than a mere 2 per cent. Amongst the lower quartile of non-manual workers, real household disposable income remained virtually constant for this period and for the upper quartile it actually increased slightly (Central Statistical Office 1983: 73).

Unemployment is also creating havoc, not only in the lives of 'Boys from the Black Stuff'. Like real income, unemployment is very unevenly distributed between regions, social classes, age-cohorts, and ethnic groups. Thus, according to estimates by Peter Kellner (*New Statesman*, 22.10.82: 7) based on data provided by the government's Office of Population Censuses and Surveys, *one man in three* is currently unemployed in Liverpool, Newcastle, Manchester, and Birmingham. This contrasts sharply with the *one man in ten* currently unemployed in the south-east suburban areas of Surrey, Middlesex, and Essex. This broad North versus South distinction conceals wide variations *within* regions. In London for example, the unemployment rate in parts of Islington, Hackney, Lambeth, Southwark, and Tower Hamlets was almost four times as great as in parts of Barnet, Bexley, Croydon, Harrow, Hillingdon, and Kingston. Furthermore, economic marginalization is more acutely felt by the young and by ethnic minorities, many of whom are concentrated in already declining and deteriorating inner-city areas. Thus in October 1982, more than one male in four aged under 20 years was unemployed in England and Wales compared with one male in seven aged over 20 years. Similarly, young women fare worse than their elder sisters: just under one in four under 20 compared with one in ten over 20 years older were unemployed (Department of Employment 1983: S29). Ethnic minorities also experience higher rates of unemployment. According to a recent Home Office research publication, the black unemployment rate (registered and unregistered) in London in 1975 was about 12.3 per cent compared with a white rate of only 5.5 per cent. Extrapolating from this and other data, the author concluded that 'the unemployment rate for young blacks may be as much as three times the rate for young whites' (Stevens 1979: 16).

When politicians blandly talk about 'The Nation' with its back to the wall pulling together with Churchillean strength to overcome adversity, they say nothing about the grossly uneven and unjust contribution extracted from different sections of 'This Nation'. It is clear from the above data, which is only a small portion of that available, that *some* are paying the price for the *rest of us* – the final brutal irony being that those shouldering the burden now will not be among the main beneficiaries in the future should the British economy rise like a pheonix out of its present burnt-out industrial infrastructure.

The government has reason to feel anxious about the possible effects of the uneven distribution of unemployment and falling living standards. There is a well-worn orthodox view that unemployment leads to crime, and although Mrs Thatcher and her colleagues may well argue that unemployment is no excuse for rioting or committing any other crime, they also have reason to believe, maybe quietly, that some sub-populations are potentially more dangerous than others. Politics, like sociology, is not an exact science. Increasing people's oppression by reducing their living standards, and imposing intolerable levels of unemployment without compensatory welfare benefits or future hope may not necessarily lead to riotous assembly or criminal mayhem, but it *might*.

Glimpsing this haunting possibility, successive British governments, and particularly the present one, have taken prudent precautions. One of these has been to pursue rigorously a policy of 'non-interference' with the judiciary's autonomy, even though Their Honours' sentencing practice has exacerbated overcrowding in prisons, a problem many a Home Secretary's heart has bled for – in public! This apparently negligent posture could be adopted by the government because the judiciary is an institution of proven, even if unwitting reliability, particularly when it comes to buttering the powerful's side of any conflict (Griffiths 1977). Under the government's attentive gaze but motionless body, the judiciary has, in effect although not necessarily with intention, set about imposing discipline upon the unemployed and unemployables, thus nipping their criminal propensities where it really hurts. As an infamous Watergate conspirator cannily observed: 'get them by the balls, and their hearts and minds will follow'.

The depths to which the government has these 'common-sense' informed anxieties can be plumbed by dipping into some recent Home Office publications. Thus Gladstone, writing in the *Research Bulletin* states that 'there does seem to be some reason to fear that the high rate of unemployed young people forecast for the next twenty years may exert a considerable pressure towards crime' (1979: 40). In the same publication the following year, Smith argued that 'largely due to increased numbers of offenders brought before the courts, over the last thirty years the average daily prison population in England and Wales has more than doubled' (1980: 18). A report of the House of Lords Select Committee on Unemployment concluded that:

> 'We believe unemployment to be among the causes of ill-health, mortality, crime, or civil disorder. Although this is an area where irrefutable proof is virtually impossible, we find the evidence highly indicative and we are satisfied that the link is sufficiently probable to allow the drawing of certain conclusions. We regard the connection as more than plausible.'   (House of Lords 1982)

A banal and mundane orthodoxy 'lives': more unemployment leads to more crimes, this leads to more offenders being brought before the court, and this leads, like day following night, to more people being imprisoned. The government demonstrated clearly, although covertly, their awareness of these links when they wrote in the *Observations on the Fifteenth Report of the Expenditure Committee* (1980: 1)

'Between 1968 and October 1979 the prison population rose from nearly 32,500 to 42,500. Earlier this year it rose to 44,800 and continues to be not much below this level . . . the main factor in the general year-by-year trend has been the steady increase in the absolute numbers of offenders coming before the courts. Despite some recent levelling-off in the upward trend in recorded crime *a continuing rise is likely in the figures of crime and offenders*, and without counteracting policies, further increases in the prison population must be expected [my italics].'

This quote is important not only because it reveals the government's anxiety about the possible rising crime rate, but because it conceals the reasons the government considers cause this rise. Yet it is clear from the earlier quotes, and of course common-or-garden political sense reinforced by astute advisers, that the government is aware of the possible threat posed to social order by the dramatic increase in unemployment and particularly its higher incidence among the young and/or those belonging to an ethnic minority, living in decaying inner-city areas, and coming from a working class (increasingly a misnomer) background.

Thus the growth of unemployment, which is itself a reflection of deepening economic crisis, has been accompanied by an increase in the range and severity of state coercion, including the rate and length of imprisonment. This increased use of imprisonment was not a direct response to any rise in crime, but was rather an ideologically motivated response to the *perceived* threat of crime posed by the swelling population of economically marginalized persons. Whether this perception was based on 'fact' is unclear for the literature on unemployment and crime (Box and Hale 1982; Tarling 1982) comes to an ambiguous conclusion. But what is clear is that this perception was *real* in its consequences. Unemployment levels have and are having an effect on the rate and severity of imprisonment *over and above* the effect produced by changes in the volume and pattern of crime (Box and Hale 1982). The unemployment-effect on prison population is not as a result of the courts mechanically responding to increased 'work-load'; it is essentially produced by the judiciary acting in terms of its beliefs on the relationship between unemployment and crime and what might deter potential unemployed persons from committing crimes. These beliefs prepared a sufficiently large proportion of judges and magistrates to respond to deteriorating economic conditions in a predictable way. When unemployment and the volume of recorded crime increased simultaneously – as they did over the last five years – the judiciary interpreted this as the 'devil making work for idle hands'. Consequently, they responded by increasing the severity of penal sanctions, particularly because, in their view, it would prevent some idle hands committing more crimes, or getting up to no good politically.

It is as though the judiciary were a barometer of anxiety levels felt by the superordinate class whenever class antagonisms deepen during times of economic crisis. Although this effect would not be unexpected, given *who* constitute the British judiciary (Griffiths 1977: 28–9), it is none the less important to spell out this process and at the same time correct the unfortunate tendency present in some radical criminology to slip into the imagery and logic of conspiracy theory.

Doubtless many radical criminologists would be reluctant to concede the point, but there is, according to Pottieger (1980) a close similarity between the theoretical structure of radical analysis and structural-functionalism. Once this similarity is recognized, it might be possible to resolve some tensions resident in the radical analysis of 'unemployment and imprisonment' by learning from some structural-functionalists' mistakes. Thus, one major problem with much structural-functional analysis was identified by Merton (1957); it consists, he argued, in the failure to make distinct the difference between objective observable consequences (functions) and actors' subjective dispositions (motives).

Some radical criminologists have also made this error and the outcome is that critics, including two friendly to the radical enterprise (Spitzer 1980; Steinert 1977), have accused them of putting forward a conspiratorial account of how society is maintained particularly through centrally directed and finely orchestrated social control organizations. Clearly there is an obvious temptation for radical criminologists to argue that because imprisonment can be viewed as functional for the maintenance of existing class relations, those with the power to do so must be consciously manipulating the imprisonment rate. But as Reasons and Kaplan (1975) argue, a radical analysis can proceed entirely on the basis of *unintended consequences* without making any inference concerning the motives of magistrates or judges. However, if the increased use and severity of imprisonment during periods of increased unemployment has the unintended consequence of firming up class domination at a time when power-relations are potentially threatened, then there still remains the problem of explaining why judges and magistrates unwittingly bring about this outcome.

It is in answer to this question that the orthodox view – unemployment leads to crime leads to imprisonment – plays a crucial role. It is not that members of the judiciary conspire to instil more discipline into the unemployed as a means of defusing their potential threat to social order, but that when it comes to sentencing, each judge and magistrate, as a matter of routine practice, takes into account a number of legal and *extra-legal* factors. If, as is likely, many of the judiciary believe that unemployment leads to more crime – and the chances are that during periods of rising unemployment the level of recorded serious crime and especially its amplification in the media (Chibnall 1977; Hall *et al.* 1978) will confirm this – then extending the use and severity of imprisonment, in an attempt to increase its deterrent and incapacitation effect, will appear to them as nothing less than a normal and rational response any sensible person would take. In the aggregate, these individual decisions form a pattern. Radical criminologists, following the logic of structural functional analysis, view this pattern as helping to support an economic and social system threatened by one of its contradictions. But clearly this objective consequence was not intended by the individuals whose decisions brought it about. Rather, they merely implemented their belief that unemployment causes crime by imposing more and longer sentences in the hope that this would reduce the crime problem. Thus, if the decisions of individual judges and magistrates are kept distinct from the unintended consequences which flow from them when aggregated, it is possible to avoid falling into the trap of advocating a conspiracy theory to account for the relationship between rising unemployment and rising rates of imprisonment.

This does not necessarily mean that during times of rising unemployment the judiciary increase the severity of penal sanctions only against the unemployed; they may well extend imprisonment across the spectrum of persons found guilty, particularly as the majority of these are bound to be working class and/or ethnically oppressed. None the less, when passing sentences, the judiciary are likely to make fine distinctions even within these subordinate groups. If there is judicial anxiety during times of deteriorating economic conditions, then it would be those convicted persons perceived to be actually or potentially disruptive who would feel the harsher side of judicial discrimination. It is possible that even within the unemployed population the judiciary would see crucial distinctions.

For example, unemployed males are more likely to be perceived as problematic, because in western culture work is not only believed to be the typical way in which males are disciplined but it is also their major source of identity and thus the process by which they build up a stake in conformity. Consequently when males are removed from, or denied access to work, it is widely believed that they will have various anarchistic responses amongst which criminal behaviour is likely to figure quite strongly. These cultural meanings of work attributed to males are likely to have effects on how unemployed males are processed in the criminal justice system.

In contrast, because of institutionalized sexism, unemployed females can, and for the most part do, slip back into or take up the wife/mother social role and hence become subject to all the informal controls of *being* in the family, thus making criminalization and imprisonment, as a form of social control, an unlikely resource to be utilized by the judiciary. Furthermore, given the view held by a large proportion of the population that female employment leads to delinquent 'latch-key' children, it is unlikely that judges and magistrates will favour imprisoning unemployed mothers, for they will be seen as fulfilling their stereotypical gender-role and hence playing their informal part in delinquency control. Removing them to prison would interfere with this vital social service. Indeed, the gender-role of keeping the family together becomes all the more import-ant during times of economic crisis and high unemployment; rapidly increasing the rate of imprisonment for females, particularly adult females, during such times would jeopardize the 'social reproductive' process, and thus further impair the chances of longer-term economic recovery (Braithwaite 1980: 204). Whilst it is unlikely that the judiciary will necessarily be aware of this macro-functional relationship, the aggregation of their individual decisions not to imprison unemployed females unwittingly brings it about!

Young unemployed males will also be perceived as potentially or actually more dangerous than older males simply because their resist-ance to adversity will have been less worn away by barren years of accommodative strategies to inequalities in the distribution of income and life chances (Parkin 1971: 60–9). They will have experienced less discipline at the work place, and their physical prowess and energy, attributes often considered prerequisites for 'conventional' crime, will still be in prime condition. Consequently, it can be expected that the association between unemployment and imprisonment will be greater for a population of younger compared with older males.

Finally, there are reasons why ethnic minorities, particularly young males, would be treated more harshly by the judiciary. Not only is the unemployment rate amongst this group double or even treble that of its white counterpart (Stevens 1979), but their demographic characteristics also signal potentially high levels of criminal behaviour. They are disproportionately aged between 15 and 25 years old. As a group, black British are then doubly vulnerable, first to higher levels of unemploy-ment and second, higher levels of criminality because that is 'youth's speciality'. In addition, black youth is politically marginalized and there-fore unwilling and incapable of attempting to struggle for change of the system from the inside. As Lea and Young argue:

'The growth of a generation of young people in the decaying inner-cities, vast numbers of them with little or no experience of work and employment, is . . . not simply a set of social problems and depriva-tions, it is also a crisis for the political process. The local networks of trade union branches, trades councils and Labour Party branches, the traditional institutions of organized working-class politics, no longer function as channels for the political organization of a generation of young people whose experience of work and production, and the patterns of life that come with it, is minimal.'

(Lea and Young 1982b: 14)

When racial discrimination is added, and when there have already been urban riots in which Britons of West Indian origin and unemployed figured prominently (Field and Southgate 1982) – and even more so in the highly sensationalized media presentation – there are a whole bundle of reasons why the government would view ethnic minorities as in need of discipline.

The judiciary would not necessarily have to be credited with this degree of macro-sociological insightfulness! Individual judges and magistrates merely have to view many young employed offenders, particularly if they are also black, as likely to commit further serious criminal acts, and that would justify, in their learned opinion, imposing a sentence of imprisonment. The government then only has to throw up its arms in despair that the prison population is growing and then quietly allow the prison-building programme to proceed so that the swelling number of prisoners can be accommodated.

Recent British research to examine the empirical support for the above arguments has been conducted by Box and Hale (1982). They analysed unemployment, conviction, and imprisonment rates and sever-ity in England and Wales for the period 1949–79. They demonstrated that although the crime rate had a positive effect on the use and severity of imprisonment, unemployment rates also had an *independent* effect, particularly on young males. Thus it appears that for every 1,000 increase in youth unemployment 23 additional young males get sent to prison *after the effect of crime rates and court workload have been controlled.* This research reinforces and extends other, mainly North American research which has also demonstrated a relationship between unemploy-ment and prison population (Brenner 1976; Dobbins and Bass 1958; Grabosky 1979; Greenberg 1977; Jankovic 1977; Robinson, Smith, and

Wolf 1974; Stern 1940; Vogal 1975; Yeager 1979). It does not however subscribe to the view that prison population size rises and falls directly in line with economic cycles, so that labour is jettisoned when it is needed and imprisoned when depression reduces the demand for labour. A comparison of the average daily prison population with the total number of persons unemployed (now approximately 45,000 in England and Wales compared with 3 millions) reveals the naivity of this view. None the less, Box and Hale consider their evidence to be consistent with another view: during times of economic crisis, state coercion increases in response to the perceived threat, real or imagined, of public disorder including crime waves. The judiciary, being an integral part of the state control apparatus, makes its contribution to this increased level of coercion by imprisoning more, particularly those typifying the actually, or potentially, disruptive problem populations. This judicial response is one the state, by adopting a posture of non-interference with the independence of the judiciary, gratefully allows to occur. It is however only one coercive trump card the state conceals up its sleeve, and there-fore the judiciary should not carry an excessive burden in radical analysis for solving ideological and material crisis of capitalist contradictions.

Criminal statistics for England and Wales do not provide data on the employment status or ethnic origins of persons convicted, but there is indirect evidence that young unemployed and ethnic minorities are more adversely affected by present judicial practices (Gladstone 1979; McLintock 1976). For example, persons sent to prison for defaulting on a fine are usually those lacking the economic resources to pay it; the publicized martyr who refuses to pay a fine on principle is a rare specimen amongst the hum-drum, fine-defaulting population. Courts are not incapable of predicting defaulters, so when they impose a fine on an unemployed or poor offender for a crime not deserving imprisonment immediately, they have a pretty good idea that they are in fact imposing indirectly a prison sentence. This practice appears to have increased over the last decade, particularly for young offenders (see *Table 8*). Imprison-ment for fine defaulting rose by over 300 per cent for both young males and females, whereas it only rose by 34 per cent and 88 per cent for their respective elders. Since unemployment is more concentrated amongst the young and the ethnic minorities it would not be unreasonable to infer that the unemployed young, including West Indians, figure prominently in the population of fine defaulters in prison.

Evidence on sentencing and employment status is more readily available from North America, and there the picture is clearer, although not without foggy patches. Thus Box and Hale (1982: 23) cite ten recent American studies on unemployment status and judicial outcome. Of these, seven reported that unemployed, economically marginalized, convicted persons were more likely to be dealt with severely, even when other relevant variables, such as current offence and prior record had been controlled. Box and Hale also document numerous studies on ethnic status and sentencing decisions. The evidence overwhelmingly supported the view that ethnic and racial minorities were discriminated against by the judiciary. Unfortunately these numerous studies did not always attempt to unravel the interaction between ethnic status and employment status. Clearly these are highly related, but it seems clear from those studies exploring this distinction that employment status has an independent effect on judicial outcome.

No wonder that in both America (Irwin 1977) and England (Banks 1978) there is evidence of demographic changes within the prison population. Prisons are getting younger (Baldock 1980) and blacker. For example, Christianson (1981) points out that in the US, between 1973 and 1979 the incarceration rate per 1,000 for whites rose from 46.3 to 65.1. The comparable black rates were 368 and 544. Not only are these rates higher, but the rate of incarceration for black offenders has risen faster. Consequently, the black 'share' of the prison population, although there are no prizes for this achievement, rose during the last decade. Of course a part of this 'racial disproportionality' in prisons will be accountable for by the higher rate of black crime, but even after accounting for this, there are still more black prisoners than would be expected (Blumstein 1982).

Unfortunately, there are no comparable data on the black population in British prisons, but it could be inferred from arrest patterns that blacks in Britain receive harsher penal treatment. For example, in the Metropolitan Police District in 1975, blacks represented only 4.2 per cent of the total population. Yet they constituted 37.1 per cent of those arrested for violent theft and 28.7 per cent of those arrested for robbery (Stevens and Willis 1979: 32) – the relevance of these particular data being that nearly one-half of those convicted for these offences receive a prison sentence and the rate of incarceration for these same offences has increased during the last decade. The outcome is obvious. According to reliable sources, a guesstimate that 40 per cent of young persons in prison are black 'errs on the side of caution'. Of course, until the cloak thrown over this type of 'sensitive' data by the Official Secrets Act is penetrated, or better still, removed, guesstimates are the name of the game. But the above one is not far out, which means that blacks are *ten* times more prevalent in the young prisoners' population than the general population.

It is no mere coincidence that as prisons are getting younger and blacker, so the rate and duration of unemployment among the young and black continues to increase. For it is on the unemployed and unemployable that the long arm of the law falls like a dead weight. Of course, offenders are being imprisoned because they committed crimes as well as the fact that they are unemployed, unprivileged, and possibly ethnically oppressed. But when the crimes of the prison population – which mainly involves property offences – are compared with the crimes of the non-imprisoned, powerful offending population, it becomes quite clear that the government's 'law and order' campaign and its judicial ally's sentencing practice are not that concerned to control serious crime. Rather they are more concerned to instil discipline, directly and indirectly, on those people who are no longer controlled by the soft-discipline-machine of work and who might become growingly resentful that they are being made to pay the price for economic recession. Whilst the powerful are getting away with crimes whose enormity appears to sanctify them, the powerless are getting prison.

And justice for all?

From the perspective adopted in this book, there are two – at least – major problems with the above government penal policy and current judicial sentencing practices.

In the first place, this 'law and order' campaign is not a response to democratic pressures from below. That pressure is certainly there. Inner-city lower-class residents are increasingly terrified of street crime, vandalism, and burglary. Numerous studies, both in America and Britain have documented the agoraphobic extremes this fear has induced (Balkin 1979; Hartnagel 1979). The elderly are very afraid of street crime and burglary and want more protection (Clarke and Lewis 1982; Yin 1980). Women in general have a greater fear of being criminally victimized, particularly sexually (Gordon *et al.* 1980). Some require protection, but others, under the sobering influence of feminism, realize they have to reclaim the night for themselves rather than wait for the state to act against patriarchy. Ethnic minorities are certainly clamouring for police protection from racist 'inspired' violent assaults and arson; they are also demanding less police brutality and harassment visited upon them! Prisoners have been demanding 'less prison', not only because it brutalizes and criminalizes many prisoners, but because it is irrelevant for a substantial proportion of persons incarcerated (Fitzgerald 1977).

But the government's current 'law and order' policy has little to do with these various constituencies' interests. Rather it has its own reasons, fears, and rationale for firming up the state's defences by increasing police and prison manpower, increasing their technological capacity, and extending their powers of arrest and detention without at the same time providing democratic forms of control. Thus the Criminal Attempts Act, 1981, was 'intended' to repeal the widely condemned 'sus' laws. But the strengthened law of 'attempt' can be stretched as a result of this act to cover attempted theft of unknown materials from unknown persons, as well as attempting to steal a parked car. Mere presence, particularly if your 'face does not fit' or your skin colour is the 'wrong shade' in a street with parked cars, could, through an officer's eyes, constitute an attempt. Through this act, police discretion has been extended rather than curtailed, and it is the powerless on whom this discretion will fall heavily. The Criminal Justice Act, 1982, also strengthened the state's armoury. This act undermined the Children's and Young Persons' Act, 1969. It not only restored to the judiciary the power to commit young persons to prison, a power the earlier act had severely restricted – at least in principle – but it also extended the age limit downwards from 17 to 15 years. The new 'youth custody' sentence introduced by the 1982 Act reflects a very strong desire to move wayward adolescents from the 'caring' hands of social workers and probation officers to the calloused hands of prison officers. The Police and Criminal Evidence Bill, 1982, is another example of the state attempting to shore up its powers. It is simply one in a line of legal manoeuvres whose latent consequence, no matter what the stated intentions, will be to increase the power of the police to invade the individuals' privacy (not lawyers, journalists, priests, or doctors) and detain them until evidence is 'found'. Indeed, the effect of the act can be predicted from the effect of the Anti-Terrorism and Prevention Act, which gave police in Northern Ireland powers similar to those now granted to the mainland police.

The target crime (or otherwise) problem in the present 'law and order' campaign reflects the government's (and the interests of those groups they represent) anxieties, real or imagined, fancied or fabricated. This anxiety is fed by fear of youthful rebellion, riot or resistance, a fear reinforced by the knowledge that this group bears the major burden of the present economic recession, and by the belief that such groups under current conditions of deprivation are prone to innovative criminal responses.

There may be some happy coincidence with the 'crime problem' as defined by the government and citizens. But it is more fortuitous than the latter determining the former's policies. When it is not fortuitous, it is likely to be the consequence of 'consciousness manipulation' (Sinden 1980). Thus the increased criminalization of social security 'scroungers' appears to enjoy a degree of public support. However, this is not because 'scroungers' deprive tax-payers of more money than do other respectable scroungers, such as tax-avoiders and evaders. Indeed, recent estimates in a *World in Action* programme (February 1983) place Department of Health and Social Security fraud at £108 millions per year compared with £4,000 millions lost through tax non-payment or avoidance. However, public opinion on this issue is more formed by government officials, who through media amplification, create 'folk devils' out of society security 'scroungers'. The public, less able to gauge accurately the pecuniary loss inflicted by tax-evasion, are provoked into a 'moral panic'. In its turn, the government then appears to be responsive to public concern, whereas in reality its purpose is to impose discipline and fear into the unemployment recipients of state benefits (and those multitudes who might soon join them) because they, and not respectable middle-class employed or corporate tax-evaders, are perceived to be more problematic and potentially disruptive.

This brings us to the second problem, from the perspective adopted in this book, with the government's and judiciary's 'law and order' posturing. The target population for being criminalized is wide of the mark. Police and prisons are being strengthened and expanded not to control or contain crimes of the powerful – these remain, as ever, undiscussed, unrecognized and uncontrolled. The target population is relatively young males (and increasingly females). Thus, during the decade ending 1981, receptions into prison under sentence increased by 64 per cent for males under twenty-one years of age compared with only a 34 per cent increase for older males. Similarly the number of young females sentenced to prison rose by a massive 117 per cent compared with a large but smaller increase of 88 per cent for older women. So young people (amongst whom the unemployed and/or ethnically oppressed are over-represented) have shouldered the major burden of courts sentencing more people to prison. This is not because these young people have been convicted of many more crimes; admittedly these have increased during the last decade, but they have not however, increased anywhere near as fast as the increase in the number sent to prison, and the peak for adolescent conviction rates appears to be 1977. Depending on the sex and age of sub-groups, it has remained constant or slightly dipped since then. Furthermore, the increased number of persons imprisoned cannot be explained simply by the increased number of convictions; *the proportion* of all convicted persons sentenced to imprisonment (including borstals, and detention centres) has increased. It is clear from the above data that the judiciary are imprisoning proportionately more convicted young persons than older persons now than they were a decade ago.

The crimes this group of young imprisoned offenders commit are mainly 'street' crimes, such as robbery, and 'conventional crimes', such as burglary and theft, within which taking away and driving is the single largest offence. For example, of the 27,782 young males received into prison under sentence in 1981, 3,274 (12 per cent) were guilty of taking and driving away a car. Why this should receive such a harsh sentence is not apparent. In addition, there were 11,620 (42 per cent) guilty of burglary, including 'attempted' burglary, and 1,084 (4 per cent) guilty of robbery. Of course, many of these crimes are *absolutely* serious, but by concentrating on the criminalization of some sub-populations committing them (and those 'considered' to be committing them), the police and courts fail to apply the law universally or 'fairly', thus exacerbating degrading housing conditions, unemployment, and racial discrimination. They also fail to deter and incapacitate more respectable offenders who then remain free in the community to victimize others, in ways *relatively* more serious than the victimization committed by imprisoned offenders. This is not to argue that no present prisoners deserve to be there. There are many heinous offences, particularly against the person, for which the culprit richly deserves imprisonment. Clearly there is no support here for abolishing prison for murderers, attempted murderers, persons causing grievous bodily harm, rapists, and other acts of violence against the person. But such offenders form a small minority of persons sent to prison. Thus, in 1981 only 4,695 (17 per cent) out of 27,782 young convicted males, and 5,373 (15 per cent) out of 36,368 adult convicted males were sent to prison for convictions of violence against the person, including rape.

The government's 'law and order' campaign and the judiciary's sentencing practice are not responses to crimes of the powerful, or crime problems as defined by the electorate, although there may be some fortunate and accidental coincidence with the latter. They are essentially responses to their own fears of growing social indiscipline. As a consequence the powerful commit devastating crimes and get away with it, whilst the powerless but 'potentially dangerous' commit less serious crimes, but get prison. Thus prisons function not only to demoralize and fracture potential resistance to domination, but they also supply ideological fodder by way of providing a massive legitimation to the portrait of crime and criminals so artfully and cynically constructed by legislators and those who influence them. In providing this service, they also further weaken potential working-class resistance by instilling in them a fear of 'conventional criminals', which is not entirely irrational. In turn, this leads to an increased demand for more and more state imposed 'law and order'. In this way the powerless are manipulated to look upward, like children for protection from those around or beneath them. Whereas, if they understand just how much the powerful criminally victimize them, they would not be so hopelessly dependant on a protector, who, like the person Ms Riding Hood encounters, turns out to be a predator.

With Holland as a notable exception (Downes 1982; Steenhuis, Tigges, and Essers 1983; Tulkens 1979) justice in Britain, the US, and most other industrialized countries is not so much blind as perverted. The autonomy of the criminal justice system, constitutionally congealed as 'separation of powers', is left untampered with by those with the power, but not the will, to redirect it. Those with the will, but not the power are unable to alter the situation without much more organizational and solidaristic action. Of course, in a truly democratic society, citizens should have the right to criticize effectively those with the power to arrest, prosecute, and imprison. The criminal justice personnel should be accountable not only for *who* they criminalize, but *why*, and in *whose* interests. There will only be justice for all when the answers, respectively, are: 'those who objectively criminally victimize citizens most', which does not mean relying on dubious opinion polls, but instead demands a programme of sensitizing people to the numerous ways in which they are victimized but remain relatively ignorant of their own victimization, or are seduced into seeing such processes as 'disasters', 'accidents', or 'unavoidable incidents'; 'because that is what citizens are demanding', which does not mean intuiting collective will, but establishing institutional democratic procedures through which people's demands can be communicated to elected, responsive, responsible, and removable political leaders; and 'it is in the interests of us all equally and is not covertly masking differential benefits accruing to the powerful, privileged, and wealthy. These are not utopian demands. Rather they reside essentially within the democratic ideal. They are therefore only demands that principles espoused in public by our political leaders are translated into practice. We have for too long ignored crimes of the powerful, allowed the poor to be imprisoned scapegoats, and encouraged criminal justice personnel to act subversively. Justice has suffered, and so have we all.

References

ADLER, F. (1975) *Sisters in Crime*. New York: McGraw-Hill.
―――― (1977) Interaction between women's emancipation and female criminality. *International Journal of Criminology Penology*, **5**: 101–12.
AL-ISSA, I. (1980) *The Psychopathology of Women*. New Jersey: Prentice-Hall.
AMERICAN NATIONAL COMMISSION ON PRODUCT SAFETY (1971) *Report*. Washington, DC: Government Printing Office.
AMIR, M. (1967) Victim precipitated forcible rape. *Journal of Criminal Law, Criminology and Police Science* **58**: 493–502.
―――― (1971) *Patterns of Forcible Rape*. Chicago: Chicago University Press.
ANDENEAS, J. (1966) The general preventive effects of punishment. *University of Pennsylvania Law Review* **114**: 949–83.
ANDERSON, E. A. (1976) The 'chivalrous' treatment of the female offender in the arms of the criminal justice system: a review of the literature. *Social Problems* **23**: 350–57.
APFELBERG, B. (1964) A psychiatric study of 250 sex offenders. *American Journal of Psychiatry* **100**: 762–70.
ARMSTRONG, G. (1977) Females under the law – 'protected but equal'. *Crime and Delinquency* **23**: 107–20.
ASBESTOS ADVISORY COUNCIL (1980) *Report of the Asbestos Advisory Council*. Health and Safety Commission, London: HMSO.
ASHFORD, N. A. (1976) *Crisis in the Workplace: Occupational Disease and Injury*. Cambridge, Mass.: MIT Press.

AULTMAN, M. G. and WELLFORD, C. F. (1979) Towards an integrated model of delinquency causation. *Sociology and Social Research* **63**: 316–27.

AUSTIN, R. (1981) Liberation and female criminality in England and Wales. *British Journal Criminology* **21**: 371–74.

—— (1982) Women's Liberation and increases in minor, major and occupational offences. *Criminology* **20**: 407–30.

BAAB, G. W. and FURGESON, W. R. (1967) Texas sentencing practices: a statistical study. *Texas Law Review* **45**: 471–503.

BAILEY, M. (1978) The Bingham Report and Sanction Busters. *Times* July 1: 4.

BALDOCK, J. (1980) Why prison's population has grown larger and younger. *Howard Journal* **19**: 142–55.

BALDWIN, R. and KINSEY, R. (1982) *Police Powers and Politics*. London: Quartet.

BALKIN, S. (1979) Victimization rates, safety and fear of crime. *Social Problems* **26**: 343–58.

BANKS, C. (1978) A survey of the south-east prison population. Home Office Research Unit, *Research Bulletin* **5**. London: Home Office.

BARNETT, H. (1981) Corporate capitalism, corporate crime. *Crime and Delinquency* **27**: 4–23.

BARRON, R. D. and NORRIS, G. M. (1976) Sexual divisions and the dual labour market. In D. Barker and S. Allen (eds) *Dependence and Exploitation in Work and Marriage*. London: Tavistock.

BAYLEY, D. (1979) Police function, structure and control in western Europe and North America. In N. Morris and M. Tonry (eds) *Crime and Justice: An Annual Review of Research* Vol. 1. Chicago: Chicago University Press.

BECKER, H. S. (1967) Whose side are we on? *Social Problems* **14**: 239–47.

BEDAU, H. A. (1964) Death sentences in New Jersey. *Rutgers Law Review* **19**: 1–55.

BENN, S. I. and PETERS, R. S. (1959) *Social Principles and the Democratic State*. London: Allen and Unwin.

BENN, T. (1981) *Arguments for Democracy*. London: Jonathan Cape.

BEQUAI, A. (1978) *White-Collar Crime: A Twentieth Century Crisis*. Lexington: Heath.

BERNSTEIN, I. N., KELLY, W. R., and DOYLE, P. A. (1977) Charge reduction: an intermediate stage in the process of labelling criminal defendants. *Social Forces* **56**: 362–84.

BIENEN, L. (1977) Rape II. *Woman's Rights Law Reporter* **3**: 90–137.

BINDER, A. and SCHARF, P. (1982) Deadly force in law enforcement. *Crime and Delinquency* **28**: 1–23.

BINGHAM, T. H. (1978) *Report on the Supply of Petroleum and Petroleum Products to Rhodesia*. London: HMSO.

BISHOP, C. (1931) *Women and Crime*. London: Chatto and Windus.

BLAU, P. M. and SCOTT, W. R. (1962) *Formal Organizations*. London: Routledge.

BLOCK, A. (1977) Aw! your mother's in the mafia – women criminals in progressive New York. *Contemporary Crisis* 1: 5–22.

––––––– (1980) Searching for women in organised crime. In S. K. Datesman and F. R. Scarpitti (eds), *Women, Crime and Justice*. New York: Oxford University Press.

BLUMSTEIN, A. (1982) On the racial disproportionality of United States' prison population. *Journal Criminal Law and Criminology* 73: 1259–281.

BLUNDELL, W. E. (1978) Equity funding: 'I did it for the jollies'. In J. M. Johnson and J. D. Douglas (eds), *Crime at the Top*. New York: Lippincott.

BOHMER, C. (1974) Judicial attitudes toward rape victims. *Judicature* 57: 303–07.

BORDUA, D. J. and REISS, A. J. (1967) Environment and organisation: a perspective on the police. In D. J. Bordua (ed.) *The Police*. New York: Wiley.

BOWKER, L. H. (1981) Gender differences in prisoner subcultures. In L. H. Bowker (ed.) *Women and Crime in America*. New York: Macmillan.

BOX, S. (1981a) *Deviance, Reality and Society* 2nd ed. London: Holt, Rinehart and Winston.

––––––– (1981b) Where have all the naughty children gone? In National Deviancy Symposium, *Permissiveness and Control*. London: Macmillan.

BOX, S. and HALE, C. (1982) Economic crisis and the rising prisoner population in England and Wales, 1949–1979. *Crime and Social Justice* 16: 20–35.

––––––– (1983a) Liberation and female criminality in England and Wales revisited. *British J. Criminology* 22: 35–49.

––––––– (1983b) Liberation or economic marginalization: the relevance of two theoretical arguments to female crime patterns in England and Wales, 1951–1980. *Criminology* (forthcoming).

BOX, S. and RUSSELL, K. (1975) The politics of discreditability: disarming complaints against the police. *Sociological Review* 23: 315–46.

BRAITHWAITE, J. (1979a) *Inequality, Crime and Public Policy*. London: Routledge.

––––––– (1979b) Transnational corporations and corruption: towards some international solutions. *International Journal of Sociology and Law* 7: 125–42.

––––––– (1980) The political economy of punishment. In E. L. Wheelwright and K. Buckley (eds) *Essays in the Political Economy of Australian Capitalism*, Vol. 4. Sydney: ANZ Books.

––––––– (1981a) Inegalitarian consequences of egalitarian reforms to control corporate crime. *Temple Law Quarterly* (forthcoming).

––––––– (1981b) Challenging just deserts: the sentencing of white-collar criminals. *Journal of Criminal Law and Criminology* (forthcoming).

––––––– (1983) *Corporate Crime in the Pharmaceutical Industry*. London: Routledge.

BRAITHWAITE, J. and GEIS, G. (1981) On theory and action for corporate crime control. (unpub. paper).

BRENNER, M. H. (1976) *Estimating the Social Costs of National Economic*

Policy: Implications for Mental and Physical Health, and Criminal and Aggression. Washington, DC: Joint Economic Committee, Congress of the United States.

BRIDGES, L. and GILROY, P. (1982) Striking Back. *Marxism Today* (June): 34–5.

BROWN, D. (1971) *Bury My Heart at Wounded Knee.* New York: Holt, Rinehart and Winston.

BROWN, G. W. and HARRIS, T. (1978) *Social Origins of Depression.* London: Tavistock.

BROWNMILLER, S. (1975) *Against Our Will.* London: Secker and Warburg.

BRUCK, C. (1975) Women against the law. *Human Behaviour* 4: 24–33.

BUNDRED, S. (1982) Accountability and the metropolitan police: a suitable case for treatment. In D. Cowell, T. Jones, and J. Young (eds) *Policing the Riots.* London: Junction.

BURGESS, A. W. and HOLMSTROM, L. L. (1974) *Rape: Victims of Crisis.* Maryland: Brady.

BURNHAM, D. (1973) 3 of 5 slain by police here are black. *New York Times* (Aug 26): 50.

CARSON, W. G. (1970) White collar crime and the enforcement of factory legislation. *British Journal Criminology* 10: 383–98.

———— (1974) Symbolic and instrumental dimensions of early factory legislation. In R. Hood (ed.) *Crime, Criminology and Public Policy.* London: Heinemann.

———— (1980) The institutionalization of ambiguity: early British factory acts. In G. Geis and E. Stotland (eds), *White Collar Crime: Theory and Research.* London: Sage.

———— (1981) *The Other Price of Britain's Oil.* London: Martin Robertson.

CARSON, W. G. and MARTIN, B. (1974) *The Factory Acts.* London: Martin Robertson.

CAUDILL, H. M. (1977) Dead laws and dead men: manslaughter in a coal mine. *Nation* 226: 492–97.

CENTRAL STATISTICAL OFFICE (1982) *Social Trends 12.* London: HMSO.

———— (1983) *Social Trends 13.* London: HMSO.

CENTER FOR RESEARCH ON CRIMINAL JUSTICE (1977) *Iron Fist and the Velvet Glove: An Analysis of the U.S. Police.* California: Centre Research Criminal Justice.

CERNKOVICH, S. A. (1978) Evaluation of two models of delinquency causation. *Criminology* 16: 335–52.

CHAMBLISS, W. J. (1964) A sociological analysis of the law of vagrancy. *Social Problems* 12: 46–67.

———— (1978) *On The Take: From Petty Crooks to Presidents.* Indiana: Indiana University Press.

———— (1981) The criminalization of conduct. In H. L. Ross (ed.), *Law and Deviance.* London: Sage.

CHAMBLISS, W. J. and SEIDMAN, R. B. (1971) *Law, Order and Power.* Reading: Addison-Wesley.

CHANCELLOR OF EXCHEQUER (1980) *The Government's Expenditure Plans 1980/81 to 1983/4.* London: HMSO (Cmnd. 7841).

CHAPMAN, J. R. and GATES, M. (eds.) (1978) *The Victimization of Women*. New York: Sage.

CHAPPELL, D. (1976) Forcible rape and the criminal justice system. *Crime and Delinquency* **22**: 125–36.

CHESLER, P. (1972) *Women and Madness*. New York: Avon.

CHESNEY-LIND, M. (1973) Judicial enforcement of the female sex-role: the family court and the female delinquent. *Issues in Criminology* **8**: 51–70.

———(1974) Juvenile delinquency: the sexualization of female crime. *Psychology Today* **7**: 43–6.

———(1977) Judicial paternalism and the female status offender. *Crime and Delinquency* **23**: 121–30.

———(1978) Chivalry reexamined: women and the criminal justice system. In L. H. Bowker (ed.) *Women, Crime and the Criminal System*. Mass.: Lexington.

CHETLEY, A. (1979) *The Baby Killer Scandal*. London: War On Want.

CHIBNALL, S. (1977) *Law and Order News*. London: Tavistock.

CHOMSKY, N. and HERMAN, E. S. (1979a) *The Washington Connection and Third World Fascism*. Nottingham: Spokesman.

——— (1979b) *After the Cataclysm*. Nottingham: Spokesman.

CHRISTENSEN, J., SCHMIDT, J., and HENDERSON, J. (1982) The selling of the police: media, ideology and crime control. *Contemporary Crises* **6**: 227–39.

CHRISTIANSON, S. (1981) Our black prisons. *Crime and Delinquency* **27**: 364–75.

CLARK, J. P. and TIFFT, L. L. (1966) Polygraph and the interview validation of self-reported deviant behaviour among juveniles. *American Sociological Review* **27**: 826–34.

CLARK, K. B. (1965) *Dark Ghetto*. New York: Harper and Row.

CLARK, L. and LEWIS, D. (1977) *Rape: the Price of Coercive Sexuality*. Toronto: Women's Press.

CLARKE, A. H. and LEWIS, M. J. (1982) Fear of crime among the elderly. *British Journal Criminology* **22**: 49–62.

CLINARD, M. B. (1952) *The Black Market: A Study of White Collar Crime*. New York: Holt, Rinehart and Winston.

——— (1964) *Anomie and Deviant Behaviour*. New York: Free Press.

——— (1978) *Cities With Little Crime*. Cambridge: Cambridge University Press.

CLINARD, M. B. and YEAGER, P. C. (1980) *Corporate Crime*. New York: Free Press.

CLINARD, M. B., YEAGER, P. C., BRISSETTE, J. M., PETRASHEK, D., and HARRIS, E. (1979) *Illegal Corporate Behaviour*. Washington, DC: US Government Printing Office.

CLOWARD, R. A. and OHLIN, L. (1961) *Delinquency and Opportunity*. New York: Free Press.

CLOWARD, R. A. and PIVEN, F. F. (1979) Female protest: the channeling of female innovation resistance. *Signs* **4**: 661–69.

COCHRANE, P. (1978) Sex crimes and pornography revisited. *International Journal Criminology and Penology* **6**: 307–17.

COGGAN, G. and WALKER, M. (1982) *Frightened For My Life: An Account of Deaths in British Prisons*. London: Fontana.

COHEN, A. K. (1955) *Delinquent Boys*. New York: Macmillan.

COHEN, L. E. and STARK, R. (1974) Discriminatory labelling and the five-finger discount. *Journal of Research Crime and Delinquency* 11: 25–39.

COHEN, M. D. (1971) The psychology of rapists. *Seminars Psychiatry* 3: 307–27.

COHEN, S. and TAYLOR, L. (1976) *Prison Secrets*. London: NCCL/RAP.

COHEN, S. and YOUNG, J. (1980) *Manufacture of News*. London: Constable.

COLLINS, R. (1975) *Conflict Sociology*. New York: Academic Press.

CONGER, R. D. (1976) Social control and social learning models of delinquent behaviour. *Criminology* 14: 27–40.

CONKLIN, J. E. (1977) *Illegal But Not Criminal*. New Jersey: Spectrum.

CONWAY, A. and BOGDAN, C. (1977) Sexual delinquency: the persistence of a double standard. *Crime and Delinquency* 23: 131–42.

COOK, W. (1967) Policemen in society: which side are they on? *Berkeley Journal of Sociology* 12: 117–29.

COOTE, A. and CAMPBELL, B. (1981) *Sweet Freedom*. London: Fontana.

COURT, J. H. (1976) Pornography and sex crimes, *International Journal of Criminology and Penology* 5: 129–57.

COUSSINS, J. (1977) *The Equality Report*. London: National Council for Civil Liberties Rights for Women Unit.

COX, B., SHIRLEY, J., and SHORT, M. (1977) *The Fall of Scotland Yard*. London: Penguin.

CRESSEY, R. D. (1953) *Other People's Money*. New York: Free Press.

—— (1969) *The Theft of a Nation*. New York: Harper and Row.

CRITES, L. (ed.) (1976) *The Female Offender*. Lexington: Lexington Books.

CULLEN, F. T., GOLDEN, K. M. and CULLEN, J. B. (1979) Sex and delinquency. *Criminology* 17: 301–10.

CULLEN, F. T., LINK, B. G., and POLANZI, C. W. (1982) The seriousness of crime revisited. *Criminology* 20: 83–102.

CURTIS, L. A. (1974) Victim precipitation and violent crime. *Social Problems* 21: 594–605.

CUTLER, J. (1982) Cover-up on asbestos victims. *New Statesman* 10th Oct.: 4.

DATESMAN, S. K. and SCARPITTI, F. R. (1977) Unequal protection for males and females in the juvenile court. In T. N. Ferdinand (ed.) *Juvenile Delinquency* Beverley Hills: Sage.

—— (1980) *Women, Crime and Justice*. New York: Oxford University Press.

DATESMAN, S. K., SCARPITTI, F. R., and STEPHENSON, R. (1975) Female delinquency: an application of self and opportunity theories. *Journal Research Crime and Delinquency* 12: 107–23.

DAVIS, A. J. (1970) Sexual assaults in the Philadelphia prison system. In J. Gagnon and W. Simon (eds), *The Sexual Scene*. Chicago: Aldine.

DECROW, K. (1974) *Sexist Justice*. New York: Vintage.

DEMING, R. (1977) *Women: The New Criminals*. Nashville: Thomas Nelson.

DENZIN, N. K. (1977) Notes on the criminogenic hypothesis: a case study of the American liquor industry. *American Sociological Review* 42: 905–20.

DEPARTMENT of EMPLOYMENT (1983) *Employment Gazette* (January): S29.

DERSHOWITZ, A. M. (1961) Increasing community control over corporate crime: a problem in the law of sanctions. *Yale Law Journal* 71: 289–306.

DIAMOND, I. (1980) Pornography and repression: a reconsideration. *Signs* 5: 686–701.

DIRKS, R. L. and GROSS, L. (1974) *The Great Wall Street Scandal*. New York: McGraw-Hill.

DOBASH, R. E. and DOBASH, R. (1981) *Violence Against Wives*. London: Open Books.

DOBBINS, D. A. and BASS, B. (1958) Effects of unemployment on white and negro prison admissions in Louisiana. *Journal Criminal Law and Criminology* 48: 522–25.

DONNERSTEIN, E. and HALLAN, J. (1980) The facilitating effects of erotica on aggression against women. *Journal Personality and Social Psychology* 39: 269–77.

DOUGLAS, J. D. and JOHNSON, J. M. (eds) (1977) *Official Deviance*. New York: Lippincott.

DOWIE, M. (1977) Pinto Madness. *Mother Jones* 2: 18–34.

DOWNES, D. (1982) The origins and consequences of Dutch penal policy. *British Journal Criminology* 22: 325–62.

DRUCKER, D. (1979) The common law does not support a marital exception for forcible rape. *Women's Rights Law Report* 5: 181–99.

DURKHEIM, E. (1898/1951) *Suicide*. New York: Free Press.

DUSTER, T. (1970) *The Legislation of Morality*. New York: Free Press.

DWORKIN, A. (1974) *Woman Hating*. New York: Dutton.

EDWARDS, S. (1981) *Female Sexuality and the Law*. London: Martin Robertson.

ELLIOT, D. A. and AGETON, S. S. (1980) Reconciling race and class differences in self-reported and official estimates of delinquency. *American Sociological Review* 45: 95–110.

EPSTEIN, S. D. (1979) *The Politics of Cancer*. New York: Anchor.

ERICKSON, K. T. (1976) *Everything in its Path*. New York: Simon and Schuster.

ERICKSON, M. L. and SMITH, W. B. (1974) On the relationship between self-reported and actual deviance. *Humboldt Journal of Social Relations* 2: 106–13.

ERMANN, M. D. and LUNDMAN, R. L. (eds) (1978) *Corporate and Governmental Deviance*. Oxford: Oxford University Press.

—— (1982) *Corporate Deviance*. New York: Holt, Rinehart and Winston.

ETZIONI, A. (1961) *A Comparative Analysis of Complex Organizations*. Glencoe: Free Press.

FARBERMAN, H. A. (1975) A criminogenic market structure: the automobile industry. *Sociological Quarterly* 16: 438–57.

FARLEY, L. (1980) *Sexual Shakedown*. New York: Warner.

FEINMAN, C. (1979) Sex role stereotypes and justice for women. *Crime and Delinquency* **25**: 87–94.

FELDMAN-SUMMERS, S. and PALMER, G. C. (1980) Rape as viewed by judges, prosecutors and police officers. *Criminal Justice & Behaviour* **7**: 19–40.

FIELD, S. and SOUTHGATE, P. (1982) *Public Disorder*. Home Office Research Study No. 72. London: HMSO.

FISHER, G. and RIVIL, E. (1971) Psychological needs of rapists. *British Journal of Criminology* **11**: 182–85.

FISSE, W. B. (1971) The use of publicity as a criminal sanction against business corporations. *Melbourne University Law Review* **8**: 250–79.

FITZGERALD, M. (1977) *Prisoners in Revolt*. London: Penguin.

FITZGERALD, M. and SIM, J. (1979) *British Prisons*. Oxford: Blackwell.

FITZMAURICE, C. and PEASE, K. (1982) Prison sentences and population: a comparison of some other European countries. *Justice of the Peace* **146**: 575–79.

FOSTER, T. W. (1975) Make believe families: a response of women and girls to the deprivations of imprisonment. *International Journal of Criminology and Penology* **3**: 71–8.

FOX, J. and HARTNAGEL, T. F. (1979) Changing social roles and female crime in Canada: a time series analysis. *Review Canadian Sociology and Anthropology* **16**: 96–104.

FRIEDMAN, H. M. (1979) Some reflections on the corporation as a criminal defendant. *Notre Dame Lawyer* **55**: 173–202.

FROSCH, J. and BROMBERG, W. (1939) The sex offender – a psychiatric study. *American Journal Orthopsychiatry* **9**: 761–76.

FULLER, J. G. (1962) *The Gentlemen Conspirators*. New York: Grove.

FYFE, J. J. (1978) *Shots Fired* (unpubl. PhD). State University of New York at Albany.

────── (1981) Observations on police deadly force. *Crime and Delinquency* **27**: 376–89.

────── (1982) Blind justice: police shootings in Memphis. *Journal of Criminal Law and Criminology* **73**: 707–22.

GALLIHER, J. F. (1971) Explanations of police behaviour. *Sociological Quarterly* **12**: 308–18.

GEARY, R. (1980) *Deaths in Prison*. London: NCCL.

GEBHARD, P., GAGNON, J. H., POMEROY, C. V., and CHRISTENSON, C. V. (1965) *Sex Offenders*. New York: Harper & Row.

GEIS, G. (1967) The heavy electrical equipment anti-trust cases of 1961. In M. B. Clinard and R. Quinney (eds) *Criminal Behaviour Systems*. New York: Holt, Rinehart and Winston.

────── (1975) Victimization patterns in white-collar crime. In I. Drapkin and E. Viano (eds) *Victimology* Vol. V. Lexington: Lexington Books.

────── (1978) Deterring corporate crime. In M. D. Ermann and R. L. Lundman (eds) *Corporate and Government Deviance*. New York: Oxford University Press.

GEIS, G. and MEIER, R. F. (eds) (1977) *White Collar Crime*. New York: Free Press.

GEIS, G. and STOTLAND, E. (eds) (1980) *White Collar Crime: Theory and Research*. Beverley Hills: Sage.

GIALLOMBARDO, R. (1966) *Society of Women: A Study of a Woman's Prison*. New York: Wiley.

GIBBONS, D. (1977) *Society, Crime, and Criminal Careers* 3rd Ed. New Jersey: Prentice-Hall.

GIBBONS, H. B., MORRISON, J., and WEST, J. (1970) The confessions of known offenders in response to a self reported delinquency schedule. *British Journal of Criminology* **10**: 277–80.

GIBSON, L., LINDEN, R., and JOHNSON, S. (1980) A situational theory of rape. *Canad. Journal of Criminology* **22**: 51–65.

GILROY, P. (1982) The myth of black criminality. *Socialist Register*. London: Merlin.

GIORDANO, P. G. and CERNKOVICH, S. A. (1979) On complicating the relationship between liberation and delinquency. *Social Problems* **26**: 465–81.

GLADSTONE, F. (1979) Crime and the crystal ball. Home Office Research Unit, *Research Bulletin No. 7*. London: Home Office.

GOFF, C. H. and REASONS, C. (1978) *Corporate Crime in Canada*. Ontario: Prentice-Hall.

GOLD, M. (1966) Undetected delinquency behaviour. *Journal of Research Crime and Delinquency* **3**: 27–46.

GOODMAN, W. (1963) *All Honourable Men*. Boston: Little, Brown.

GORDON, M. T., RIGER, S., LeBAILLY, R. K., and HEATH, L. (1980) Crime, women, and the quality of urban life. *Signs* **5**: S144–S160.

GRABOSKY, P. N. (1979) Economic conditions and penal severity: testing a neo-Marxian hypothesis. (Unpub. paper).

GRAHAM, J. M. (1972) Amphetamine politics on Capital Hill. *Society* **9**: 14–23.

GREEN, E. (1961) *Judicial Attitudes in Sentencing*. London: Macmillan.

GREEN, M. J. (1972) *The Closed Enterprise System*. New York: Grossman.

GREENBERG, D. F. (1977) The dynamics of oscillatory punishment processes. *Journal Criminal Law and Criminology* **68**: 643–51.

GREENBERG, S. and ADLER, F. (1974) Crime and addiction: an empirical analysis of the literature, 1920–1973. *Contemporary Drug Problems* (Summer): 221–70.

GREER, G. (1975) Seduction is a four-letter word. In L. G. Schultz (ed.), *Rape Victimology*. Illinois: C. C. Thomas.

GRIFFIN, S. (1973) The politics of rape. *Oz* **41**: 27–31.

GRIFFITHS, J. A. (1977) *The Politics of the Judiciary*. London: Fontana.

GRINSPOON, L. and HEDBLOM, P. (1975) *The Speed Culture*. London: Harvard University Press.

GROSS, E. (1978) Organizational sources of crime: a theoretical perspective. In N. K. Denzin (ed.) *Studies in Symbolic Interaction* Greenwich CT.: JAI Press.

GROTH, A. N. and BIRNBAUM, J. (1979) *Men Who Rape*. New York: Plenum.

GUNNINGHAM, N. (1974) *Pollution, Social Interest and the Law*. London: Martin Robertson.

GUTMAN, H. G. (1961) Trouble on the railroads in 1873–1874. *Labor History* **2**: 225–37.

——— (1962) Reconstruction in Ohio. *Labor History* **3**: 10–19.

GUTTMACHER, M. S. (1951) *Sex Offenses: the Problem, Causes and Prevention*. New York: Norton.

HACKLER, J. C. and LAUTT, M. (1969) Systematic bias in measuring self-reported delinquency. *Canadian Review Sociology and Anthropology* **6**: 92–106.

HAGAN, J., SIMPSON, J. H., and GILLIS, A. R. (1979) The sexual stratification of social control: a gender-based perspective on crime and delinquency. *British Journal of Sociology* **30**: 25–38.

HALL, J. (1952) *Theft, Law and Society* rev. ed. Indianapolis: Bobbs-Merrill.

HALL, S., CRITCHER, C., JEFFERSON, T., CLARKE, J., and ROBERTS, B. (1978) *Policing the Crisis: Mugging, The State, and Law and Order*. London: Macmillan.

HALLER, M. H. (1976) Historical roots of police behaviour: Chicago 1890–1925. *Law and Society Review* **10**: 303–12.

HARDING, R. W. and FAHEY, R. P. (1973) Killings by Chicago police, 1969–1970. *Southern California Law Review* **46**: 284–315.

HARDT, R. H. and PETERSON-HARDT, S. (1977) On determining the quality of the delinquency self-report method. *Journal of Research Crime and Delinquency* **14**: 247–61.

HARRING, S. (1976) The development of the police institution in the U.S. *Crime and Social Justice* **5**: 54–9.

HARRING, S. and McMULLIN, L. (1975) The Buffalo police 1872–1900: labour unrest, political power and the creation of the police institution. *Crime and Social Justice* **4**: 5–14.

HARRING, S., PLATT, T., SPEIGLMAN, R., and TAKAGI, P. (1977) The management of police killings. *Crime and Social Justice* **8**: 34–43.

HARRIS, A. (1977) Sex and theories of deviance. *American Sociological Review* **42**: 3–16.

HARTNAGEL, T. F. (1979) Perceptions and fear of crime. *Social Problems* **58**: 177–93.

HARTUNG, F. E. (1950) White-collar offenses in the wholesale meat industry in Detroit. *American Journal Sociology* **56**: 25–34.

HASKELL, M. R. and YABLONSKY, L. (1974) *Crime and Delinquency*. Chicago: Rand McNally.

HASKINS, G. (1960) *Law and Authority in Early Massachusetts*. New York: Macmillan.

HAY, D. (1975) Property, authority and criminal law. In D. Hay *et al.*, *Albion's Fatal Tree*. London: Allen Lane.

HEALTH AND SAFETY COMMISSION (1980) *Health and Safety Commission Report 1978/79*. London: HMSO.

HEALTH AND SAFETY EXECUTIVE (1980) *Health and Safety: Manufacturing and Service Industries, 1978*. London: HMSO.

HEILBRONER, L. R. (ed.) (1972) *In the Name of Profit*. New York: Doubleday.

HENSON, S. D. (1980) Female as totem, female as taboo: an inquiry into the freedom to make connections. In E. Sagarin (ed.), *Taboos in Criminology*. London: Sage.

HEPBURN, J. R. (1976) Testing alternative models of delinquency. *Journal of Criminal Law and Criminology* **67**: 450–60.

HERSCHBERGER, R. (1970) *Adam's Rib*. New York: Harper and Row.

HEWITT, P. (1982) *The Abuse of Power*. London: Martin Robertson.

HILLS, S. L. (1971) *Crime, Power and Morality*. Scranton: Chandler.

———— (1980) *Demystifying Social Deviance*. New York: McGraw-Hill.

HINDELANG, M. J. (1973) Causes of delinquency: a partial replication and extension. *Social Problems* **18**: 471–87.

———— (1976) *Criminal Victimization in Eight American Cities*. Cambridge, Mass.: Balinger.

———— (1978) Race and involvement in common law personal crimes. *American Sociological Review* **43**: 93–109.

———— (1979) Sex differences in criminal activity. *Social Problems* **27**: 143–56.

HINDELANG, M. J., GOTTFREDSON, M., and GAROFALO, L. (1978) *Victims of Personal Crimes*. Cambridge, Mass.: Ballinger.

HINDELANG, M. J., HIRSCHI, T., and WEIS, J. G. (1979) Correlates of delinquency. *American Sociological Review* **44**: 995–1014.

HIRSCHI, T. (1969) *Causes of Delinquency*. California: University of California Press.

HOFFMAN-BUSTAMENTE, D. Y. (1973) The nature of female criminality. *Issues in Criminology* **8**: 117–37.

HOLMSTROM, L. L. (1975) Rape: the victim and the criminal justice system. *International Journal Criminology and Penology* **3**: 101–10.

HOLMSTROM, L. L. and BURGESS, A. W. (1975) Rape: the victim goes on trial. In I. Drapkin and E. Viano (eds) *Victimology* Vol. III. Mass.: Lexington.

———— (1978) *The Victim of Rape*. New York: Wiley.

HOME OFFICE (1982) *Criminal Statistics, England and Wales, 1981*. London: HMSO.

HOPKINS, A. (1978) *Crime, Law and Business*. Canberra: Australian Institute of Criminology.

———— (1980a) Controlling corporate deviance. *Criminology* **18**: 198–214.

———— (1980b) Crimes against capitalism – an Australian case. *Contemporary Crises* **4**: 421–32.

HOROWITZ, I. L. (1977) *Genocide: State-Power and Mass Murder*. 2nd ed. New Jersey: Transaction Books.

HORWITZ, A. and WASSERMAN, M. (1979) The effect of social control on delinquent behaviour: a longitudinal test. *Sociological Focus* **12**: 153–70.

HOUSE OF COMMONS HOME AFFAIRS COMMITTEE (1980) *Deaths in Police Custody*. London: HMSO.

HOUSE OF LORDS (1982) *Report from the Select Committee on Unemployment*. London: HMSO.

HUMPHREY, D. (1972) *Police Power – Black People.* London: Panther.

HURD, G. (1979) The television presentation of the police. In S. Holdaway (ed.) *The British Police.* London: Edward Arnold.

IANNI, F. (1974) *A Family Business.* London: Routledge.

INCIARDI, J. and SIEGEL, H. (1977) *Crime: Emerging Issues.* New York: Praeger.

INSTITUTE OF RACE RELATIONS (1979) *Police Against Black People.* London: Institute Race Relations.

IRWIN, J. (1977) The changing social structure of the men's prison. In D. F. Greenberg (ed.) *Corrections and Punishment.* London: Sage.

JACKSON, S. (1978) The social context of rape: sexual scripts and motivation. *Women's Studies International Quarterly* 1: 27–38.

JACOBS, D. and BRITT, D. (1979) Inequality and police use of deadly force. *Social Problems* 26: 403–12.

JACOBY, N., NEHEMLIS, P., and ELLS, R. (1977) *Bribery and Extortion in World Business.* New York: Macmillan.

JAMES, J. and THORNTON, W. (1980) Women's liberation and the female delinquent. *Journal of Research Crime and Delinquency* 17: 230–44.

JANKOVIC, I. (1977) Labour market and imprisonment. *Crime and Social Justice* 9: 17–31.

JENSEN, G. F. and EVE, R. (1976) Sex differences in delinquency. *Criminology* 13: 427–48.

JOHNSON, A. G. (1980) On the prevalence of rape in the U.S. *Signs* 6: 136–46.

JOHNSON, B. (1976) Taking care of labour: the police in American politics. *Theory and Society* 3: 89–117.

JOHNSON, J. M. and DOUGLAS, J. D. (eds) (1978) *Crime at the Top.* New York: Lippincott.

JOHNSON, R. E. (1979) *Juvenile Delinquency and its Origins.* Cambridge: Cambridge University Press.

JONES, C. (1973) Attribution of fault to rape victim as a function of respectability of the victim. *Journal Personality and Social Psychology* 26: 415–19.

JUDGE, A. (1972) *A Man Apart: the British Policeman and His Job.* London: Arthur Barker.

JUDSON, C. J., PANDELL, J., OWENS, J., MCINTOSH, J., and MATSCHULLAT, D. (1969) A study of the California jury penalty in first degree murder cases. *Standford Law Review* 21: 297–341.

KENNEDY, E. (1978) The tragedy at tower no 2. *New York Times Magazine* (Dec. 3): 54–7 ff.

KETTLE, M. and HODGES, L. (1982) *Uprising: the Police, the People and Riots in Britain's Cities.* London: Pan.

KLASS, A. (1975) *There's Gold in Them There Pills.* Harmondsworth: Penguin.

KLEIN, D. (1973) The etiology of female crime: a review of the literature. *Issues in Criminology* 8: 3–30.

—— (1981) Violence against women: some considerations regarding its causes and its elimination. *Crime and Delinquency* 27: 64–80.

KLEIN, D. and KRESS, J. (1976) Any woman's blues: a critical overview of women, crime and the criminal justice system. *Crime and Social Justice* 5: 34–47.

KLOCKERS, C. B. (1980) The Dirty Harry Problem. *Annals* 452: 33–47.

KOBLER, A. L. (1975) Police homicide in a democracy, and Figures (and perhaps some facts) on police killing of civilians in the U.S., 1965–1969. *Journal Social Issues* 31: 163–84, 185–91.

KNAPP COMMISSION (1973) *Report on Police Corruption.* New York: Braziller.

KRISBERG, B. (1975) *Crime and Privilege.* New Jersey: Spectrum.

KROHN, M. D. and MASSEY, J. L. (1980) Social control and delinquency behaviour: an examination of the elements of the social bond. *Sociological Quarterly* 21: 529–43.

KRUTTSCHNITT, C. (1980) Social status and sentences of female offenders. *Law and Society Review* 15: 247–65.

LaFREE, G. D. (1980) Variables affecting guilty pleas and convictions in rape cases. *Social Problems* 58: 833–50.

LAMBERT, J. R. (1972) *Crime, Police and Race Relations.* London: Oxford University Press.

LANE, R. (1967) *Policing the Society: Boston, 1822–1885.* Cambridge, Mass.: Harvard University Press.

―――― (1979) Urbanization and criminal violence in the 19th Century. In H. Graham and T. Gurr (eds), *Violence in America.* Beverley Hills: Sage.

LEA, J. and YOUNG, J. (1982a) Race and crime. *Marxism Today* (August): 38–9.

―――― (1982b) The riots in Britain 1981: urban violence and political marginalization. In D. Cowell, T. Jones, and J. Young (eds) *Policing the Riots.* London: Junction Books.

LeGRAND, C. E. (1973) Rape and rape laws: sexism in society and law. *California Law Review* 61: 919–41.

LEIGH, L. H. (1982) *The Control of Commercial Fraud.* London: Heinemann.

LEMERT, E. M. (1967) *Human Deviance, Social Problems and Social Control.* New Jersey: Prentice-Hall.

LEONARD, E. B. (1982) *Women, Crime and Society.* New York: Longman.

LEONARD, W. N. and WEBER, M. G. (1970) Automakers and dealers: a study of criminogenic market forces. *Law and Society Review* 4: 407–24.

LEVI, M. (1981) *The Phantom Capitalists.* London: Heinemann.

LIAZOS, A. (1972) The poverty of the sociology of deviance: nuts, sluts and perverts. *Social Problems* 20: 103–20.

LIEBOW, E. (1967) *Tally's Corner.* Boston: Little, Brown.

LINDEN, R. and FILLMORE, C. (1981) A comparative study of delinquency involvement. *Canadian Review Sociology and Anthropology* 18: 433–61.

LOTZ, O. R. and HEWITT, J. D. (1977) The influence of legally irrelevant factors on felony sentencing. *Sociological Inquiry* 47: 39–48.

LOVING, N. and OLSON, L. (eds) (1976) *National Conference on Women and Crime.* Washington, DC: National League of Cities.

LUNDMAN, R. J. (1979a) Shoplifting and police referral; a re-examination. *Journal of Criminal Law and Criminology* **69**: 395–401.

——— (1979b) Organizational norms and police discretion. *Criminology* **17**: 159–71.

MACANDREW, C. and EDGERTON, R. B. (1970) *Drunken Comportment*. London: Nelson.

MACKINNON, C. A. (1979) *Sexual Harassment of Working Women*. New Haven: Yale University Press.

MCCAGHY, C. H. (1968) Drinking and deviance disavowal: the case of child molesters. *Social Problems* **16**: 43–9.

——— (1976) *Deviant Behaviour: Crime, Conflict, and Interest Groups*. New York: Macmillan.

MCCAGHY, C. H. and DENISOFF, R. S. (1973) Pirates and politics. In R. S. Denisoff and C. H. McCaghy (eds), *Deviance, Conflict and Criminality*. Chicago: Rand-McNally.

MCCLEARY, R., O'NEIL, M. J., EPPERLEIN, T., JONES, C., and GRAY, R. H. (1981) Effects of legal education and work experiences on the perceptions of crime seriousness. *Social Problems* **28**: 276–89.

MCCORD, W. (1958) The biological basis of juvenile delinquency. In J. Roucek (ed.) *Juvenile Delinquency*. New York: Philosophical Library.

MCCORMICK, A. E. (1977) Rule enforcement and moral indignation: some observations on the effects of criminal anti-trust conviction upon societal reaction processes. *Social Problems* **25**: 30–8.

——— (1979) Dominant class interests and the emergence of anti-trust legislation. *Contemporary Crises* **3**: 399–417.

MCLINTOCK, F. H. (1976) Unemployment and criminality. In United Nations Social Defense Research Institute, *Economic Crisis and Crime*. Rome: UNSDRI.

MCMARTHY, C. (1972) Deciding to cheapen the product. In R. L. Helbroner (ed.) *In the Name of Profit*. New York: Doubleday.

MCMULLAN, M. (1961) A Theory of corruption. *Sociological Review* **9**: 181–201.

MALAMUTH, N. (1980) Testing hypotheses regarding rape: exposure to sexual violence, sex differences, and the normality of rapists. *Journal of Research in Personality* **14**: 121–37.

MANNHEIM, K. (1965) *Comparative Criminology*. London: Routledge & Kegan Paul.

MANNING, P. K. and REDFINDER, L. T. (1977) Invitational edges of corruption: some consequences of narcotic law enforcement. In P. E. Rock (ed.) *Politics and Drugs*. New Jersey: Dutton.

MARK, R. (1973) *The Dimbleby Lecture*, BBC television.

——— (1977) *Policing a Perplexed Society*. London: Allen and Unwin.

——— (1978) *In the Office of Constable*. London: Collins.

MARTIN, J. P. and WEBSTER, D. (1971) *Social Consequences of Conviction*. London: Heinemann.

MARTIN, R. (1934) *Defendants and Criminal Justice*. University of Texas Bulletin, No. 3437: Bureau of Research in the Social Sciences.

MATHIESEN, T. (1974) *The Politics of Abolition*. London: Martin Robertson.

MATZA, D. (1964) *Delinquency and Drift.* New York: Wiley.
—— (1969) *Becoming Deviant.* New Jersey: Prentice-Hall.
MEDEA, A. and THOMPSON, K. (1974) *Against Rape.* New York: Farrar, Straus and Giroux.
MERTON, R. (1938) Social structure and anomie. Reprinted in *Social Theory and Social Structure* (1957). New York: Free Press.
MEYER, M. W. (1980) Police shootings at minorities: the case of Los Angeles. *Annals* **452**: 98–110.
MILLER, W. R. (1977) Police authority in London and New York City, 1830–1870. *Journal of Social History* **8**: 81–101.
MILLMAN, M. (1975) She did it all for love: a feminist view of the sociology of deviance. In M. Millman and R. M. Kanter (eds) *Another Voice.* New York: Vintage.
MILLS, C. W. (1956) *The Power Elite.* Oxford: Oxford University Press.
MILTON, C. (1977) *Police Use of Deadly Force.* Washington, DC: The Police Foundation.
MINOR, W. W. (1977) A deterrence-control theory of crime. In R. F. Meier (ed.) *Theory in Criminology: Contemporary Views.* London: Sage.
—— (1978) Deterrence research: problems of theory and method. In J. A. Cramer (ed.) *Preventing Crime.* London: Sage.
MITFORD, J. (1977) *The American Prison Business.* London: Penguin.
MOFFIT, D. (ed.) (1976) *Swindled! Classic Business Frauds of the Seventies.* New Jersey: Dow Jones.
MORGAN, P. (1978) *Delinquent Fantasies.* London: Temple Smith.
MORGENTHAU, R. (1969) Equal justice and the problem of white-collar crime. *Conference Record Board* **6**: 17–20.
MORRIS, A. and GELSTHORPE, L. (1981) False clues and female crime. In A. Morris with L. Gelsthorpe (eds) *Women and Crime.* Cropwood Conference Series No. 13, University of Cambridge: Institute of Criminology.
MORRIS, R. R. (1964) Female delinquency and relational problems. *Social Forces* **43**: 82–9.
MULLER, M. (1974) *The Baby Killer.* London: War On Want.
MYERS, M. A. (1979) Offended parties and official reactions: victims and the sentencing of criminal defendants. *Sociological Quarterly* **20**: 529–40.
—— (1980) Personal and situational contingencies in the process of convicted felons. *Sociological Inquiry* **50**: 65–74.
NADER, R. (1965) *Unsafe at Any Speed.* New York: Grossman.
NADER, R. and GREEN, M. (eds) (1973) *Corporate Power in America.* New York: Gross.
NAGEL, I. (1981) Sex differences in the processing of criminal defendants. In A. Morris with L. Gelsthorpe (eds) *Women and Crime.* Cropwood Conference series No. 13, University of Cambridge: Institute of Criminology.
NAGEL, S. (1969) *The Legal Process from a Behaviour Perspective.* Homewood, Ill.: Dorsey.
NAGEL, S. and WEITZMAN, L. (1971) Women as litigants. *Hastings Law Journal* **23**: 171–98.

NEEDLEMAN, M. L. and NEEDLEMAN, C. (1979) Organizational crime: two models of criminogenesis. *Sociological Quarterly* 20: 517–28.

NELSON, S. and AMIR, M. (1975) The hitch-hiker victim of rape: a research report. In I. Drapkin and E. Viano (eds) *Victimology* Vol. V. Mass.: Lexington.

NEWMAN, D. J. (1957) Public attitudes toward a form of white collar crime. *Social Problems* 4: 228–32.

NETTLER, G. (1974) *Explaining Crime.* New York: McGraw-Hill.

NYE, I. F., SHORT, J. F., and OLSON, V. J. (1958) Socioeconomic status and delinquent behaviour. *American Journal of Sociology* 63: 381–89.

OAKLEY, A. (1972) *Sex, Gender and Society.* New York: Harper and Row.

——— (1980) *Subject Women.* London: Fontana.

O'CONNOR, J. (1973) *The Fiscal Crisis of the State.* New York: St. Martin's Press.

——— (1975) Productive and unproductive labour. *Politics and Society* 5: 297–336.

PARKIN, F. (1971) *Class, Inequality and Political Order.* London: McGibbon & Kee.

PARSONS, T. (1963) A sociological approach to the study of organizations. In *Structure and Process in Modern Societies.* New York: Free Press.

PAYAK, B. (1963) Understanding the female offender. *Federal Probation* 28: 7–12.

PEARCE, F. (1976) *Crimes of the Powerful.* London: Pluto.

PLATT, A. (1969) *The Child Savers.* Chicago: Chicago University Press.

——— (1978) Street crime – a view from the left. *Crime and Social Justice* 9: 26–34.

POLICE COMPLAINTS BOARD (1980) *Report of the Police Complaints Board (1980).* London: HMSO.

POLLAK, O. (1950) *The Criminality of Women.* Connecticut: Greenwood.

POOLE, E. D. and REGOLI, R. M. (1979) Parental support, delinquent friends and delinquency. *Journal Criminal Law and Criminology* 70: 188–93.

PROP (1979) *Don't Mark His Face: Hull Prison Riot (1976).* London: PROP.

PRESIDENT'S COMMISSION ON LAW ENFORCEMENT AND ADMINISTRATION OF JUSTICE (1967) *Task Force Report: Crime and Its Impact – An Assessment.* Washington DC: US Government Printing Office.

QUINNEY, R. (1974) *Critique of Legal Order.* Boston: Little, Brown.

——— (1977) *Class, State and Crime.* London: Longman.

RADA, R. T. (1978) *Clinical Aspects of the Rapist.* New York: Grune & Stratton.

RAINWATER, L. (1970) *Behind Ghetto Walls.* Chicago: Aldine.

RANS, L. L. (1978) Women's crime: much ado about . . . ? *Federal Probation* 42: 45–9.

REASONS, C. E. and KAPLAN, R. L. (1975) Tear down the walls? Some functions of prison. *Crime and Delinquency* 21: 360–72.

RECKLESS, W. C. and KAY, B. A. (1967) *The Female Offender.* Washington, DC: US Government Printing Office.

REED, J. P. and REED, R. S. (1975) 'Doctor, lawyer, indian chief': old rhymes and new on white-collar crime. *International Journal of Criminology and Penology* 3: 279–93.

REIMAN, J. H. (1979) *The Rich Get Richer and the Poor Get Prison.* New York: Wiley.

REINER, R. (1978) The police in the class structure. *British Journal of Law and Society* 5: 166–84.

—— (1980) Fuzzy-thoughts: the police and law-and-order politics. *Sociological Review* 28: 377–413.

REISS, A. J. (1971) *The Police and the Public.* Yale: Yale University Press.

REYNOLDS, G. W. and JUDGE, A. (1968) *The Night the Police Went on Strike.* London: Weidenfeld and Nicholson.

ROBERTS, S. V. (1971) Crime rates of women up sharply over men's. *New York Times* (June, 13): 1, 72.

ROBIN, G. D. (1963) Justifiable homicide by police officers. *Journal of Criminal Law, Criminology and Police Science* 54: 225–31.

—— (1977) Forcible rape: Institutionalised sexism in the criminal justice system. *Crime and Delinquency* 23: 136–53.

ROBINSON, C. D. (1978) The deradicalization of the policeman. *Crime and Delinquency* 24: 129–51.

ROBINSON, W. H., SMITH, P., and WOLF, J. (1974) *Prison Population and Costs.* Washington, DC: Library of Congress.

ROCK, P. (1977) Review Symposium on C. Smart, Women, Crime and Criminology. *British Journal of Criminology* 17: 392–95.

RODMELL, S. (1981) Men, women and sexuality: a feminist critique of the sociology of deviance. *Women's Studies International Quarterly* 4: 145–55.

ROGERS, K. (1973) For her own protection . . . *Law and Society Review* 7: 223–46.

ROSENBLATT, E. and GREENLAND, D. (1974) Female crimes of violence. *Canadian Journal of Crime and Corrections* 16: 173–80.

ROSS, E. A. (1907) *Sin and Society.* Boston: Houghton Mifflin.

ROSSI, P. H., WAITE, E., BOSE, C. E., and BERK, R. E. (1974) The seriousness of crimes: normative structure and individual differences. *American Sociological Review* 39: 224–37.

ROTHSCHILD, D. P. and THORNE, B. C. (1976) Criminal consumer fraud: a victim oriented analysis. *Michigan Law Review* 74: 661–707.

RUSSELL, D. (1975) *The Politics of Rape.* New York: Stein & Day.

RUSSELL, F. (1975). *A City in Terror, 1919, the Boston Police Strike.* New York: Viking.

SANDERS, W. B. (1980) *Rape and Women's Identity.* Beverley Hills: Sage.

SANDHU, J. (1977) *Juvenile Delinquency: Causes, Control, and Prevention.* New York: McGraw-Hill.

SANDHU, J. and IRVING, L. H. (1974) Female offenders and marital disorganization: an aggressive and retreatist reaction. *International Journal of Criminology & Penology* 2: 35–43.

SCARMAN, L. G. (1982) *The Scarman Report.* Harmondsworth: Penguin.

SCHRAG, P. and DIVOKY, D. (1981) *The Myth of the Hyperactive Child.* Harmondsworth: Penguin.

SCHRAG, P. G. (1971) On Her Majesty's Secret Service: protecting the consumer in New York City. *Yale Law Journal* 80: 1529–603.

SCHRAGER, L. S. and SHORT, J. F. (1977) Toward a sociology of organizational crime. *Social Problems* 25: 407–19.

—— (1980) How serious a crime? Perceptions of organizational and common crimes. In G. Geis and E. Stotland (eds) *White-Collar Crime: Theory and Research*. New York: Sage.

SCHUR, E. M. (1973) *Non-Radical Intervention*. New Jersey: Spectrum.

—— (1979) *Interpreting Deviance*. New York: Harper and Row.

—— (1980) *The Politics of Deviance*. New Jersey: Spectrum.

SCHWARTZ, M. D. and CLEAR, T. R. (1980) Towards a new law on rape. *Crime and Delinquency* 26: 129–51.

SCHWENDINGER, H. and SCHWENDINGER, J. (1974) Rape myths. *Crime and Social Justice* 1: 18–27.

—— (1975) Defenders of order or guardians of human rights? In I. Taylor, P. Walton, and J. Young (eds) *Critical Criminology*. London: Routledge.

—— (1976) A review of rape literature. *Crime and Social Justice* 6: 79–85.

—— (1980) Rape victims and the false sense of guilt. *Crime and Social Justice* 13: 4–18.

SCOTT, M. B. and LYMAN, S. M. (1968) Accounts. *American Sociological Review* 33: 46–62.

SCRATON, P. (1982) Policing and institutionalized racism on Merseyside. In D. Cowell, T. Jones, and J. Young (eds) *Policing the Riots*. London: Junction Books.

SCULL, A. T. (1977) *Decarceration*. New Jersey: Spectrum.

SCUTT, J. A. (1978) Debunking the theory of the female 'masked' criminal. *Australian and New Zealand Journal of Criminology* 11: 23–42.

SEBBA, L. and CAHAN, S. (1975) Sex offenses: the genuine and the doubted victim. In I. Drapkin and E. Viano (eds) *Victimology* Vol. V. Mass.: Lexington.

SEYMOUR, W. N. (1973) Social and ethical considerations in assessing white-collar crime. *American Criminal Law Review* 11: 821–34.

SHACKLADY-SMITH, L. (1978) Sexist assumptions and female delinquency: an empirical investigation. In C. and B. Smart (eds) *Women, Sexuality and Social Control*. London: Routledge.

SHAWCROSS, W. (1979) *Side-Show: Kissinger, Nixon and the Destruction of Cambodia*. London: Andre Deutsch.

SHERMAN, L. W. (ed.) (1974) *Police Corruption*. New York: Anchor.

SHERMAN, L. W. and LANGWORTHY, R. H. (1979) Measuring homicide by police officers. *Journal of Criminal Law and Criminology* 70: 546–60.

SHORTER, E. (1977) On writing the history of rape. *Signs* 3: 471–82.

SHOVER, N. (1980) The criminalization of corporate behaviour: federal surface coal mining. In G. Geis and E. Stotland (eds) *White Collar Crime: Theory and Research*. Beverley Hills: Sage.

SHOVER, N. and NORLAND, S. (1978) Sex roles and criminality: science or conventional wisdom? *Signs* 4: 111–25.

SHOVER, N., NORLAND, S., JAMES, J., and THORTON, W. E. (1979) Gender roles and delinquency. *Social Forces* **58**: 162–75.

SILVERMAN, M. and LEE, P. R. (1974) *Pills, Profits and Politics*. Berkeley: University of California Press.

SIMON, R. J. (1975) *Women and Crime*. Mass.: Heath.

——— (1976) Women and crime revisited. *Social Science Quarterly* **56**: 648–63.

SIMON, R. J. and SHARMA, N. (1979) Women and crime: does the American experience generalize? In F. Adler and R. J. Simon (eds) *The Criminology of Deviant Women*. Boston: Houghton.

SIMON, W. and GAGNON, J. H. (1977) The anomie of affluence: a post-Mertoniab conception. *American Journal Sociology* **82**: 356–78.

SIMONS, R. L., MILLER, M. G., and AIGNER, S. M. (1980) Contemporary theories of deviance and female delinquency: an empirical test. *Journal of Research into Crime and Delinquency* **15**: 42–57.

SINDEN, P. G. (1980) Perception of crime in capitalist America: the question of consciousness manipulation. *Sociological Focus* **13**: 75–85.

SMART, C. (1976) *Women, Crime and Criminology*, London: Routledge.

——— (1977) Criminological theory: its ideology and implications concerning women. *British Journal of Sociology* **28**, 89–100.

——— (1979) The new female criminal: reality or myth? *British J. Criminology* **19**: 50–9.

SMART, B. and SMART, C. (eds) (1978) Accounting for rape. In *Women, Sexuality and Social Control*. London: Kegan Paul.

SMITH, A. S. (1961) The incredible electrical conspiracy. *Fortune*, (Apr.) 132–80.

SMITH, D. (1980) Reducing the custodial population. Home Office Research Unit, *Research Bulletin No. 9*. London: Home Office.

SMITH, D. A. (1979) Sex and deviance: an assessment of major sociological variables. *Sociological Quarterly* **21**: 183–96.

SMITH, D. A. and VISHER, A. C. (1980) Sex and involvement in deviance/crime: a quantitative review of the empirical literature. *American Sociological Review* **45**: 691–701.

SKOLNICK, J. H. (1966) *Justice Without Trial*. New York: Wiley.

SMITH, D. C. (1974) *'We're Not Mad, We're Angry'*. Vancouver: Women's Press.

SMITHYMAN, S. C. (1979) Characteristics of 'undetected' rapists. In W. H. Parsonage (ed.) *Perspectives on Victimology*. London: Sage.

SNIDER, D. L. (1978) Corporate crime in Canada: a preliminary report. *Canadian Journal Corrections* **20**: 142–68.

SOBLE, R. L. and DALLOS, R. E. (1974) *The Impossible Dream: The Equity Funding Scandal*. New York: Putnam's.

SPITZER, S. (1975) Towards a Marxian theory of crime. *Social Problems* **22**: 368–401.

——— (1980) 'Left-wing' criminology: an infantile disorder? In J. A. Incardi (ed.) *Radical Criminology: The Coming Crisis*. Beverley Hills: Sage.

STARK, R. (1972) *Police Riots*. California: Wadsworth.

STARK, R. and McEVOY, J. (1970) Middle class violence. *Psychology Today* 4: 52–4.

STAW, B. M. and SZWAJKOWSKI, E. (1975) The scarcity-munificence component of organizational environments and the commission of illegal acts. *Administrative Science Quarterly* 20: 345–54.

STEENHUIS, D. W., TIGGES, L. C. M., and ESSERS, J. J. A. (1983) The penal climate in the Netherlands. *British Journal Criminology* 23: 1–16.

STEFFENSMEIER, D. J. (1978) Crime and the contemporary woman: an analysis of changing levels of female property crime, 1960–1975. *Social Forces* 57: 566–84.

——— (1980a) Assessing the impact of the women's movement on sex-based differences in the handling of adult criminal defendants. *Crime and Delinquency* 76: 344–57.

——— (1980b) Sex differences in patterns of adult crime, 1965–1977: a review and assessment. *Social Forces* 58: 1080–108.

——— (1981) Patterns of female property crime 1960–1978: a postscript. In L. Bowker (ed.) *Women and Crime in America.* New York: Macmillan.

——— (1983) An organizational perspective on sex-segregation in the underworld: building a sociological theory of sex differences in crime. *Social Forces* (forthcoming).

STEFFENSMEIER, D. J. and COBB, M. (1981) Sex differences in urban arrest patterns, 1934–1979. *Social Problems* 29: 37–50.

STEFFENSMEIER, D. J. and JORDON, C. (1978) Changing patterns of female crime in rural America, 1962–1975. *Rural Sociology* 43: 87–102.

STEFFENSMEIER, D. J. and KRAMER, J. H. (1980) The differential impact of criminal stigmatization on male and female felons. *Sex Roles,* 6: 1–8.

STEFFENSMEIER, D. J. and STEFFENSMEIER, R. H. (1980) Trends in female delinquency. *Criminology* 18: 62–85.

STEFFENSMEIER, D. J., STEFFENSMEIER, R. H., and ROSENTHAL, A. S. (1979) Trends in female violence, 1960–1977. *Sociological Focus* 12: 217–27.

STEFFENSMEIER, D. J., ROSENTHAL, A. S., and SHEHAN, C. (1980) World War II and its effects on the sex-differential in arrests: an empirical test of the sex-role equality and crime proposition. *Sociological Quarterly* 21: 403–16.

STEFFENSMEIER, D. J. and TERRY, R. M. (1973) Deviance and respectability: an observational study of reactions to shoplifting. *Social Forces* 41: 417–526.

STEINERT, H. (1977) Against a conspiracy theory of criminal law a propos Hepburn's social control and the legal order. *Contemporary Crisis* 1: 437–40.

STERN, G. M. (1976) *Buffalo Creek Disaster.* New York: Random House.

STERN, L. T. (1940) The effects of the depression on prison commitments and sentences. *Journal Criminal Law, Criminology and Police Science* 31: 696–711.

STEVENS, P. (1979) Predicting black crime. Home Office Research Unit, *Research Bulletin No. 8.* London: Home Office.

STEVENS, P. and WILLIS, C. F. (1979) *Race, Crime and Arrests*. London: Home Office.

—————— (1981) *Ethnic Minorities and Complaints Against the Police*. Research and Planning Unit Paper, No. 5. London: Home Office.

STODDARD, E. R. (1968) The 'informer code' of police deviancy. *Journal of Criminal Law, Criminology and Police Science* **59**: 202–14.

STONE, C. D. (1975) *Where the Law Ends: Social Control of Corporate Behaviour*. New York: Harper and Row.

STOTLAND, E. (1977) White-collar criminals. *Journal of Social Issues* **33**: 179–96.

SUMNER, C. (1976) Marxism and deviance theory. In P. Wiles, (ed.) *Crime and Delinquency in Britain* vol. 2. London: Martin Robertson.

SUNDAY TIMES INSIGHT TEAM (1979) *Suffer the Children*. London: Futura.

SUTHERLAND, E. (1940) White-collar criminality. *American Sociological Review* **5**: 1–12.

—————— (1945) Is 'white collar crime' crime? *American Sociological Review* **10**: 132–39.

—————— (1949) *White-Collar Crime*. New York: Holt, Rinehart and Winston.

SWARTZ, J. (1975) Silent killers at work. *Crime and Social Justice* **3**: 15–20.

SWIGERT, V. and FARRELL, R. (1976) *Murder, Inequality and the law*. Mass.: Heath.

—————— (1981) Corporate homicide: definitional processes in the creation of deviance. *Law and Society Review* **15**: 161–82.

SYKES, G. M. and MATZA, D. (1957) Techniques of neutralization: a theory of delinquency. *American Sociological Review* **22**: 664–70.

SZASZ, T. (1970) *Ideology and Insanity*. New York: Anchor.

—————— (1977a) *Psychiatric Slavery*. New York: Free Press.

—————— (1977b) *The Theology of Medicine*. Oxford: Oxford University Press.

TAKAGI, P. (1974) A garrison state in 'democratic' society. *Crime and Social Justice* **1**: 27–33.

TARLING, R. (1982) Unemployment and crime. *Research Bulletin No. 14*. London: Home Office.

TAYLOR, I. (1982) *Law and Order*. London: Macmillan.

TAYLOR, I., WALTON, P. and YOUNG, J. (1973) *New Criminology*. London: Routledge.

TAYLOR, L. (1976) The significance and interpretation of replies to motivational questions: the case of sex offenders. In P. Wiles (ed.) *Crime and Delinquency in Britain*. London: Martin Robertson.

TEILMANN, K. S. and LANDRY, P. H. (1981) Gender bias in juvenile justice. *Journal of Research into Crime and Delinquency* **16**: 47–80.

THIO, A. (1975) A critical look at Merton's anomie theory. *Pacific Sociological Review* **18**: 139–58.

—————— (1978) *Deviant Behaviour*. Boston: Houghton-Mifflin.

THOMAS, C. W. and HYMAN, J. M. (1978) Compliance theory, control theory and juvenile delinquency. In M. D. Krohn and R. L. Akers (eds) *Crime, Law and Sanctions*. London: Sage.

THOMAS, C. W., HYMAN, J. M., and SIEVERES, C. M. (1975) Juvenile court intake: an analysis of discretionary decision making. *Criminology* **12**: 413–32.

THOMAS, J. E. and POOLEY, R. (1980) *The Exploding Prison.* London: Junction Books.

THOMPSON, E. P. (1975) *Whigs and Hunters.* London: Allen Lane.

THORNTON, W. E. and JAMES, J. (1979) Masculinity and delinquency revisited. *British Journal of Criminology* **19**: 225–41.

TITTLE, C. R. and VILLEMEZ, W. J. (1977) Social class and criminality. *Social Forces* **56**: 474–502.

TONER, B. (1977) *The Facts of Rape.* London: Arrow.

TUCK, M. and SOUTHGATE, P. (1981) *Ethnic Minorities, Crime and Policing.* Home Office Research Study No. 70. London: Home Office.

TULKENS, H. (1979) *Some Developments in Penal Policy and Practice in Holland.* London: Barry Rose.

TURK, A. (1969) *Criminality and Legal Order.* Chicago: Rand-McNally.
——— (1981) *Political Criminality.* New York: Sage.

UNGAR, S. J. (1973) 'Getting away with what you can'. In L. R. Heilbroner (ed.) (1972) *In the Name of Profit.* New York: Doubleday.

VANDIVIER, K. (1972) Why would my conscience bother me? In R. L. Heilbroner (ed.) (1972) *In the Name of Profit.* New York: Doubleday.

VANICK, C. (1977) Corporate tax study, 1976. In D. M. Ermann and R. J. Lundman (eds) (1978) *Corporate and Governmental Deviance.* Oxford: Oxford University Press.

VAUGHAN, D. (1980) Crime between organizations: implications for victimology. In G. Geis and E. Stotland (eds) (1980) *White Collar Crime: Theory and Research.* Beverley Hills: Sage.

VEDDER, C. B. and SOMMERVILLE, D. B. (1970) *The Delinquent Girl.* Springfield, Ill.: Charles C. Thomas.

VOGAL, R. (1975) Prison reform in social perspective. *The Texas Observer,* **67**: 3–5.

WALLERSTEIN, J. S. and WYLE, C. J. (1947) Our law-abiding law breakers. *Probation* April: 107–12.

WARD, D. A. and KASSEBAUM, G. C. (1966) *Women's Prison: Sex and Social Structure.* London: Weidenfeld and Nicolson.

WEIS, J. G. (1976) Liberation and crime: the invention of the new female criminal. *Crime and Social Justice* **6**: 17–27.

WEIS, K. and BORGES, S. S. (1973) Victimology and rape: the case of the legitimate victim. *Issues in Criminology* **8**: 71–116.

WEIS, K., BORGES, S. S., and WEIS, S. (1975) Victimology and the justification of rape. In I. Drapkin and E. Viano (eds) *Victimology* Vol. V. Mass.: Lexington.

WEISS, R. (1978) The emergence and transformation of private detective industrial policing in the U.S., 1850–1940. *Crime and Social Justice* **9**: 35–48.

WEST, D. J., ROY, C., and NICHOLS, F. L. (1978) *Understanding Sexual Attacks.* London: Heineman.

WHEELER, S. (1976) Trends and problems in the sociological study of crime. *Social Problems* **23**: 525–33.

WIDOM, C. S. (1978) Toward an understanding of female criminality. *Progress in Experimental Personality Research* 8: 245–308.
——— (1979) Female offenders: three assumptions about self-esteem, sex-role identity and feminism. *Criminal Justice and Behaviour* 6: 365–82.
WILSON, J. Q. (1975) *Thinking About Crime.* New York: Basic Books.
WINICK, C. (ed.) (1978) *Deviance and Mass Media.* New York: Sage.
WINSLOW, R. W. (1969) *Crime in a Free Society.* Belmont, California: Dickenson.
WOLFGANG, M. E. (1958) *Patterns of Criminal Homicide.* Philadelphia: University of Pennsylvania Press.
——— (1980) *National Survey of Crime Severity.* University of Pennsylvania (mimeographed).
WOLFGANG, M. E. and FERRACUTI, F. (1967) *The Subculture of Violence.* London: Tavistock.
WOLFGANG, M. E., FIGLIO, R. M., and THORNBERRY, T. (1975) *Criminology Index 1945–1972.* New York: Elsevier.
WOLFGANG, M. E. and RIEDEL, M. (1973) Race, judicial discretion and the death penalty *Annals* 407: 119–33.
WOOD, P. L. (1973) The victim in a forcible rape case: a feminist view. *American Criminal Law Review* 11: 335–54.
WOODWARD, K. and MALAMUD, P. (1975) Now, the violent woman. *Newsweek* (October 6).
WRIGHT, M. (1982) *Making Good: Prison, Punishment and Beyond.* London: Burnett.
WRONG, D. (1961) The oversocialized conception of man in modern sociology. *American Sociological Review* 26: 183–93.
YEAGER, M. G. (1979) Unemployment and imprisonment. *Journal of Criminal Law and Criminology* 70: 585–88.
YIN, P. P. (1980) Fear of crime among the elderly. *Social Problems* 27: 492–504.
YODER, S. A. (1979) Criminal sanctions for corporate illegality. *Journal of Criminal Law and Criminology* 69: 40–58.
YOUNG, T. (1981) Corporate crime: a critique of the Clinard Report. *Contemporary Crisis* 5: 323–36.
ZIMRING, F. E. and HAWKINS, G. J. (1973) *Deterrence.* Chicago: Chicago University Press.

Subject index

Name index